EUROPE'S
APPRENTICESHIP

¶Libellus/ qui Informatio puerorum appellatur
cū modico apparatu nouiter cōpilat⁹/ Incipit.

TITLE-PAGE OF BOOK PRINTED BY R. PYNSON
(LONDON, 1500) FOR AN OXFORD BOOKSELLER

G. G. COULTON

Fellow of St. John's College, Cambridge

EUROPE'S APPRENTICESHIP

A SURVEY
OF MEDIEVAL LATIN
WITH EXAMPLES

THOMAS NELSON AND SONS LTD
LONDON EDINBURGH PARIS MELBOURNE
TORONTO AND NEW YORK

First published, 1940

CONTENTS

v

CONTENTS

TO THE
MEDIEVAL ACADEMY
OF AMERICA

THIS SMALL VOLUME IS DEDICATED
IN GRATEFUL RECOGNITION

PREFACE

THE only part of this volume which can claim originality is the first section. This was completed in nearly its present form, some seven years ago, as a contribution to the question of monastic learning in the coming fourth volume of my *Five Centuries of Religion*. But it became obvious that the necessary fulness of detail would over-weight that volume and, again, would render it impossible for periodical publication ; yet, on the other hand, it was not long enough to form a separate and inde-pendent volume. I have therefore caught gladly at the opportunity to make it the first and principal section of this present book. Since its whole value depends upon exact documentation, full references are supplied in the Appendix.*

The second section aims at supplying such brief details of medieval education as may be needed to throw light upon the first and third.

The last section has presented, of course, an embarrass-ing wealth of choice. Chronological arrangement (with slight exceptions) was obviously needed. I have thus travelled from the Vulgate Bible down to one of the last medieval mission-preachers. Within those dozen centuries, it seemed best to emphasize four periods :

* These correspond to numerals in my text. I use [square brackets] throughout, (a) for *approximate* dates, and (b) for explanatory words inserted into the translations.

(1) the Vulgate Bible, (2) the Revival of A.D. 1000–1150, (3) the Age of Innocent III., and (4) the Eve of the Reformation. As to subjects, I have leaned towards those which throw direct light upon medieval education, Church faith and discipline, or primitive manners and customs. Primitive, that is, not in the strict sense as being peculiar to that age, but as more characteristic of general western society in those days than in ours. Care has been taken, again, to present a sufficient variety of style both in prose and in verse. Some of the orthographic or grammatical errors may well be due to careless medieval scribes; a few, again, may possibly lie at the door of the present printers and Editor, under difficulties of time and eyesight. But, on the whole, it is hoped that the extracts may fulfil the purpose for which they were chosen, and afford a collection all the more truly representative by reason of its motley character.

I am much indebted to Professor G. R. Potter for valuable assistance in proof revision, and to Mr. E. P. Goldschmidt for the loan of the two blocks which illustrate this volume.

G. G. COULTON

SECTION I
THE LATIN BACKGROUND

CHAPTER I

MAINLY ABOUT MONKS

INCREASING attention is paid nowadays to Medieval
Thought, and at Messrs. Nelson's invitation I have con-
tributed a volume on that subject to their Discussion
Books. There, on the very threshold, I was confronted
with the difficulty of explaining, with any scientific
precision, the atmosphere in which those thinkers worked.
For many years past I have felt that past injustices have
given place in our generation, here and there, to reactions
which exaggerate almost equally in the favourable
direction. I have felt more and more, as the evidence
accumulated under my hand, that there is a dangerous
half-truth in the common cliché : " Medieval England
had three vernaculars—English, French, and Latin."
Three languages, yes, but not three vernaculars : for
there is nearly always one definite mother-tongue,
which is seldom really dethroned.

More than fifty years ago I had the good fortune to
tramp for half a day in Switzerland with a companion
who turned out to be the youngest then member of the
Belgian Parliament. He laid great emphasis upon the
disadvantage, in some ways, of the bi-lingual conditions
in his country. There are millions (he said) who speak
two languages with almost equal facility. In nearly
every case there is a natural preference for one or the

other, but nearly always there is something lacking in clearness of speech, and therefore of thought. Everywhere they are content with approximations : *ils parlent partout à peu près* : one language blunts the other, and when the edge is taken off our speech there is a certain loss of precision in the mind also. That is the text of this first section of the present volume. I am convinced that historians have taken too little account hitherto of the limitations in Latin speech, and consequently in freedom and energy of thought, during that period. Everybody admits that scholastic philosophy, in its later decadent stages, was sadly lacking in sense of proportion : that time and energy were wasted upon trifles which might more profitably have been spent in verification of the very foundations of European belief. But it is not sufficiently recognized that all this may be said, to some extent, even concerning the heyday of medieval philosophy. In proportion as this suggestion is novel, it must be supported by weight of evidence ; and therefore I am marshalling here all the indications that I have noted in the last few years, with chapter and verse. Full references will be found in the Appendix to this present volume * ; and thus the section will at least afford a foundation for future discussion, and a challenge to further and fuller examination. It is, of course, a mere fraction of the total evidence available, but it may supply material for a rough *ad interim* conclusion. If we can first see Latin and the vernaculars in their due pro-

---

* Except in the case of evidence discovered only at the last moment, in the Visitations of Lincoln Diocese between 1510 and 1531. These are as yet unprinted, but Professor Hamilton Thompson's generosity has allowed me to see them by anticipation. The religious houses will there be found in alphabetical and chronological order, so that my citations can be checked at once.

portions, we are then in a better position to judge Medieval Thought.

Nobody would dream of denying that nearly all the most learned literature was written in Latin, not only in the Middle Ages but often for some time afterwards. Nor, again, that this was the official language of the Universities, dominant also in law and in medicine, and a frequent means of international communication by word of mouth. There is plenty of proof, as will be seen, that a man might easily learn enough Latin to forget, wholly or partially, his native tongue.[1] But that last consideration is secondary to the main question. We need first to reckon how great was this stock of Latin which the ordinary cleric was supposed to acquire, and how much, again, was acquired by the scholar who stood a long way above the crowd. What these men lost elsewhere while they were gaining their Latin will come in for later inquiry.

It may clear the ground to lead off with a consideration which has never, to my knowledge, been properly emphasized. In the inmost thoughts even of the most learned men, the mother-tongue seems always, or nearly always, to have remained uppermost. St. Aelred of Rievaulx ranks high among twelfth-century scholars. His pupil and biographer, Walter Daniel, thus describes his last moments.[2] "These words constantly sounded from his mouth in our ears : ' Hasten, hasten !' This he oftentimes reinforced with the name of Christ, and indeed in English, because in that tongue Christ's name is contained in a single syllable and hath in some wise a sweeter sound. He would say therefore (to use his own words) ' Hasten, *for Crist luve*.' " This testimony, moreover, gains further significance from the far-fetched

15

explanation which Daniel seeks for such a simple occurrence. Two generations later came Berthold of Regensburg, a learned Franciscan whom Roger Bacon celebrates as the greatest preacher of his century. It has been noted that he spoke more naturally in his native German than in Latin, and apparently used the vernacular even in his sermons to monks and friars.[3] A little later, the great Dominican mystic, Heinrich Suso, scholastic philosopher though he was, tells us why he wrote his "Little Book of Eternal Wisdom" in the vernacular. "And therefore [the author of this book] wrote his meditations down ; and he wrote them in German, because they had thus come unto him from God."[4] St. Bridget of Sweden apparently wrote her *Revelations*, about 1363, at Rome ; long before this, she had founded a whole new Order of monks and nuns, and had prescribed its Rule. One might have expected her, if any woman, to think in the language of the service books and the Holy Scriptures ; yet her revelations were communicated to her from heaven in the Swedish tongue, and only translated later into Latin by her confessor. Johann Busch, who wrote about A.D. 1450, was one of the great monastic reformers of his century. In his autobiography, he gives the long prayer which he composed for himself, "which also I have been wont to recite even in German, especially when I do not celebrate [Mass]." It is in the German tongue that he gives the words of this prayer in his book.[5] Moreover, he tells us the same of his own master, Johann Cele of Deventer, who had been Gerhard Groot's pupil, and was himself rector of the most famous grammar school in Europe[6] : "In order to renew more frequently the affection of prayer in himself he would sometimes pray, either mentally or vocally, at one time

THE LATIN BACKGROUND

in Latin and another in German, and sometimes in both."
Busch gives three specimens, a German of eleven lines,
a Latin of four, and a mixed prayer of three. We have
here what Professor R. W. Chambers notes concerning
the English mystics of the fourteenth and fifteenth centuries : they " wrote sometimes in Latin, but also in
English, because either to them, or to the enclosed sisters
for whom so often they wrote, English was the language
of passionate and instinctive utterance." [7]   Erasmus's
last recorded words were in Dutch : " Lieber God." [8]

A sidelight on this is afforded by the words of Ekkehard IV. of St. Gallen.[9] Writing of conditions in the
early eleventh century, he says : " Men who are only half-
teachers are wont thus to teach their boys [in Latin
composition] saying : ' See first how we ought to speak
in most choice German idiom to anyone, and then turn
those words in the same order into Latin.' " An eminent
scholar like Ekkehard might reprobate this method ;
but his words are conclusive as to the temptation among
ordinary folk. The model monastery of Murbach, in
816, aimed at a high standard here. Its Statutes run :
" Those of [the brethren] who are teachers [*scholastici*]
follow the use of Latin rather than of rustic speech.
For by such confabulation men sometimes penetrate
deeper into the knowledge of the Scriptures than by
reading ; also they learn the art of composition, and their
sense is sharpened for learning." [10]

This is perfectly intelligible ; the written evidence
accords with what we should have expected from human
nature, and it is borne out by modern experience. I
have heard a distinguished Roman Catholic professor
complain of his difficulties in teaching seminarists. So
long as they were on purely traditional ground (he said)

it was easy enough ; the clichés passed without effort from the teacher to the pupil. But the moment it was a question of expressing modern ideas, or of adapting the old to the modern mentality, the difficulties began, and sometimes became almost insuperable. This is borne out by the printed criticisms of three able and energetic teachers of our own generation. A veteran professor of Maynooth, Dr. Walter McDonald, devotes several pages of his autobiography to this subject.[11] He writes : " I am convinced that our lack of success [in educating the young Irish clergy] is due, in a very great measure, to the use of Latin in our schools." The advantages, he feels, are outweighed by the disadvantages. He thinks things had been better in the Middle Ages, and that they are better even nowadays at Rome itself than in Ireland. Yet, even so, " the use of Latin as a school language is one of the most potent of the causes that have been retarding the progress of theological science in Rome as elsewhere. Would either [Science or History] be what it is if those by whom they have been developed had continued to teach and write in Latin ? Does not the era of progress date from the time when the questions raised by both began to be discussed in the language of ordinary life ? " And, even in theology, " it is not in any dead language that one can press the kind of argument that carries conviction where such difficulties are real. Newman could write Latin as well as most ; but how straitened he would have been—that subtle wit of his and keen intellect made stiff and blunt—if he had had to express himself in any other language than that which he had been using from infancy ! " And Dr. McDonald appeals for corroboration to one of the most earnest of his colleagues in France, the Abbé Hogan : also to

" *The Training of a Priest*, written by the Rev. John Talbot Smith, LL.D., and published with an Introduction by that saintly man, the late Bishop of Rochester, Dr. McQuaide." One chapter of this volume, "The Language of the Seminary," does indeed bear out all, and perhaps more than all, of that which the Maynooth professor has said. We must remember, of course, that there was a far greater body of Latin speech and writing in the Middle Ages than in modern Ireland or America ; but it is difficult to say that there was proportionately more then (considering the whole of Europe, both town and country) than there was in the city of Rome from (say) 1470 to 1870. It would seem fair, therefore, to suspect something like the same difficulties in medieval Europe which we know to have existed in more modern Rome.

But, while speaking here of the Middle Ages, we must, for the moment, definitely exclude the earlier generations, the so-called Dark Ages. For, at the very threshold of this subject, we are met with the paradox that the worst Latin was written in those earlier days when Latin was most frequently spoken. The times and places of most unclassical Latin, when once the barbarian invasions had passed over Europe, were not the farthest removed from Augustus and from his city of Rome, but the nearest. Latin had to die out as a real vernacular before it was revived in literature. The struggle between these two currents—the unconscious and the self-conscious Latin, we may call them—lasted for many generations, and the different stages were not contemporaneous in different lands. While whole centres of learning like Lyons and Bordeaux, or a few individual scholars here and there in other places, kept up the study and imitation of the Classics, a whole new literature had grown up, Christian and anti-pagan, which was destined to sway the western world for centuries. Its original aim was practical; no man could afford to neglect the offer of salvation; therefore none could ignore the Christian Scriptures and liturgy. The East, and the West at first to some extent, possessed these in Greek: but Latin was the real business language of the whole West, even more than English is now that of our whole Empire. In Gaul, for instance, all cultivated people studied it; the trader could not get on without it; and many even among the peasants and artisans had some smattering of it. It thus became the natural language of that liturgy which had begun as a manual of truly congregational worship; and for the same reason, at a very early date, the Hebrew and Greek scriptures were translated into this popular business tongue, in order that the people of the West might read their Bible just as Chrysostom and other eastern saints insisted on its being universally read in the East. The old " Italian " and " African " Latin versions, and that " Vulgate " which St. Jerome presently built upon them, combined the simplicity of common speech with fresh literary elements, very powerful in themselves and most pregnant for the future, which came in from Greek and Hebrew; the translators were thus not only borrowers but creators also. The classics were still read to some extent, if only by a few scholars; and much of the true classical spirit still came in at second hand through writers like Augustine and Jerome, who were always eagerly studied and who had themselves been steeped in ancient literature. The breaking-point in France between unconscious and self-conscious Latin has been admirably described by Gaston Paris in his *Esquisse historique de la littérature française au moyen âge* (1907,

p. 23). " It was the contact with the *Barbari* which made the *Romani* fully conscious of this distinction. They realized that, if their speech was not *lingua barbara*, yet it was not altogether *lingua latina* ; therefore they called it *lingua romana*, to which name the clergy added the scornful adjective *rustica*. . . . This language, which was the natural means of communication with the conquerors, and which those latter soon learned, gained thus in importance ; yet three centuries had yet to pass before the Church decided to prescribe its use in the priests' familiar homilies."

After the break-off of the direct classical tradition, we may note three stages, clearly marked, in the study of Latin : First, the revival under Charles the Great ; next, that which culminated in the twelfth century ; and, thirdly, the Renaissance of the fourteenth and fifteenth centuries. In the " Dark Ages " Latin was truly a consolidating force. Yet in this period, though classical books were preserved in monastic libraries, the only safe places of deposit in that welter of wars and social unrest, they were less and less studied or systematically imitated. Here again we have to note a paradox : this comparative ignorance helped to maintain purity of transmission. " The works of classical literature, for the very reason of the imperfect comprehension of earlier Latin by the clergy, were more safely kept than they would have been if the knowledge of classical Latin had remained general. Thus these works, at a date when men had not yet invented the method of separating words, were laboriously transcribed without knowledge of their contents ; and the scribe was therefore far less tempted into arbitrary changes and interpolations. Therefore, until the ninth century, texts were kept pure from arbitrary distortion : this does not begin until men begin to separate the words, and to understand the language better." [12] Side by side with this growing ignorance of the old, ran a living current of new literature, inspired mainly by the Bible, the Bible-commentators, and the Liturgy. " The vital forces [of ancient civilization] were carefully nursed by Christianity, when once it had gained the upper hand ; the new Christian literature contended on even terms with the ancient Roman, and gained so complete a victory within a few centuries that, from the middle of the sixth century, ' Latin Literature ' is practically coextensive with ' Christian Literature.' " [13] With the vitality of youth, it had youth's crudities ; its force lay to a great extent in its wide appeal to all classes, from the prince to the peasant. But such vulgarization always implies a certain loss of precision ; the thing becomes *vulgaris* in both senses of that word, as being common to the multitude and as stooping to the multitude. Apart from those writings which were consciously influenced by assiduous study and imitation—if not of the classics, at least of such semi-classics as Augustine, Jerome, and Boëthius—the Latin of A.D. 550–810 was commonly very barbarous in style. The chroniclers of (say) 1250, although Antiquity then lay nearly a thousand years behind and the Renaissance had not yet dawned, wrote not only far more clearly, but incomparably more correctly, than Bishop Gregory of Tours in 576. Italian histories like that of Benedict of Monte Soracte [1000] and Novalese [1050] read like the work of blundering schoolboys beside the English chroniclers of the early twelfth century. The Spanish (or Gaulish) abbess, Aetheria, describing her travels in the Holy Land [385] is perhaps even less faithful to

grammatical inflexions than Gregory : in the very first
paragraph of her book we find *planissima* for *planissimam* ;
habebat for *habebantur* ; *per valle illa* for *per vallem illam*.
Pope Zacharias I. (751) was capable of writing very
ungrammatical Latin ; so also was Hadrian I. (786).
The bad grammar of John XII. has become proverbial ;
the Roman synod of 963 mocked at him for writing
" excommunico vos da Deum Omnipotentem, ut non
habeatis licentiam nullum ordinare et missam celebrare."
The monastic and episcopal charters of the Dark Ages
are far more incorrect when drawn up in countries of
Romance than in those of Teutonic speech. In 718, at
Farfa, we find " constat nos Barbatus et Valerianus
clerici . . . vendidisse . . . ad pretium placitum et diffinitum
auri solidos appretiatos numero viii." In 750, Gisolf,
duke of Lombardy, grants to the monks of Monte
Cassino a charter ending " scripto praecepto ipse per
Bertari notario. Actum in hunc sacrum Benebentanum
nostrum Palatio, mense Septembrio." At Cluny, in
855 : " Ego in Dei nomen, Gondoenus, clericus, rogitus
escripsit." [14] At Monte Cassino, in [960] " per hanc
cartula obligamus nos et nostris heredibus vobis."
Among the worst are the Piedmontese charters, where
the scribes revel in datives or ablatives plural, evidently
for sheer love of their succulent terminations ; repeatedly
we find such a phrase as *nos jugalibus* for *nos conjuges*.
But worst of all, perhaps, are the Sardinian ; for here,
as late as the end of the eleventh century, we find a
language almost closer to vernacular Italian than Latin :
e.g. " si quis ta carta destruere aud sterminare ea boluerit "
for " si quis istam cartam destruere aut exterminare eam
voluerit." [15] It is true, there are indications that grammar
schools were far more general in Italy than in other

countries ; and a few Italians were among the best of
the Dark Age writers ; but this schooling must have
made liberal concessions to popular speech, since the
average of correctness was very low in Italy, as apart
from fluency, where no doubt the average was high.
Again, though the Spaniards were probably fluent in
speech, they wrote with corresponding carelessness in
grammar. For instance, the Prior of the Cluniac house
of Our Lady of Nájera, composing an official report in
about 1210 to the Abbot of Cluny, " writes less correct
Latin than we should find in a document written at the
same date in France. The writer blunders more than
once over his cases ; *e.g.* he writes : *a domno Aldefonso
regis, ex quemdam burgensem,* etc." [16] If it would be
difficult or impossible to match that in contemporary
France, still more definitely may we claim this for
England. A glance through any of the volumes of
Dugdale's *Monasticon* will show that Anglo-Saxon or
Norman-Saxon Latin, however clumsy, never sinks to
the level of these papal and monastic, or quasi-monastic,
documents in the Latin countries.[17] Only one explanation seems possible : that these Teutonic or Celtic out-
siders wrote better because they had learned the language
by fierce and patient application, instead of sucking it
in easily with their mother's milk. In our own day a
Welsh-speaking Welshman, if his abilities and his
education favour him, will often use correcter English
than his equal on this side of the border. It was partly
because Bede [720] lived so far from Rome that he wrote
so much better than any Roman of his day. It was
among Irish and Anglo-Saxons at this time, and the
Germanic districts evangelized by Celtic and English
monks, that scholarship glowed most steadily among the

embers; so that, though the early English charters sometimes show traces of that wild exuberance of style which was popular in Ireland, they generally show a far more respectable Latin than their continental contemporaries. And it was from them that the impulse came which led Europe, intellectually speaking, out from the Dark Ages into the light. The movement centres round Charles the Great [800]. " In Italy, at that time, decay had long since set in ; and here it was all the deeper because, since the days of Gregory the Great, the sciences, in the special sense of that word, had met with contempt. Here, men were concerned with gaining dominion over the world, and the aims which they followed were predominantly practical ; they cared little for literary matters " ; moreover, the Saracen invasions were a numbing canker.[18] But Charles was a man of extraordinary breadth and driving power ; and he set himself, in his own words, " to revive the study of letters, wellnigh extinguished through the neglect of our ancestors." With the Englishman Alcuin, who has been called with some truth his Minister of Education, he undertook not only to raise the level of clerical culture but (as a scribe at St. Gallen expressed it) to make war upon faulty texts as he had made war upon his enemies in the field.[19] It was he who made the first serious effort to produce a pure text of the Vulgate ; and he procured from Monte Cassino a model text of St. Benedict's Rule, which he sent round to great monasteries as a standard. Under his successors, there was a remarkable revival of learning at some of the great monasteries—Tours, Fulda, St. Gallen, Fleury—and nothing of what had been gained during his reign was lost again, however it might be forgotten at some times and places. But there was still plenty of room for progress, and the next step came with that great revival which can be roughly associated with the year A.D. 1000, and which produced Ralph Glaber's famous " white robe of churches." This culminated in certain cathedral schools, Chartres and Orléans in especial, where the Latin classics were better cultivated than at any other time until the Renaissance.

The fact is that the more correct Latin which was written in the ninth century, and still more definitely the far correcter Latin of the twelfth, were to a great extent artificial languages. The old natural language had died down almost into a patois : as Lot says : " in the seventh and eighth centuries, and even at the end of the sixth, nobody in Gaul knew how to spell Latin, simply because nobody pronounced it correctly " (p. 107 ; *cf.* p. 148). To quote again from Lot (p. 150) : " Its part is that of an auxiliary language. Men write it, but do not speak it ; or again, if they do speak it (*e.g.* at a Council) it is after the fashion of modern conventional languages, *Esperanto*, or *Ido*, which well-meaning folk struggle to use at a Congress and forget when they go out. Latin was no longer anybody's mother-tongue. It was no longer living ; it survived itself in ghost-life." The new scholarship was vigorous ; but it was more self-conscious and less instinctive. Thus, though this attained great success in its highest manifestations, and a very fair average of success in the best days of monasteries and universities, yet it had always the weakness of every movement that depends on self-conscious labour ; dullards and sluggards were tempted to content themselves with the mere show of knowledge. Moreover, even among those who would willingly have done better, there was often a lack of opportunity ; so that, throughout this lower stratum of so-called Latin scholarship, almost any ignorance was possible. The evidence for this is overwhelming. While even the best medieval scholars can be found falling back upon the mother-tongue, the "submerged tenth" among the clergy sometimes failed to rise above the standard of a modern preparatory school. The indications come from too many different countries and ages to be explained away.

Let us first take the evidence of translations, all the more valuable because it is fortuitous ; and because it crops up at so many different times and places.

The monk, of all men, might be expected to be thoroughly at home in Latin, considering that it was essential to his true profession—the *Opus Dei* par excellence—to spend many hours a day chanting in that language. Yet, in every generation, from Bede in [720] down to the Reformation, we find the authorities assuming a great deal of Latin ignorance, and making special translations for the use of ignorant brethren.

Bede [720] insisted on the need of translating the Lord's Prayer and Apostles' Creed for the sake not only of the laity "but also of clerics or monks who are ignorant of the Latin tongue." Therefore, he adds, he himself has translated them "for the sake of many priests, who are often unlearned." [20] Not long after this, a translation of St. Benedict's Rule was begun at St. Gallen, which certainly stood then among the half-dozen most flourishing and learned monasteries in Europe.[21] The Rule was translated into Anglo-Saxon also ; and a good many versions were made in the later Middle Ages.[22] Notker, one of the greatest of these St. Gallen scholars, wrote a considerable number of translations ; and his letter to Bishop Hugo of Sion

(998–1017) implies that he intended them for clergy as well as laity.[23] In 1119, Philippe de Thaon " translated into verse, for Anglo-Norman clergy, the ecclesiastical *computus* [for calculating the Easter cycle and other feasts] ; an idea which seems singular, and which proves, moreover, the insufficiency of the clergy of those days in those subjects which they ought to have known best and, to begin with, in the Latin language." [24] Adam of Prémontré [1160] ridicules those of his day who sneer at the sermon unless it be " all in Latin, and (what is more ludicrous) unless it be spoken in pompous and unusual language. They say ' the man felt well and acutely in his mind ; but what he said is less sound and acceptable, because he resorted to this vulgar speech in his delivery ' : yet they themselves understand not a single word of what is said, unless it be expounded to them in the vernacular." [25] Innocent IV. [1250] seems plainly to contemplate cases where monks, and, still more probably nuns, take the vows without ever realizing that the Rule forbids flesh-eating.[26]

In 1254 the General of the Dominicans sent round a circular letter to the Order, with the proviso that it was to be expounded in the vulgar tongue to the novices and the friars who knew no Latin.[27] True, the *lay brethren* of all monastic Orders were generally ignorant of Latin ; but the Dominican friars, in 1254, were on the whole the most learned religious of their time. Turning from them to the Benedictines and Augustinians, we find that, about this same time, Archbishop Odo Rigaldi of Rouen [1250] frequently insists that a monastery shall possess the Rule in French as well as Latin, or that his own injunctions shall be translated into French, to make sure that all the monks understand them.

Yet Rouen was one of the most civilized dioceses in Europe, at what would be generally singled out as the golden age of the Medieval Church. And in this the Archbishop was simply following the injunctions of Gregory IX. in 1235—Gregory IX., St. Francis's friend and protector—who had decreed : " Seeing that, in many monasteries, the Rule is understood by few persons when it is read, we command that the reading from the Rule in Chapter, on account of the lesser members, be expounded on the spot in the vulgar tongue." This precept was repeated by an English Provincial Chapter in [1279]. [28]

Robert of Greatham [1270] translated the gospels of the Mass into French, for the sake of some " who hear and read the gospels, and who understand not that which the text saith." The context also implies that some of these are clerics.[29] Hermann v. Minden, Provincial of the Teutonic Dominican Province (1286–90), sent certain formal " admonitions " to a nunnery. These begin by enjoining that they must have a correct copy of the constitutions of the Order, " which should be frequently read and sometimes expounded in the vulgar tongue." [30]. In 1290, Nicholas IV. issued a body of statutes for the Cluniac Order ; the twenty-first of these provides that no document be sealed with the common seal of any monastery " unless it have first been read in the chapter-house before all the brethren in the vulgar tongue as well as in Latin." [31] A little earlier, the Abbot-General of the Premonstratensian Order tried to put a stop to the abuse by which novices were admitted while insufficiently instructed in grammar and unable to speak Latin properly.[32] In 1302, the Bishop of Winchester prescribed that business documents should be read to the nuns of Romsey "in lingua intelligibili." In 1286, his injunctions to them had been in French.[33] The abbot of Aurillac, drawing up statutes in 1303 for the prior and monks of Saillans, took care to translate them also into French, " to give and understand clearly the manner of France" to those monks. So, again, with those which he drew up for another dependent priory, Aspres.[34] In 1304, the more important of the bishop of Speyer's injunctions to two nunneries are to be expounded to the sisters in the vulgar tongue.[35] It was about this time, apparently, that a manual for use of the laity at Mass, in English, was adapted for the Cistercians of Rievaulx " to make it useful for both those monks who could read, and those who could not.[36] Clement V., at the Council of Vienne (1311) decreed : "when the Rule is read in Chapter, let it be expounded in the vulgar tongue, for the sake of the younger monks, by the president of the Chapter or by some other to whom he shall commit this duty." This was repeated, almost in so many words, by Benedict XII. in his statutes for the reform of the Cluniac Order (1337).[37] In 1315, the newly-built college at Paris for students from the different houses of the Premonstratensian Order was divided into separate lodgings according to the separate nations from which the brethren came ; an implication that they spoke sometimes, at least, their separate languages.[38] About 1330, the prior of the great monastery of St. Geneviève at Paris translated the Rule into French for the benefit of some of his more ignorant brethren : "I know" (he says) " that a good many of you—*plusieurs*—do not well understand the Latin tongue, and yet ye must needs understand our Rule." [39] The canonist, John of Acton, writing shortly before the Black Death, repeats the injunction of Vienne (which by his time had become incorporated in Canon Law), only changing " for the sake of the younger " into " for the sake of the simple," and adding an illuminating commentary of his own.⁴⁰ " For," he writes, " simplicity or a mean acquaintance with letters—*modica litteratura*—does not seem blameworthy in a monk, since ' a good monk hardly maketh a good clerk.' ⁴¹ But I know not whether the Possessionate Religious ⁴² take this to heart ; for though these have some members who are teachable and able to profit in study, yet they do greatly abhor to contribute from the goods of their monastery, (however it may abound in wealth and may possess fat palfreys and other luxuries) in order to send such students to the university, or to give them an exhibition to that end. But I believe rather that this proceedeth not from their zealous insistence upon devout contemplation, (as with St. Augustine whom I have just quoted) but rather from envy and gall, lest some in their monastery should become wiser or better than the rest, and so rebuke, by the authority of Scripture, the strange errors of these others who are sometimes illiterate "—*idiotarum*. Here we have the satire of a secular cleric who criticized the monks freely ; but his interpretation of the papal decree is borne out by the increasing frequency of similar provisions. In 1312, when the prior of Canterbury Cathedral came into St. Augustine's abbey and read the Pope's bull to the brethren assembled there, he proposed to " expound it in the vulgar tongue " ; at next day's sitting, again, the Abbot told the Prior " to make the above-mentioned proclamations in the mother-tongue."⁴³ The articles of inquiry for English Benedictine visitors [1360] ask : " Is the Rule read publicly in chapter, and expounded for the sake of the younger brethren in the vulgar tongue, if necessary ? " And, again, " Do the brethren, in their parliament and in their accusations in chapter and their corrections and other colloquies and solaces talk at least French or Latin, as commanded in the statute of Northampton ? " Again, the Provincial Chapter of 1343 (or 1346) prescribes conversational amenities as a safeguard against the " frequent matters of contention or murmuring " : one of these is " that the pronoun *tu*, or *thou* in English speech, . . . be henceforward altogether omitted " between brother and brother. This was repeated in 1444, when the different papal and conciliar statutes were formed into an official code for the Province. In the same code it was prescribed that the Benedictine students at Oxford " should preach frequently both in Latin and in the vulgar tongue . . . at least four times a year in each tongue." [44] The Augustinian General Chapter [1400] prescribed regular inquiry " whether there be any of the brethren who understand not the Canon of the Mass or the words of Consecration.[45] Martin, prior at Melk, pleading in 1433 before the Fathers of Bâle for efficacious monastic reform, instances first the difficulty of finding visitors whose heart was in their work. He proceeds : " There is yet another thing, no less lamentable, that in these dioceses [of Austria] there are very few Abbots to be found—*rarissimi inveni-untur*—who have a competent knowledge of Latin— *qui competentis sint litteraturae*—but they are utterly stupid and ignorant, so that many—*plerique*—cannot deliver two proper sentences in succession, however brief, in the Latin tongue, although the Rule saith : *The abbot should be learned in God's law, so that he may be able to bring forth things new and old.* Nay, whensoever they are called together by the Bishop or his Vicar for any conference, one speaketh for all in the vulgar tongue." [46]

In 1441 the Benedictine Chapter at Nürnberg decreed that the proclamation of the Council of Basel against flesh-eating in monasteries " should be publicly read in refectory at meal-times during Lent, and explained in the vernacular." [47] Cardinal Nicholas Cusanus [1450] deposed the abbot of St. Michael at Hildesheim " by reason of his complete ignorance of the Latin tongue." [48] The same cardinal, in his Provincial Council of Mainz (1451), complained that men were smuggled into canonries who could not speak Latin.[49] The Spanish synod of Aranda (1473) decreed that no man should be ordained who did not comprehend the Latin speech.[50] The *Livre de Sapience*, printed at Geneva in 1478 and edited by a Cluniac monk, advertised itself as intended for the use of the " simples prestres qui n'entendent ni le latin ni les escriptures," as well as " pour le salut des simples gens lays." In 1530, at Montier-la-Celle in Champagne, the monks were evidently accustomed to speak of their drinking-vessels not in Latin but in French.[51]

Moreover, one of the most frequent of episcopal injunctions to monasteries, during the century before the Reformation, is that they should hire a master to give the novices and younger monks some sort of instruction in Latin. This was, in fact, one of Benedict XII.'s explicit statutes ; yet it is not uncommon to find visitors reporting, as at the great cathedral abbey of Durham about 1390, " there is no cloister-master to teach the monks in the rudiments of learning, to wit, grammar, logic and philosophy." The clerics deputed to help the priest-monks at their Masses were " almost illiterate, unable to say the *confiteor* or the *misereatur.*" [52] There was no Latin-master at Norwich Cathedral in 1514, or at the almost equally great monastery of Walsingham in 1526.[53] At a visitation of Norwich Cathedral, in 1520, one of the monks was bidden to read, and it was found that he " understood nothing." If such injunctions are rare or non-existent in the case of the smaller abbeys and ordinary priories, this was probably because such houses were scarcely seriously expected to conform to the statute. In the visitations by bishops of Lincoln, between 1420 and 1436, we find six injunctions for English translation to the monks, " lest any of you should be able to plead ignorance of the same." [54] And, about this same time, Latin chartularies were translated into English, for business use, not only on behalf of the nuns of Godstow but also for the great abbey of Oseney, at the very gates of Oxford.[55] In 1519, Bishop Bothe held a synod of the clergy of his diocese (Hereford). He drew up a series of articles for their reform, and caused one of his senior clergy to translate them into the vulgar tongue, " for the easier and fuller understanding thereof." [56]

In the case of nuns, these translations are less surprising than in that of the monks. Professor R. W. Chambers has recently pointed out that English was the natural language for the hermits of the twelfth century ; and that Capgrave [1440] wrote his life of St. Gilbert in English " for the solitarye women which unneth can undyrstand Latin." So, again, about the same time, one of the Sheen Carthusians compiled a vernacular Life of Christ for a nun ; and on a later page Professor Chambers gives seven similar instances.[57] At no period was the average nun a good Latinist : it seems certain now that the *Ancien Riwle* was first written in English. In the later Middle Ages, disciplinarians fell back more and more frankly upon the vernacular for the religious education of nuns. From the mid-fifteenth century onwards, we find an increasing number of versions for the special use of cloistered women. The orthodox ecclesiastical translators are very plain-spoken here. As one of them puts it, " they learn no Latin in their youth " ; another : " Women of Religion, in reading books of Latin, be excused of great understanding " ; and yet another : " Forasmuch as many of you, though ye can sing and read, yet ye cannot see what the meaning thereof is." Finally, Bishop Fox of Winchester, in 1517, caused the Rule to be translated for the use of nuns, and gave as his reason : " The reading [among nuns] is always done in the Latin tongue, whereof they have no knowledge nor understanding but be utterly ignorant of the same." Until the reforms of Abbot Thomas de la Mare [1350] the nuns of Delapré " were in great part illiterate, and said no services, but instead of each of the Church hours they repeated certain Paternosters and Ave Marias." The convent had no service-books ; Thomas endowed them by taking six or seven volumes from the St. Albans precentor's store.[58] The evidence collected by Professor Eileen Power fully bears out her conclusion : " The majority of nuns during this period [of the later Middle Ages] knew no Latin. . . . Even in the greatest houses, where the nuns were drawn from the highest social classes and might be supposed to be best educated, the knowledge of Latin was dying out." [59] We have very clear evidence on this point from Bishop Fox of Winchester, the Founder of Corpus Christi College at Oxford.

In 1517, he caused the Rule to be translated into English
for nunneries, because in these "the reading is always
done in the Latin tongue, whereof they have no knowledge nor understanding, but are utterly ignorant of
the same." [60]

The foregoing evidence is strongly corroborated by
the official visitations of Lincoln diocese on the verge of
the Reformation, which the generosity of Professor
Hamilton Thompson has enabled me to see in transcript.
These will soon be printed by the Lincoln Record
Society, the houses visited being arranged alphabetically
and chronologically. Thus my statements can be easily
verified.

At Dorchester, in 1517, the Rule was read aloud in
English once a year, and every Saturday in Latin. One
canon complained that it ought to be expounded in
English. At Oseney, in 1520, the visiting Bishop notes,
as though by exception, that he preached his sermon
to the brethren in Latin : but to one of them, imprisoned
for contumacy, and to the assembled chapter, " exhorta-
tionem saluberrimam partim latine partim vulgari elo-
quio fecit." In 1520, the Bishop preached to the Godstow
nuns in English. In 1520 Bishop Atwater made his
statutory visitation at Bicester Priory. "He delivered a
most salutary exhortation to the Prior and the brethren
in the vulgar tongue." So again at Daventry ; so
did Bishop Longland at Burnham nunnery (p. 131), and
Atwater at Catesby. At Ashby, in 1520, the Vicar-
General preached *in vulgari*; in 1530, *partim latine, partim
in vulgari*. At Stixwold (1525) Longland preaches
sermone vulgari, and evidently the witnesses speak English.
At Fotheringhay (1530) long English speeches by witnesses are recorded. At Elstow (1531) the answers

of all the nuns to the Bishop's inquiries are reported in English. At Higham Ferrers (1520) the rule of Latin speech in refectory has fallen into abeyance. A Fellow of Lincoln College, Oxon, has to make a public apology to the Bishop for disobedience ; this is in English. In these, as in other visitations, it sometimes transpires that there is no grammar-master. At Caldwell priory, in 1530, the episcopal visitation showed that " they have no instructor in grammar " ; " and because the Sacrist, Dom William Newport, confessed that he could not construe the Lord's Prayer, therefore the Lord Bishop removed him from his office." Of all monks, the Sacrist has perhaps least excuse for not knowing Latin.

CHAPTER II

NUNS, LAYFOLK, AND PARSONS

WE must not infer, I think, that nuns in 1500 were less instructed than in 1200. They may possibly have been less familiar with Latin at the latter than at the former date ; but, pretty certainly, the main cause for this multiplication of translations was the growing conviction in all but the most conservative minds that the old system, after long trial, was manifestly breaking down. Men were beginning to realize that real excellence in a second language is very difficult for every man ; in most cases it is insuperably difficult. Nothing can entirely efface the first impressions of childhood ; and we may apply here the Italian proverb : " She who professes more to us than a mother, is a deceiver." The Church, in imposing upon western Europe one single learned language, had as difficult a task as to impose clerical celibacy or to check clerical capitalism and luxury : the old Adam often proved unconquerable. We may safely use the word *impose*, since there are traces of this policy already in the eighth century, and it becomes commanding and undisguised in the eleventh. At Charles the Great's Synod of Frankfort, in 794, the 52nd decree ran " That God is not such as may be prayed to in three languages only "—by which Hebrew, Greek, and Latin seem clearly meant. What is implied here becomes evident in 1079, when we find the hierarchy had insisted upon the maintenance of a linguistic *status quo* which had at first been reached by spontaneous evolution, aided by no more than natural encouragement from the clergy. In that year, 1079, the King of Bohemia besought Gregory VII. to allow the translation of the Latin liturgy into that Slavonic tongue which the people could comprehend ; and the great Pope answered him in the tone of " ye know not what ye ask." He writes : " For it is clear to those who reflect often upon it, that not without reason has it pleased Almighty God that Holy Scripture should be a secret in certain places, lest, if it were plainly apparent to all men, perchance it would be little esteemed and would be subject to disrespect ; or it might be falsely understood by those of mediocre learning, and lead to error." [1] This pronouncement gains added significance from the fact that at an earlier date, when Rome and Constantinople had striven in rivalry for ecclesiastical supremacy in newly-Christianized Bulgaria (879), Rome had won these converts to her side by permitting them to use a liturgy in their own Slavonic tongue ; but " this permission was withdrawn as soon as her position in this district was firmly established." [2] Gregory VII., therefore, did no more than confirm, with the full weight of his authority, a prejudice which can be traced a long way farther back. When, for instance, Notker of St. Gallen sent some of his translations to the humanistic Bishop of Sion, he was fully conscious that this was a bold departure. He wrote to the Bishop : " I know that you will shrink from them as being unusual ; but little by little they will begin to commend themselves to you, and you will soon manage to read them [*praevalebis ad legendum*], and will recognize how quickly we can understand by means of our mother-tongue what can be understood only with difficulty, or not at all, in a foreign language." [3] We shall see presently how, long after the date at which the vernacular had become a tolerable or even excellent medium for translations, this same prejudice against any vulgarization of the learned language was very powerful. The Church, which had so long been foster-mother, felt a good nurse's natural jealousy. She magnified her office. Latin was the language in which the Bible and the Liturgy had survived, with almost the only other books in which western Europe had been interested during and after the barbarian invasions ; and, as Rashdall says, " the grossest ignorance of the Dark Ages was not due to the strength of the ecclesiastical system but to its weakness." [4] Therefore it was natural that the Church, in her immensely strong organization of the later Middle Ages, should have struggled to retain her grasp even when this threatened to become a strangle-hold. This academic jealousy rather increased as time went on ; or, at any rate, the friction increased. The words *litterae, litteratus, litteraliter* are generally referred exclusively to Latin ; even *legere* and the English *rede* seem sometimes to bear that exclusive meaning. The difficulties of translators are brought out in Miss M. Deanesly's *Lollard Bible*, pp. 23, 74–5, 101–108, 329 (*cf.* p. 161). At the end of the fourteenth century, we not only find John Purvey forced to an elaborate apology for unlocking the Bible from this sacred language, but Trevisa arguing at even greater length against the pundits who cried *Sacrilege !* upon his translation of Higden's chronicle. The author of that Gospel version published by Miss A. Paues is humbly apologetic ; and even Sir David Lyndsay feels bound to excuse himself in his *Buke of the Monarche* [1540].

For, by this time, the question had become inextricably entangled with religious prejudices. During many centuries there had been a class-dictatorship in literature ; Latin scholarship had been almost exclusively clerical ; therefore it was natural that the clergy should hold up the warning text of *pearls before swine* in defence against all encroachments.[5] In this they were greatly helped, no doubt, by the general attitude of the laity themselves, who had made little resistance against the gradual drift of the liturgy away from their comprehension ; or, more properly speaking, against their own drift away from this liturgy of immemorial antiquity. St. Francis, we know, possessed Latin only " after a fashion " in early manhood.[6] Brother Simon of Assisi never learned Latin at all.[7] The Lady Margaret, founder of two colleges, " had a little perceiving [of Latin], specially by the rubric of the ordinal for the saying of service, which she did well understand." [8] The lay brethren of the Cistercians were forbidden to learn Latin after entering the Order ; so also were the Franciscan nuns.[9]

We find that even a nobleman, religious enough to have taken the monastic vows as a lay-brother, was so ignorant of Latin as not to understand the Hours of the Blessed Virgin.[10] Among the Dominicans, the lay-brethren needed to know no more Latin than the *Paternoster* and *Credo* ; as for grace after meals, " let them who know it say the *miserere mei Deus*." [11] On the other hand, a document of 1387 shows that, among fourteen laymen of the upper class called as witnesses in an important case, eleven were described as *litterati*.[12] But Winchester was then specially

41

well off for scholars.[13] In any case, it was a revival rather than a survival. The gulf between the laity and the Liturgy (except, of course, so far as the general sense and the main intention were concerned) had been very deep for centuries past. Lot's frank description is not really exaggerated (page 121) : "never did the Church allow the Liturgy to follow the evolution of the language. The inevitable danger of becoming less and less comprehensible to the faithful layfolk, even to those who spoke 'Romance' languages, seemed less grave to her than any modification, however slight, in the form of the consecrated words. Moreover, the divorce between the officiant and the public worked only insensibly : the faithful long continued to hold dialogues with the priest before men perceived that they were talking to each other without understanding." And he adds : "Nowadays the faithful have the translation facing the Latin text in their Mass-books. But the singing-clerks have nothing of the kind ; yet this does not prevent their chanting, sometimes for their whole life long, without understanding anything of what they say, or even feeling the need of comprehension."

The *Lay-Folk's Mass-Book* (1150, translated into English about 1300) "shows clearly that the Gospel was read only in Latin, and that the layman, though not understanding it, was taught to hear it with the greatest reverence." This dualism, strange to modern notions, was encouraged by the growing emphasis laid upon all the sacraments *ex opere operato* ; *i.e.* their effect even upon an entirely passive recipient ; upon all who do not consciously and deliberately strive against the sacramental effect. It was in unison with this belief, when the gulf between the Latinist and the Latinless classes became more and more sensible, that the priest should ascribe similar virtues, *ex opere operato*, to mere attendance at Mass ; and, just as the Bible text of *pearls before swine* justified the layman's exclusion from this Latin Holy of Holies, so the parable of *the deaf adder* was cited for his consolation while he waited outside at the gate. The fifteenth-century manual of devotion entitled *Merita Missae* teaches that " the laity are to stand [at the Gospel] out of reverence ; and they will receive grace by simply hearing the Gospel without understanding it, just as an adder is affected by the charm pronounced over her, though she does not understand the words." [14] One of the most popular anecdotes for preachers was that which is first recorded by Cæsarius of Heisterbach [1230]. A lady, a confirmed invalid, constantly called for help upon St. Thomas of Canterbury. Her pet bird thus picked up the words by rote ; and, one day, as a kite swooped down upon him, he cried, " St. Thomas, help me ! " The kite fell dead to the ground.[15]

So much, then, for the indirect evidence drawn from these translations ; valuable even in its indirectness because it is so undesigned. Let us pass on now to consider the more direct evidence. Here, we may have to make allowance in many cases for the character and prejudices of the witness ; but in others the person is altogether above suspicion ; and others again are perfectly cold and impersonal ; not voices but facts. Their unanimity will probably strike the reader much as it has struck me.

Charles the Great was scandalized by that Latin which monks, with the best intentions, wrote in their official letters to him : " while pious devotion dictated the sentiments, the unlettered tongue was unable to express them aright. Hence there has arisen in our minds the fear lest, if the skill to write were thus lacking, so too would the power of rightly comprehending the Sacred Scriptures be far less than was fitting." [16] Again, in one of his capitularies of the year 802, he felt bound to prescribe that priests should be examined to see " whether they knew how to change special Masses, whether for the living or for the dead, in a reasonable way [*rationabiliter*] and so as to suit either sex, in the singular number or in the plural." [17] Charles's minister, Alcuin, wrote to the great English monasteries of Wearmouth and Jarrow, at a time when English scholarship was at a comparatively high level, prescribing that, when the Rule of St. Benedict was read, " it should be expounded in your own tongue, in order that it may be understood by all." [18] At the end of this same century, our King Alfred complained how " the churches throughout the whole of England stood filled with treasures and books, and there was also a great multitude of God's servants [*Godes thiowa*] but they had very little knowledge of the books ; for they could not understand anything of them, because they were not written in their own language." [19] In [884], Pope Marinus rebuked Sico, Bishop of Capua, as a man " ignorans studia litterarum." [20] William of Malmesbury, doubtless with a certain contemptuous exaggeration, described our pre-conquest English clergy as having lapsed into ignorance. " Contented with a hasty smattering of [Latin] letters, they scarce stammered the words of the Sacraments ; he who knew grammar was a marvel and a miracle to the rest." Here, of course, " know grammar " means the ability to read a classical author with any ease. [21] Here, no doubt, we must make for William's contemptuous rhetoric that allowance which is demanded by Professor Stenton's recent studies ; moreover, our country had not yet come into the stream of the Cluniac revival. Let us turn, therefore, to Cluny itself, at almost the height of its fame and efficiency, as displayed in the *Customal* of about 1070.

Here, although so much of the monk's work was in choir, careful provision is made for illiteracy. Theoretically, the Psalter was chanted by heart. But, as modern monks will tell us, this often amounts, at the best, only to being able to keep company with others who are chanting the same words ; few could repeat a psalm as they can repeat the Creed. In the Middle Ages, there was evidently a considerable residuum who never approached to this theoretical standard. So, in this Cluny customal, it is provided that two monks may absent themselves from the conventual Mass for kitchen-work, " and especially if any of them are illiterate " [*idiotae*]. We may assume that enough came under this category to supply a series of shifts ; otherwise those two, or their few fellows, would very seldom hear Mass at all. Again, one monk presided at the redistribution of clothes after the yearly washing by the fullers : " Let him sit so that he may watch lest any brother, especially one illiterate [*idiota*] should be so negligent as to take others than those whereon his own name is inscribed ; for this also is a decree of our fathers, that none should omit the inscribing of his name with ink on his woollen shirt and with thread on his drawers." [22] Similar precautions are to be found in the later *Customal* of Abingdon, at a time when it was among the most efficient of English houses [1250].[23] One of the most important of the conventual officials was the almoner. Yet here, again, there is careful provision for ignorance : " he shall be excused from none of the conventual duties unless he be illiterate "—*nisi illiteratus fuerit*.[24] The constitutions of the great German reform of Hirschau [1070] make similar allowances for illiterate [*idiotae*] monks.[25]

Abbot Daniel of Holme was a favourite of King Stephen, who, " if he had known how to sing Mass, would have made him Archbishop of Canterbury." [26] It is true that Nicholas Brakespear, the future Pope, was refused admittance to St. Albans in early life ; and a great and exclusive monastery like the cathedral priory of Canterbury might refuse a young postulant because he could not read Latin properly, as we know to have been the case in 1324 ; [27] yet it is evident that these cannot be taken as typical. At the great abbey of St.-Bertin, in 1246, the monks had to hire an outside master for their young brethren, in face of the " want of literature " from which the majority of the community suffered.

It was in the twelfth century that the current of the Cluniac revival flowed most strongly ; and the episcopal cities of northern France were in the full stream. From this date we have the evidence of Abbot Guibert of Nogent, a younger contemporary and friend of Saint Anselm. Guibert, in his autobiography, tells us of the wonderful improvement in schools during his own day, for he lived at the beginning of this twelfth-century Renaissance. But we must take these words in connection with what he says of his boyhood : " there was scarce a single town of ordinary size that had a grammar-master, and very few cities had one." [28] In another place, he tells us how a deputation of clergy from the diocese of Laon, in 1106, went to Langres to discuss an episcopal election with the Pope. The Pope asked us, says Guibert, why we had elected this man. " Whereunto none of the priests answered, for some of them scarce knew the elements of Latin ; so that he turned to the [three] Abbots." The senior abbots compelled Guibert, the youngest, to speak for them, " for the discussion was carried on, not in the vernacular, but in Latin." [29] Scarcely less significant is the praise which Guibert lavishes upon this pope's predecessor, Urban II., as a man of most unusual accomplishments ; " for he seemed no less fertile in his command of the Latin tongue than any fluent advocate can be in his mother-tongue." [30] The very praise shows how rare and exceptional it was even for a pope to command Latin completely as a vernacular.

John Beleth, in the preface to his *Rationale Divinorum Officiorum* [1170], implies that priests also are included in his list of those who do not understand the gospels at Mass, so that " scarcely or not at all may there be found any man who understands what he reads or hears read." [31] His contemporary, Abbot Philippe de Harvengt [1170] tells us that it is possible to find priests who " not only know not to make a speech in Latin without mistakes, but perchance not even to sing their Compline correctly without assistance." [32] Two generations later, *Customals* were compiled for the two great abbeys of Westminster and St. Augustine's, Canterbury, which are almost identical on most of the main points. In both of these, it is provided that novices shall make their formal demand for admission, not in Latin, but in the French of upper-class daily life. The lay-brother, again, might use French even for the solemn formula of profession itself, though this is prescribed to be read from a slip in Latin, "if he be literate, even to a slight degree"— *si fuerit, quamvis paulisper, litteratus*—yet he may make it in French, or even, at a pinch, in English. Yet this formula, which might prove of insuperable difficulty to the young monk, in the days when the great choir of Westminster was in its freshest and greatest glory, was of a brevity and simplicity which may be judged by the corresponding French : "Je, frère N, promets estableté et chasteté et honnête conversation devant Dieu et tous ses saints ; et que je serai obédient et vivrai sans propriété tant comme j'aurai à vivre." [33] So was it also (to anticipate chronologically for a moment) at Tywardreth, where the whole dialogue is written in the Calendar in a fifteenth-century hand.

"*Prior.* What desire ye ?

Novice. To be mad Broder.

Prior. Ys hit your wyl and yow hertely desyre to be parte taker of all massis and prayers and almys dede done yn holy place, or schall be done here after ?

Novice. Ye.

Prior. Al so ys hit your wille to defende and to manteyne the righte of this holy plas to your power, whereby God and Synt Androw may be the pesabeler servyd by your worde and godewille, as a trewe broder otghte to do ?

Novice. Ye." [34]

Caesarius of Heisterbach [1230] tells of a miracle performed upon a priest who was so ignorant that he could say only one Mass, viz. that of Our Lady. [35] Humbert de Romans [1240], in his commentary on the Augustinian Rule, speaking of the admission of unworthy postulants, writes : "for it is right that Religious should be such as can understand competently the things

48

which are written in books." [36] His contemporary, Roger Bacon, when he wishes to give a universally comprehensible illustration of mere parrot-learning, writes : " just as boys gabble through the psalter which they have learnt ; and as clerks and country priests recite the church services (of which they know little or nothing) like brute beasts." [37] Another contemporary, the Franciscan Rubruquis, employs almost the same words when he comes to describe the Nestorian clergy whom he found in China. " They say their offices and have their sacred books in Syriac, but they do not know the language ; so they chant like those monks among us [in Europe] who do not know grammar." [38] It is extraordinarily significant that both these writers should pitch naturally upon this analogy as best suited to bring home to their readers an example of crass ignorance. Again, St. Thomas Aquinas writes of " the inexperience of many priests, who in some parts [of the Roman Church] are found to be so ignorant that they cannot even speak Latin ; moreover, very few can be found who have learned Holy Scripture."

Sinibaldo Fieschi (afterwards Innocent IV.) was one of the great canon lawyers of the Middle Ages. In his *Commentary on the Decretals* [1240] he comes to the question of the clergy and Latin (Lib. I., *de Elect,* rub. 6, c. 7. Ed. Turin, 1581, *f.* 19b.) He writes : " However, the man who is altogether *illiteratus* ought not to be ordained to any Order. If however he be ordained, it may then be said that he is a cleric. . . . But if [such clerics] be wanting in knowledge, and there is hope that they may improve, they may be promoted, but not if there be no hope of them, unless the church be such as cannot afford to lack their counsel and help, or unless they be monks or hermits, who need contemplation more than knowledge." [39]

In 1274, the year of St. Thomas's death, the Synod of Gerona issued the following decree (No. 25) : " That all beneficed clergy and all who are to be promoted to parish churches, and who cannot talk in Latin speech (except those whose age leaves no hope of their progress), be compelled to learn at some High School [*in studio*] by the bishop and archdeacon (where the archdeacon has been wont to possess this right) by deprivation of their benefices until they can speak Latin. But to those who are willing to study and profit in grammar, we indulge in our mercy that they may enjoy at the schools the fruits of their benefices for three years from the feast of St. John Baptist now at hand, even as though they were serving their churches, provided always that some one remains to serve the parish thus robbed of its due service. But he who, within these three years, has not cared to advance so far as to be able to speak Latin, and who has neglected to conquer his ignorance by study, let him be suspended from his benefice." The next sentence shows that there were *multi* who needed this spur to learning.[40]

The Council of Cologne, in 1260, had decreed that priests should at least know how to read and to sing God's praises. Those who cannot, must hire competent curates to do their duty.[41] In 1295 the Bishop of Winchester complained that " many ignorant and illiterate men, to the peril of their own souls, usurp the pastoral office " ; therefore archdeacons are to examine candidates on the Decalogue, the Seven Sacraments, and the Seven Deadly Sins, " and to see whether they know how to expound all these things to the layfolk in the vulgar tongue." The clerk who compiled this bishop's own register was evidently a very incorrect Latinist himself.[42]

The founder of Merton College (1264) made special arrangements for grammar teaching there, because he "perceived that the clergy of England were, for the most part, mere stammerers in the Latin tongue,"[43] and so they could not profit by the university lectures. The same complaint was made in an almost contemporaneous statute of the Cistercian General Chapter (1306); many of their young monks are sent up to the university unprepared in Latin.[44] At Cambridge, as elsewhere, there was an official grammar-school, under a "Master of Glomery," for scholars who knew too little Latin to profit by the lectures.[45] In 1441, William Byngham founded "God's House" at Cambridge in order to remedy the "decay" of "seventy [grammar] schools or more" which he had found on a recent journey from Southampton to Ripon.[46] Yet perhaps things went rather better in the southern countries, where Romance tongues were spoken, and therefore Latin came far more easily. The friar Salimbene of Parma, telling us how he entered the Franciscan Order in 1238 at the age of fifteen, boasts that he had been taught and drilled in grammar from "my very cradle."[47]

In 1284, Archbishop Pecham complained that the clergy in Wales were almost as illiterate as the layfolk.[48] In 1308 the St. Albans monks elected Hugh for their abbot, who attempted to get excused from the voyage to Rome for personal confirmation, "seeing that he feared nothing more than the Latin tongue, wherein he had but little learning"—*in qua parum doctus fuit*.[49] Bishop Guillaume Durand, in his memorial to the Council of Vienne (1311), recurs twice to this plague of clerical ignorance. He writes: "Another remedy might be employed against the ignorance of the clergy . . . that the First Tonsure be conferred upon none except such as know how to read and sing competently." Again, "that none be promoted to Orders, whether secular or regular clerics, unless they know how to sing and read well and competently according to [their art], and can understand Latin and speak it properly" [congrue]. At present, he complains, men see "insufficient and illiterate youths" promoted, by undue influence, above their betters.[50] Marsilius of Padua (1324) speaks in one place of the number of illiterati who enjoy clerical privileges; and twice, far more strongly, of illiteracy among even priests and prelates.[51] He writes: "I call God to witness, and the multitude of the faithful, that I have seen and remember to have heard very many [plurimos] priests, abbots and some prelates of the Church so paltry [diminutos] that they could not even speak according to grammar." Again, after complaining that not one bishop or archbishop in ten is a competent theologian, he adds: "But concerning the rest of the inferior prelates, abbots and priors of monasteries and other parsons of churches, I call God to witness, who is Truth Immortal, that a numerous multitude of these is lacking in life and learning sufficient [to their rank], so that very many of them cannot even utter grammatical speech [in Latin]" —sic etiam ut grammatice nesciant ipsorum quamplures congruum proferre sermonem.

In the fourteenth century, we find an early Scottish Church statute "that there be no rector or vicar who does not possess all the synodal decrees, and cannot read and understand them (since a consequence is that through their ignorance of them our officials and archdeacons are often put to trouble) and that they be brought every year to the synod ; and this we decree under a penalty of forty shillings." [52] In 1338, the Chapter of Rouen cathedral granted a franc in alms to a nun of the diocese of Thérouanne whose convent had been destroyed in the wars, and who *loquebatur bene latinum* : this was evidently a distinction in a nun.[53] Grandisson of Exeter (1357), an exceptionally energetic and efficient bishop, supplies valuable incidental evidence. He found that the grammar-school boys of his diocese were simply learning portions of the Latin services by heart, and even that imperfectly.[54] Among the Carmelites themselves, who, as friars, were notoriously more learned than the Benedictines and other older Orders, the General Chapter of 1362 drew a formal distinction between " the brethren who can talk Latin " and the rest.[55]

The emphasis with which Knighton describes the frequent ignorance of Latin among the clergy ordained just after the Black Death bears testimony not only to the exceptional difficulties of those years but also to the small reserve of Latin-readers among the three or four millions of our then population. If students at either the universities or the grammar-schools had been numerous and efficient, there could have been no such difficulty in finding candidates for the priesthood who could understand the Latin of their service-books.[56] But the contemporary Lollard, John Purvey, in his preface to the Wycliffite Bible, claims to have read a sermon of Bishop Grosseteste [1250] recommending the parish priest to " con the gross story " of the Sunday gospel " and tell it to his people, that is, if he understand Latin. . . . If forsooth he understood no Latin, go he to one of his neighbours that understandeth, which will charitably expound it to him." [57] In 1373, the Pope granted to John Aberkoldor, who was already vicar of the important parish church of Aberdeen, " if found fit after examination in Latin, a benefice with cure of souls (or without cure of souls if he were found unable to sing Latin and did not swear to learn) in the common or several gift of the abbot and convent of Arbroath." [58] The author of *Piers Plowman* [1380] paints the priest who knows better how to find a hare in the furrow than "to construe one clause well [in the Psalms] and ken it to my parishioners." [59] He also complains of the growing ignorance of " grammar " in his generation.[60] In the *Somnium Viridarii* (1376), the friar in his dispute with the knight speaks contemptuously of the village clergy, whom he calls " ânes déferrés de Limoges ou d'Auvergne." [61] In 1379, William of Wykeham founded his college at Winchester to supply adequate training in Latin, because " experience had shown . . . that students in the other arts often fell into peril through lack of good teaching and sufficient learning in grammar." [62] By rubric 58 of the foundation-charter, one of the chaplains was required to learn grammar and to be able to write, in order to assist the treasurer in transcribing Latin evidence.[63] At this Bishop's third visitation of the cathedral priory of Winchester (A.D. 1387), he complains that " some monks and brethren of the cathedral have little knowledge of Latin [*literaturae*], not understanding what they read, but being almost wholly ignorant of letters." [64] At about this same time, a manual was composed to assist the ordinary parish clergy in teaching their parishioners, by John Myrc, a canon of Lilleshall. Though it deals on every page with ministerial technicalities, it is written in English and—what is more—in rhyme. (*Early English Text Soc.* 1868.) Its prefatory lines explain that it is written for the "priest curatour" of a parish. At almost exactly the same time, again, between 1395 and 1404, the Augustinian Chapter gave instructions to its visitors to inquire in every monastery, among other things, "Whether any [of the cloisterers] does not understand the Canon of the Mass or the words of Consecration of the Host." [65] Again, the Augustinian Chapter of 1434 decreed as follows : "Seeing that the youth of our Order in these days and in divers monasteries are, as we are informed, altogether idle and disorderly and exceedingly indisciplined, let them be duly compelled to honest study in their cloisters by their superiors, according to the constitutions of Pope Benedict XII. ; and let a fit master be provided for this purpose, who is able to teach them in the trivium, and especially in grammar—*in primitivis scientiis et potissime in grammatica.*" [66] A similar statute had been passed by the Cistercians in 1306 ; and henceforth we find the Cistercian General Chapter decreeing frequently against this defect. In 1432 they ordered that each monastery should have its grammar-master, or at least that neighbouring monasteries should join to keep one. In 1445, they complain : "In these last days [of the world] abbots are compelled to admit to the vows even untaught and illiterate boys, whence it cometh to pass that many persons [in our Order] can neither understand nor read Latin [*litteras*]." Yet at the same time they stoutly maintain their papal privilege of presenting monks for ordination without examination by the Bishop ! In 1460 it is again decreed that masters be instituted to instruct the ignorant in grammar ; and, though the General Chapter records become far rarer after this date, we have abundant evidence that the Order rather went back than improved between 1460 and the Reformation.[67] By that time we get more explicit evidence again for the Augustinians. At the General Chapter of 1518, the select preacher said before his brethren : " We see not without grief of mind, and to the no small dishonour of your Order, that there are very few of you, indeed scarce any, who delight as they should in the study of good letters and of true learning."[68]

Let us now go back again to the early years of the fifteenth century. We find the prior of Cluny writing, with reference to the ordinary parish vicar of his day : " What sort of learning has he in Scripture or in Canon Law, when perhaps he does not even understand the first words of the Creed, or cannot speak Latin ? "[69] Johann Busch, the great monastic reformer [1450] mentions casually the provision which was made at his own model monastery of Windesheim : [70] " Before all our guests, as well priests as clerics [tam presbyteris quam clericis], we always put books of Holy Scripture [divine pagine] at mealtimes with their bread, in order that they may refresh their minds also while at their bodily food. But if they cannot read, then our hostellar [reads to them] from the Book of the Four Last Things, written on parchment in the vulgar tongue, which we always lay before common clerics and simple layfolk at their table." When he was present at a disputation for the Doctorate of Divinity at Leipzig, he was astonished at the time wasted on both sides by pointing out blunders in Latin.[71] Cardinal Pierre d'Ailly pleaded before the Council of Constance that the ignorance of Latin and Greek at the universities was a scandal to the Church.[72]

His contemporary Jean Gerson advised that more care should be taken in conferring Holy Orders : " Let candidates know how to speak Latin competently, and understand it." Dionysius Cartusianus [1430] represents a pluralist canon as confessing the shortcomings of his whole class.[73] He says : " We run hastily through divine service and we so gabble our reading, our prayers and our psalmody as scarce to pronounce the separate words." Again, he tells us that the priests' own service-books " are frequently and in many places incorrect." In yet another place, he repeats from Caesarius of Heisterbach the story of Becket's leniency towards the good priest who could say only one Mass.[74]

St. John Capistrano, in 1444, addressed a circular letter to the Observantine Franciscans, of whom he was then Vicar-General. He presses upon the reformed convents the necessity of further reform, especially in the matter of learning. He writes : " both priests and clerics ought to know at least so much of grammar that they can recite the divine service rightly, purely, and not inexactly ; that they can pronounce the words correctly, according both to the letter and to the intention, and that they shall at least understand the literal meaning of that which they read." The whole context of his letter implies that this standard was by no means always attained.[75] In 1446, the official visitors appointed by the General Chapter of the Augustinian Canons refused to visit the monasteries in Wales because of the unknown tongue ; and, though the General Chapter repeated its command : " Let not the unknown language stand in the way, since the Latin tongue is presumed to be common both to visitors and to visited," yet the objection could never have been raised if there had not been some reality in it.[76] The Oxford Chancellor Gascoigne [1450] attributed Cade's rebellion partly to the public indignation felt at " the unworthy promotion of evil and youthful candidates for the Church, who, as I know, are not even able to speak Latin "—*quos ego novi jam nescire loqui Latinum*.[77] At St. Albans, in 1452, " for many years past the young cloisterers had had no learned master who could teach them sufficiently in grammar " ; and Abbot Whethamstede set himself vigorously to reform this.[78] The abbot's own Latin, however, was not faultless ; Bishop Beckynton rebuked him for his pompous style and defective grammar.[79] When, in 1461, an attempt was made to deprive Philip Nogul, priest, of the chancellorship of Ferns as a man " so ignorant of letters that he cannot speak Latin properly," this was not considered sufficient in itself : the petitioner adds that he cannot speak the Irish language either, and that he is a notorious fornicator.[80]

The Observantine Franciscan, Angelo da Chivasso [1450], in his manual of Canon Law, asks, " May an altogether illiterate person—*omnino illiteratus*—be ordained ? He answers with Innocent IV.'s very guarded affirmative, and adds : This is supported by what we read [Gratian, *Decretum*, II., causa xvi., q. l., c. 36] where Joannes [Andreæ] comments : ' It is enough for a monk that he be good, even though he be illiterate.' " And Angelo quotes other glossators who decide " that illiteracy does not prohibit a Religious from promotion [to Orders]." [81]

Abbot Johann v. Trittenheim (Trithemius) wrote about 1490 : " Although it is not my business to correct these things, yet I cannot refrain from grief when I see how all the evils in the Church proceed from the ignorance of the priests." And again, "Let the Bishops see to this, who promote such ignorant and unlearned men to the priesthood. . . . They know nothing whatever of the Scriptures ; they scorn to learn. They know not how to write or speak Latin ; they have scarce learnt to expound the gospels [for Sundays and feast-days] in the vulgar tongue." [82] The great cathedral-preacher of Strassburg, Geiler v. Kaysersberg, complained of " those most ignorant confessors who cannot speak three words of Latin—a fact which is only too notorious." [83] His contemporary, Barclay, writes of university students :

> " But of gramer knowe they lytyll or no thynge,
>   whiche is the grounde of all lyberall cunnynge.
> Yet many ar besy in Logyke and in Lawe,
>   whan all theyr gramer is skarsly worth a strawe." [84]

David, Bishop of Utrecht, " had heard that, among so many who took Holy Orders, there were very few who were educated—*paucissimos esse qui litteras scirent.*" *Litterae* almost certainly means in this place, as in many others, " Latin." Therefore he conducted his own ordination examination himself, and found only three candidates out of 300 who were sufficient for their profession. He was at length compelled to pass the rest, because he found that no better could be found at the starvation wages of a sixteenth-century curate.[85] In St. Thomas More's *Comfort against Tribulation*, the nephew tells how he found himself at a great prelate's table next to " an unlearned priest, for he could speak no Latin at all," but had to talk in German. There is nothing in the tale or the context to suggest any surprise at this ignorance.[86] Elsewhere More writes : " Remember ye not how in our own time, of all that taught grammar in England, not one understood the Latin tongue ? " [87] By this he means very much what Geiler of Kaisersberg had meant in his criticism of the barbarous and un-grammatical Latin current among the clergy of his time.[88] Nor were these complaints merely from the point of view of literary purism ; it was a matter of great business importance also. The Council of Bourges, in 1528, while it recommended the imposition of heavy fines on clergy who absented themselves from diocesan synods, decreed also " that the synodal statutes now drawn up in Latin be translated into the vulgar tongue, and that synodal sermons be made in future in simpler form and in plainer speech, that the hearers may under-stand as much as possible thereof." [89] And a few years earlier, in 1511, Archbishop Warham had written to his monks of Canterbury cathedral : " Also a skilled teacher of grammar shall be provided to teach the novices and other youths grammar. For in default of such instruction it happens that most of the monks celebrating Mass and performing other divine service are wholly ignorant of what they read, to the great scandal and disgrace both of religion in general and the monastery in particular." [90] At Cranmer's visitation of Worcester cathedral priory in 1534 the Archbishop en-joins that there must be a regular teacher of Latin, " who shall every day diligently instruct and teach the younger monks in the knowledge of grammar." This was neglected, and Latimer, in 1537, had to repeat the injunction, " that he have a continual schoolmaster, sufficiently learned to teach you grammar." He summed up : " In this my visitation I evidentlie perceive the ignorance and negligence of dyvers religious persons in

this monasterie to be intolerable and not to be suffred." [91]
On page 439 of his *Educational Charters* Leach printed a
document less explicit, but very suggestive, concerning
the monks of Westminster at this time ; and about the
same time, in Germany, Wimpheling quotes a gross case
of Latin ignorance on the part of a monk who undertook
to confute Geiler v. Kaysersberg.[92] Clement VII., in
1529, dissolving St. Frideswide's monastery at Oxford,
explained in his bull that this was done in favour of
sana scientiarum studia.[93] In 1535, the abbot of Wardon
wrote to Cromwell his reasons for resignation ;
one was that his monks were contentedly ignorant.
"I caused bokes of gramer to be boughte for eche off
them, and assignidd mi brother to enstructe theim, but
ther wollde come non to him but one Richard Balldok
and Thomas Clement. Item, they be in nombre xv.
brethern, and except iii off theim non understand ne
knowe ther Rule nor the statutes off ther Religione."

It is true, the cloisterer theoretically chanted his psalms
by heart ; yet with all but the most learned in the
Middle Ages, as in modern times, this only meant that
he knew enough to sing with the rest as the psalmody
rolled along. At Norwich cathedral priory in 1526,
ten of the younger monks are found complaining " that
they are compelled by the superiors and their senior
brethren to commit to memory the psalms of the
psalter, together with anthems, responses and other
canticles, and to waste good hours in frequent recitation,
and this oftentimes when there is no need." " The
bishop felt that he must deliberate before answering
them." [94] The answer given by any antiquary of our
own day who should judge only from monastic theory,
would probably be simple and immediate ; but Bishop

Nicke, in the sixteenth century, who had to reconcile a
" somdel streit " Rule with actual practice, was diplo-
matically cautious. At Bec, in 1558, the Vicar-General
of the province admitted a modification ; the younger
monks were allowed to have books before them, instead
of chanting in the choir from memory, " as they had
formerly done, with great waste of time." [95]

For the nuns, we have a good deal of evidence. The
Clarisses' Rule provided that nuns who did not know
letters [*i.e.* Latin] should not learn them.[96] Gerson, in
his treatise of instruction to nuns, orders those who understand no Latin to form a habit of pious meditation while
they chant the psalms in choir.[97] Such nuns, it can
hardly be doubted, were the majority. In the late
thirteenth century, bishops sometimes sent their injunctions to nuns in French instead of Latin ; early in the
fourteenth, Bishop Stapeldon expects of the nuns of
Polsloe and Canonsleigh that they should speak Latin
not with grammatical inflexions, but only in isolated
words. In every generation, no doubt, there were nuns
who really understood their service-books and could
read the Bible, and sometimes we meet with sisters who
can truly be called learned. But apparently there was a
downward movement here during the later generations,
as there certainly was in numbers, in economics, and in
general discipline ; so that we may read Sir David Lyndsay with no discount beyond that which we ordinarily
take from a satirist. He writes :

" Therefore I thynk one gret dirisioun
   to heir Nunnis and Systeris nycht and day
   syngand [and] sayand psalmes and orisoun,
   nocht understandyng quhat they syng nor say,

But lyke ane stirling or ane papingay. . . .
It wer als plesand to thare spreit, in deid,
'God have mercy on me,' for to say thus,
As to say ' *Miserere Mei, Deus*.' " [98]

All this evidence goes to suggest that Dante's unfavourable verdict may be taken with no more allowance
for satirical rhetoric than we make for his criticisms of
contemporary life in other directions. In his *Convivio*
he reckons that, among the Latinists of his day, perhaps
one in a thousand loved that literature for its own sake.
As for the rest, " in report of them I say that they ought
not to be called lettered, because they do not acquire
literature for its own use, but just in so far as they may
gain money or office by it ; just as we ought not to call
him a harper who hath a harp in his house to hire out
for a price, and not to use it to play upon." Later on,
he recurs to the same subject : " We are not to call him
a real philosopher who is a friend of wisdom for profit,
as are lawyers, physicians, and almost all the members
of the Religious Orders [*quasi tutti li Religiosi*] who do
not study in order to know, but in order to get money
or office ; and if anyone would give them that which it
is their purpose to acquire they would linger over their
study no longer. And as amongst the different kinds of
friendship that which is for the sake of profit is least to
be called friendship, so these, such as I speak of, have
less share in the name of philosopher than any other folk."
Thus the long dominion of Latin was based to a great
extent on business considerations.[99] Rashdall was right in
pointing out that one of the main achievements of the universities in the later Middle Ages was that they trained
men for administrative work in Church and State.

Chapter III

TEST CASES : GROWTH OF VERNACULARS.

These judgments of contemporaries, and the general evidence confirming them, will gain even greater force if we turn now to specific and detailed cases, some of which, it will be seen, are recorded in the most cold-blooded official documents.

In 745 Pope Zacharias was scandalized to find that St. Boniface was rebaptizing those infants who had been baptized in bad Latin. The Pope quotes a specific case ; that of a Bavarian priest " who was utterly ignorant of the Latin tongue " and had said, " Baptizo te in nomine Patria et Filia et Spiritu sancta." But (says the Pope) seeing that this was done " merely from ignorance of the Roman speech," it cannot be considered as an invalid baptism.[1] There is no implication that either Boniface or the Pope looked upon such ignorance as highly exceptional ; on the contrary, both are seriously concerned with the very practical problem which it presents. Moreover, it is not likely that this is parallel with those Italian or Spanish cases, where incorrectness was partly born of fluency. Boniface, in his missionary work among the German forests, probably found himself in contact with a clergy whose culture, in its lowest stages, was almost negligible. Paulus Alvarus (Albarus) of Cordova, writing about 860, complained of Christian ignorance in contrast with Hebrew and Arab learning and literature. " Alas! the Christians know not their own law [or, by another reading, *language*] and the Latins pay no heed to their own tongue, so that, among the whole congregation of Christians, scarce one in a thousand can be found who can reasonably write letters of salutation to his brother. Yet we find an innumerable and multiple throng who give erudite explications of Chaldaic pomposities." [2] St. Peter Damian [1060] tells us of one priest who " could scarce stammer Latin syllable by syllable, and in rustic fashion." Another " could scarce read, syllable by syllable, one sentence of writing " in Latin. In his treatise, " Against the Ignorance and Carelessness of Parish Priests," he writes : " For nowadays, by reason of the sloth of the episcopal body, priests are to be found so ignorant of letters that not only they attain to no understanding of that which they read, but scarce, syllable by syllable, can they stammer out the very elements of a consecutive sentence. What indeed can that man pray for the people who himself, as a stranger, knoweth not what he saith ? (Migne, *Pathologica Latina*, clxv. coll. 126, 437, 712).

Even at the end of the twelfth century, when the revival of Latin studies was at its highest, Giraldus Cambrensis testifies to remarkable possibilities of priestly ignorance. Giraldus had a lively pen, and no doubt his stories do not lose in the telling ; but, on the other hand, he was a veteran Archdeacon, and one of his main professional duties was to examine the clergy. He twice speaks of clerical examinations as a farce.[3] He gives a very amusing description of the pidgin-Latin spoken by a certain anchorite.[4] No doubt such hermits were not professionally bound to know Latin, but priests

and monks were; and here Giraldus is the most explicit
of our purely literary witnesses. He assures us that he
speaks from personal knowledge, and gives startling
instances of the extent to which a prior could mis-
understand the language of the psalms. Again, he
describes the incapacity of two abbots to translate the
simplest passages from the Bible or the Missal : one of
them rendered the first words of the Mass Preface,
aequum et salutare (right and available to salvation) as
" the horse jumped "—*cheval saillavit*, as though it had
been *equus saltavit*.[5] Even stranger were the aberrations
of simple priests ; Giraldus gives fifteen examples, of
which two may here be quoted, not as the worst but
as the briefest and most intelligible. One priest, expounding the gospel story of the Canaanite woman, construed
the text as " the canine woman," and explained to his
flock that she was half-woman, half-dog. Another, in
face of Luke xxiv. 42, where the Latin has *de pisce
asso et favo mellis*, translated it " a piece of ass-fish and
honeyed beans," mistaking *assus* for *asinus* and *favus*
for *faba*.[6] Asked what was an ass-fish, he took refuge
in that time-honoured belief to which Andrew Marvell
alludes, according to which everything on earth has its
counterpart somewhere in the sea : therefore ass-fishes
in the ocean correspond to asses on land.[7] We might
be inclined to discount these as purely satirical—but
in fact they are equalled or outdone by official evidence.
Innocent III., at that great Lateran Council in 1215
which first proclaimed officially the dogma of tran-
substantiation, insisted strongly on the necessity of
combating priestly ignorance. It was probably an immediate consequence of this that we have the remarkable Sarum visitation of 1222. Examiners were sent

officially to seventeen livings in the gift of the Dean
and Chapter of that diocese. Five priests were found
unable to construe even the first sentence of the first
prayer in the Canon of the Mass—that is, in the essential
portion of that service. The first of these men " was
examined in the Gospel of the first Sunday in Advent,
and was found insufficient and unable to understand
what he read. Again he was tried in the Canon of the
Mass, at the words *Te igitur, clementissime Pater*, etc.*
He knew not the case of *Te*, nor by what word it was
governed ; and when we bade him look closely which
could most fittingly govern it, he replied : " *Pater*, for
He governeth all things." We asked him what *clementissime* was, and what case, and how declined ; he knew
not. We asked what *clemens* was ; he knew not . . .
he said that it seemed indecent that he should be examined
before the dean, since he was already in Holy Orders."
If it had not been for this unexceptionable business
record, we might have been inclined to dismiss as an
impossible exaggeration the similar story in St. Thomas
More's works, even though it be confessed in the face
of his adversary Tyndale. More quotes what was
evidently a proverbial case of " him that, because he
read in the Mass-book *Te igitur, clementissime Pater*,
preached unto the parish that Te Igitur was St. Clement's
father." [8] An equally interesting set of six examination
questions and answers to Norman priests, in mid-thirteenth
century, is recorded by the Archbishop of Rouen in
different places of his diary.[9] Here are some specimens.
" We examined John, a priest presented to the church of

* In 1529 the newly appointed grand prior of St. Antoine de Vienne
took his oath of fealty " on his knees, with his hands laid on the canon
Te igitur." (Maillet-Guy, *Grands Prieurs*, p. 17.)

Bernetot, in the lessons for St. Cecilia's Day : *Dixit Valerianus*, etc. Asked the signification of the words *tertio miliario*, he first answered ' the third thousand ' [*le tierz miller*] and afterwards ' I know not.' *Item*, when we asked how *transeuntibus* was declined, he said *hic et hoc transeunt*. Item, asked to decline *transire*, he said *transio, transis, transivi, transire, transiundi, transiundo, transiundum, transimus, transior, transiris*, beyond which he would say nothing more. Asked to parse *omni*, he said it was an adverb. Asked the signification of *optime*, he said ' much,' and again ' very.' " At a second examination, " asked the meaning of *annuam* he answered ' annual ' ; asked again what ' annual ' was, he said ' many times ' ; asked ' how many times ? ' he said ' every day.' "

Again, " we examined William de Wardres, in the lessons for the Feast of the Purification, beginning *illa namque salus* ; and he construed thus. *Illa* this is, *salus* salvation, *generata* engendered, *de Virgine Maria* of the Virgin Mary, *hoc est* that is, *die* the day, *quadragesimo* of the space of forty days, *Maria* O thou Mary, *genetrice* mother, *hodie* to-day, *ab ipsa* from her, *deportata* carried, *ad templum* to the temple, *ipsius* of him, *ut ipse* that he, *redemptor noster* our Father, *sit* may be, *presentatus* presented, *sic* in such a fashion, *cum substantia nostre carnis* in the substance of our flesh, *etiam* further, *adimplet* he fills, *ipsam* her. Being asked what this signified in French, he said that he understood not the sense well." And, again, Nicholas Quesnel, who had been presented to the rectory of Wynemerville, parsed *inanis* as a noun, and translated it as " an evil thing," ; he thought *ferebatur* meant " he carried." " We asked him the sense of the words *et vidit lucem quod esset bona* (Gen. i. 4) and he said ' it was a good thing to do.' " These examinations help us to understand the otherwise almost incredible decrees of Church Councils, beginning with Stephen Langton's at Oxford in 1222 : " Let the archdeacons see to it, on their visitations, . . . that priests can properly pronounce at least the words of the Canon of the Mass and the formula of baptism, and that they rightly understand this part [of the service books]." [10] In 1256, the General of the Premonstratensians " caused the General Chapter to sanction the decree forbidding any abbot or prior, thenceforward, to admit to the habit and profession any aspirant or novice who was not sufficiently instructed in grammar and could not speak Latin properly." [11]

In the fourteenth century, we come across the story of Bishop Louis de Beaumont, at Durham (1317), where the bishops were also abbots. This, as told by the contemporary chronicler, may be given here in Bishop Godwin's racy English.[12] " He was . . . so unlearned, that he could not read the bulles and other instruments of his consecration. When he should have pronounced this worde (*Metropoliticae*) not knowing what to make of it (though he had studied upon it and laboured his lesson long before) after a little pause, *Soyt pur dit* (saies he) let it goe for reade, and so passed it over. In like sort he stumbled at *in aenigmate*. When he had fumbled about it a while, *Par Saint Lowys* (quoth he) *il n'est pas curtois qui cette parolle ici escrit*, that is, *by Saint Lewis it was ungently done of him that writte this word heere*. Not without great cause, therefore, the Pope was somewhat strait-laced in admitting him. Hee obtained consecration so hardly, as in fowerteene years he could scarce creepe out of debt." Robert Stretton was chosen bishop of

Lichfield at the request of the Black Prince. After failing four separate times under examination, he was at last allowed by the Pope to be consecrated without. When Stretton made the usual public profession of canonical obedience on assuming his office (1360), "another man read his profession, since he himself could not read." [13]

In 1401, a priest who already held two chapelries wished to exchange these for the important living of Cornelimünster. The Pope granted permission, subject to examination by the Dean of St. Cunibert at Cologne, "to see whether he could read, construe and sing well, and could also speak Latin ; or, if he cannot yet sing, whether he will pledge himself to learn this within the year." [14] About 1430, St. Bernardino of Siena tells us of four priests who did not even know the formula for the consecration of the Host at Mass—*hoc est corpus meum*—and of whom one said, "I never bother about it ; I just say an *Ave Maria* over the wafer." [15] His younger contemporary, Johann Busch, came across a similar case in northern Germany and implies that it was not so very exceptional. The priest, examined by Busch in his archidiaconal capacity, could not find the words of consecration in his Missal, even after the rural dean had tried to help him out by giving him an unauthorized hint. [16] This same Busch tells us of an archbishop of his time who, after his consecration, got a chaplain to coach him, so that "with great industry, he at last learned so much that he began to understand what he read in his canonical hours and his Missal and the Canon [of the Mass] and the words of consecration." [17] The Dominican Barleta [1470] says in one of his sermons : "Ignorance is the mother of all evils, and ought especially to be avoided in the case of priests. . . . Yet, alas ! for nowadays

they are given to idleness and not to letters. . . . Here
is a droll story of a deacon who was to be ordained
priest. The Bishop, examining him as to his sufficiency,
asked : 'How many are the Church sacraments ?' He
answered, ' *tribus.*' ' *Quibus,*' asked the Bishop [in
mockery of his bad Latin]. To which he replied
' *chrismus, baptismus et missa pro defunctis.*' " [18] Erasmus,
at the end of his *Praise of Folly*, quotes a priest who, at a
theological discussion in his own presence, and with
approval on the part of some others, defended the burning of heretics by quoting St. Paul's command, *hominem
haereticum devita* (*Titus* iii. 10), under the impression that
devitare meant " deprive of life." Creighton, who judges
that Paul II. (1464–71) was " deeply imbued with the
spirit of the Renaissance," quotes a significant story from
a sub-contemporary.[19] The Pope " never spoke except
in the vulgar tongue at secret consistories and congregations and other like occasions. Once, in consistory, he
ordered a consistorial advocate, the lord Prospero
Caffarelli, to speak for him, the Pope. The advocate
broke down [*defecit*] in his speech ; whereat the pope
was wroth and would have taken his place ; but he
himself broke down likewise, and worse than the
advocate ; which was a great and ludicrous scandal."
Pico della Mirandola, in his *Oration* to Leo X. and the
Lateran Council (1511), said that he knew a bishop who
was absolutely ignorant of letters—*qui litteras penitus
ignorabat*, and who confessed that he had not yet learnt
the first prayer before Mass.[20] Sir Stephen Gaselee, on
pages 93–95 of his *Anthology of Medieval Latin*, gives
three instances from the anecdotes of Bebel and Adelphus
(1508–10), jocose and satirical in their intention but
credible enough in the light of the earlier evidence, and

indicative of the common reputation of the lower clergy in this respect. Bebel tells how he met an Italian priest at Innsbruck, and asked him about the recent events in Italy. " He turned away and said *non intelligo, non sum sacerdos ad grammaticam*. For what, then, are you a priest ? He answered : *Ad tria missa*. I, using the same gender, asked *Ad qualia ?* He replied : *De Beata Virgine, Spiritu Sancto, et pro Defunctis*. So I said : *Vade in pace cum tua tria missa*." The next of whom he tells was still more barbarous : so barbarous that the Bishop asked indignantly who had ordained him, and he answered, " You, my Lord, when I gave you those ten gulden." Adelphus, in his turn, tells us of a *bonvivant* bishop at Rome who, finding no mustard on the table, exclaimed : *O quanta patimus pro Ecclesia Dei*. A guest by his side corrected him : *Patimur*. The Bishop replied : " It matters little whether we say *patimus* or *patimur*, for both are in the genitive case." An age in which, while the standard of general education was steadily rising, such tales as these could be told against the clergy explains the still broader satire, and the great popularity in advanced circles, of the *Epistolae Obscurorum Virorum*.

The foregoing evidence is strengthened by the frequent inaccuracies in transcription and in translations. Take the acts of the first Benedictine Provincial Chapter of Canterbury and York, 1338, which survive in four MSS. from Durham monastery. These are so inaccurate that, in the first four pages of the Royal Historical Society edition, the variants printed in the footnotes show seven cases which make wrong grammar or sense ; and this is typical of all similar collections, solemnly official as they were, and written in great abbeys.[21]

The editors of the Cluny chartularies point out how, in that great collection, the copies grow more and more incorrect as time goes on.[22] Warton notes truly that " even such writers as Chaucer and Lydgate, men of education and learning, when they translate a Latin author, appear to execute their work through the medium of a French version." [23] The author of *Piers Plowman* evidently thought that the *altilia* of Matthew xxii. 4, meant " fowls," comparing it with *ales* (B. XV. 455). Even worse, he twice mistook *non mecaberis* (thou shalt not commit adultery) for *non necabis* (thou shalt not kill).[24] Concerning the efforts of very many medieval translators, we may echo Dr. Priebsch's comment : " They throw an unfavourable light upon the author's knowledge of Latin." [25] This is brought out very strongly in Petit de Julleville's *Histoire de la littérature française* (vol. II., ii., pp. 232, 260, 263–5). When great French patrons, Charles V. in especial, set themselves to recruit translators, they had great difficulty in finding men who were both competent and willing. It was only on great pressure that Raoul de Presles, one of the best of them, consented to undertake St. Augustine's *City of God* ; and, even then, the translator claimed the right of free rendering, " par manière de circonlocucion." In other men's translations which have come down to us, " numerous and often grievous blunders have been found " ; " the translators of the fourteenth century translated painfully, without always understanding either the letter or the spirit of the text that they had under their eyes." One of Charles V.'s translators, Denis Foulchat, confessed his difficulties with the *Policraticus* of John of Salisbury. " This honest fellow confessed that ' l'estrange gramoire ' and ' les sentences suspensives parfondes et obscures ' of the Latin had given him great trouble " ; that he was constantly puzzled and compelled to refer to others : even so, he was obliged to leave many passages blank. Dr. Andrew Clark writes concerning the unfinished version of the Oseney Chartulary : " I hazard the guess that the competent person who undertook the translation had, for some reason or other, to give over soon after the beginning, and that a would-be continuator, after some boggled attempts at carrying on the work, abandoned it as beyond his powers." [26] Often, again, when we turn from translations to the original compositions of all but the best scholars of their age, we shall feel what the archbishop of Canterbury felt upon reading a long letter from Prior Oxenden : " We are much displeased with that which you have intimated to us in your letter concerning the pollution of the cathedral [by bloodshed] and concerning your novices, not with due brevity but with unprofitable verbosity." [27] Latinism did much to encourage that fatal pedantry which puts sound before sense.

In this connection, we must look closely into the claim frequently made, that medieval Latin, though frankly un-Ciceronian, was remarkable for its clearness of definition and accuracy of expression. Quite apart from the occasional intricacy and confusion of the sentences, the hiatus here and the anacoluthon there, an attentive examination will reveal very startling ambiguities even in the most important official pronouncements. Gregory VII. condemned simoniacal ordinations as " null," *irrita* ; [28] and modern writers sometimes attempt to extricate him here from terrible theological difficulties by explaining that he meant only "irregular" ;

in other words, that his pronouncement rested upon the neglect of an obvious and essential distinction, which would scarcely be expected even from a beginner in Canon Law. Again, the decretal *Naviganti*, in which Gregory IX. undertook to solve one of the most thorny problems in the field of usury and which was incorporated in Canon Law under his direction, was so badly expressed that it has been even possible for a modern apologist to argue that the Pope or his amanuensis inadvertently left out the word *non*, thus handing down to posterity the exact opposite of his own solemn decision.[29] Innocent III., in one of his most important decrees at the Fourth Lateran Council, commanded the " exterminatio " of heretics ; and it is often pleaded nowadays that by this he intended only the original sense of that word, " expulsion." Yet in writers of those days the word is used at least as often in its modern sense of " destruction " ; and, though it occurs thirty-nine times in the Vulgate, in not one of these cases is its meaning confined to mere " expulsion " ; on the contrary, it is nearly always used for a word which in the original implies or actually asserts destruction.* Here, then, we have a question of life or death for tens of thousands of professing Christians, and one of the most solemn pronouncements ever made to the world by one of the most learned of popes, steeped to the lips in Canon Law. Yet, with at least half a dozen words at his command if he had meant mere expulsion—*pellere, expellere, bannire, ejicere, amovere, exturbare*—he prescribes a course which one magistrate might interpret as scarcely more than St. Paul's own *haereticum hominem devita*, while

---

* *E.g.* Psalm xxvi., 9 (Douay version), "For evil doers shall be *cut off*;" or Psalm lxxix., 14, "The boar out of the wood hath *laid it waste*."

others might with at least equal justice interpret it in the murderous sense which *devita* conveyed to the ignorant priest in Erasmus's *Praise of Folly*. *Scriptura*, again, or *Scriptura Sacra*, are phrases commonly restricted to the Canonical Scriptures, yet often not, even where the context lends real importance to the distinction. Not only this, but the Canonical Scriptures were themselves left undefined for more than a thousand years, until the Council of Trent finally decided in the teeth of the majority of preceding theologians. Or, if we turn to the famous medieval sentence *extra ecclesiam nulla salus*, we are told nowadays that neither *extra*, nor *ecclesia*, nor *nulla* can be taken in the sense which they would bear in other contexts, and which they ordinarily bore at the time when the motto was coined. *Adoratio*, again, was used in a sense which led to endless quarrels. *Divortium* was a common word—it might almost be said, the commonest word—for a process which in law is very different from strict divorce ; yet learned writers did not shrink from that word, which inevitably caused frequent confusion in the lay mind.[30] A regular official phrase for Plenary Indulgences, from at least 1300 onwards, was *indulgentia a poena et culpa* ; an Indulgence " from penalty and guilt "—yet it can remit nothing but the *penalty* : in itself it is powerless against the *guilt* of sin. Theologians explain this paradox carefully now, and they often did then ; but the multitude knows nothing of theological subtleties, and medieval writers tell us how thousands in their day mistook that phrase as fatally as the modern Protestant might mistake it ; for it was current not only in Church Latin but in the vernacular—French, *peine et coulpe*, and Italian, *perdona di colpa e di pena*. A whole discussion, of the deepest import, concerning the efficacy of prayers for the dead, turned in the thirteenth century on the highly probable supposition that when early fathers used the term *damnatus, damnatio*, they might have meant either *hell* or *purgatory*—*i.e.* that they used one word confusedly for two radically different conceptions.[31] Equally remarkable is the ubiquitous but hopelessly ambiguous phrase *major et sanior pars*. This was regularly used for elections or for collective decisions on the part of such a body as the monastic or cathedral chapter ; the decision was to go by the vote of the " greater and sounder part " of those who formed this body. To begin with, the phrase rests on a great confusion in logic : it tacitly assumes that the numerical majority will also include the weightiest individuals. Apart from this, it was hopelessly ambiguous ; for it offered no criterion whether, in case of conflict, numbers or quality were to count most. I have never yet found, or met anbody else who has found, any definition of that crucial word *sanior*. Indeed, I find my fellow medievalists generally agreed that the authorities deliberately avoided definition, preferring to let each case be fought out separately. Yet a moment's reflection will show the terrible risks of quarrel where elections and corporate decisions thus depended for their validity upon one crucial but hopelessly indefinite term. We need not go far for a concrete instance of this fatal ambiguity ; for it once caused a papal schism, which might never have been healed but that St. Bernard stepped in, and finally brought Christendom to a decision which was ethically admirable but quite irregular in law. Anacletus II. received the votes of twenty-four cardinals ; Innocent II. had fourteen votes. Thus there was no doubt as to *major* ; but then came the conflict over *sanior*. The minority claimed to be *saniores*, because they had four cardinal-bishops, as against two on the other side. The majority, on the contrary, claimed greater sanity in virtue of " their greater age, or rather seniority, which in some of them verged upon senility." [32] Vacandard himself admits that Innocent's election was not legal, though he contends for the illegality of Anacletus's on the other side. In any case the main facts stand ; after official Latin had done its best to confuse the issue, St. Bernard saved Europe by neglecting words, and insisting that the rivals should be judged not by the letter of the law but by the test of piety and personal character. Yet the Lateran Council of 1179, which removed this particular stumbling-block of of the undefined *sanior* from future papal elections, at the same time consecrated and fixed it for all others throughout the Church.[33]

Most remarkable of all is the want of a definition, or even of any official term whatever, for so important an idea as Papal Infallibility. There was a pre-Medieval Latin word, *inerrabilis*, which might have served the purpose ; but nobody used it. Among the hundreds of technical terms invented by the scholastic philosophers, nobody thought of *infallibilis*, at any rate in this connection. The word is not in Ducange's great Glossary of Medieval Latin. The lack of definition was so complete that a whole sect of modern theologians busies itself nowadays with explaining away that decree of the Council of Constance, which to the plain reader seems so clear, on this subject. Again, nobody throughout the whole Middle Ages sufficiently grasped the elementary distinction between the more important and the less important among papal utterances to think out, or to give a name to, that idea of *ex cathedra* upon which the whole theory of Infallibility now rests. Indeed, this all-important term is so vaguely defined, even to the present day, that nobody has dared to attempt an authoritative list of the papal utterances which were (as against those which were not) pronounced *ex cathedra*. It may be said without exaggeration that, of all the speculative divisions between Christians, the majority are due to lack of clear definition during the first thousand or fifteen hundred years of Christian thought. The Latin-speaking Middle Ages were content with uncertainty upon points where a few generations of vernacular discussion among the whole community, by bringing the question to a head, would have compelled definition and decision. A great modern writer, himself a statistician, has complained of authors who " treat us to tables of figures, often pursued into an extravagance of decimals which give only an illusive impression of accuracy." [34] We may say of a great deal of medieval thought that it ran into an extra-vagance of hair-splitting which gives an illusive impression of clearness.

Therefore I feel more and more strongly that medieval education did a great deal, for many centuries, to divorce men from their mother-tongue ; and thereby, from a good deal of common sense. The first book of original prose in the Scottish language is that by John of Ireland, who wrote very apologetically in his preface, "Consider- and that I was thretty yeris nurist in fraunce, and in the noble study of Paris in latin toung " ; and he contrasts " the common language of this contre " with " the tounge that I know better " ; that is, Latin. We see nowadays how an Englishman, settled on the Continent, will often lose half his own English and pick up nothing like its equivalent in French or German ; and so it must have been then with Latin. I cannot help believing that even the greatest minds in the Middle Ages lost something in width or delicacy of perception, and in suppleness of expression, by this system. The use of Latin as a world-language did indeed extend knowledge, but it diminished its intensity. I doubt whether at any university, at any time, there were half a dozen people able and willing to interchange their thoughts over the fireside with the intimacy which is possible at a modern university, either among older men or among undergraduates. It may be doubted whether any half-dozen ever met, except in the most exceptional circumstances, among whom every one was able to express all the shades of his thought as readily and completely and systematically as we ourselves can in our vernacular. And, again, even if an exceptional scholar was able thus to express himself, could he count upon the uptake ? Would every shade of meaning be as well understood as it usually is among our friends ? I doubt whether even Erasmus and Colet and More enjoyed anything like the same opportunities of intellectual interchange as (say) Lightfoot and Hort and Westcott.

Again, even if interchange were really perfect among the few first-rate Latinists, was it not a great disadvantage that a man's ordinary concepts were in one language, and his professional thinking in another ? Must it not have spoiled many chances of cross-fertilization in thought ? And, further still, must it not have encouraged the worst temptations of pedantry, when a man lives in his own burrow and despises the rest of the universe ? Several translators of the later Middle Ages voiced the same complaint, that their work was decried as a sacrilege, as a casting of pearls before swine. Under the influence of that spirit, whatever was said and written in Latin tended to narrowness. A university doctor's Latin was cramped by the conventional limitations of his profession ; and all the more fatally because he himself never suspected it. To choose an exaggerated illustration, it had some of the defects of a foreign waiter's English. The man can talk with irreproachable fluency on the technicalities of his own job, and over a narrow range of subjects outside it ; but there are considerable tracts of the language in which he is almost helpless ; and, owing to the reaction of thought and speech upon each other, that which he cannot express in words he is the less likely to think clearly in his mind. The unprogressiveness of medieval philosophy, outside metaphysics, was perhaps due almost as much to Latin as to ecclesiastical limitations or discouragements. Indeed, ecclesiastical domination itself was to an enormous extent based upon Latin ; this it was which too often enabled the priest to take away the key of knowledge, and which gave him many chances of escape when he entered not therein himself. It may be said that Latin began as an excellent servant, but that it ended as a somewhat tyrannous master. It became (to change the metaphor) a Holy of Holies in which the Bible, and to a great extent even the Liturgy, were laid up for the exclusive use of the priesthood.[35] Though Roger Bacon might exaggerate in his indignation, yet there was a deep foundation of truth in his complaint that the real study of the Bible was neglected in favour of the Sentences ; that men read the sacred books seldom consecutively, but commonly in a mere collection of snippets, so arranged as to divorce them from their context.[36] As to the

Liturgy, we have an illuminating remark from the German traveller Johann Schiltberger [1420]. He found some Christian communities even in remote Daghestan. He notes, " They have a bishopric there, and the priests are of the Order of friars, and they know no Latin, and what they sing or read is in the Tartar speech ; and this is so ordered that the layfolk are all the stronger in their faith." [37] The demands of the layfolk for vernacular versions of parts or all of the Liturgy were at last beginning to overcome all hierarchical opposition at the time when Schiltberger wrote.[38]

There were, of course, many degrees of Bible knowledge in the Middle Ages. Some men, like St. Bernard and the great mystics, especially among the early friars, evidently knew the text as well as Bunyan did.[39] In many other cases, however, the quotations and allusions show a much narrower range ; just the texts that happen to be included in the Breviary, or sometimes very little outside the Psalter and the Gospels. But all those are men whose writings have come down to us ; beneath them lay a whole multitude of clerics whose ignorance was graded down to those lowest specimens which I have quoted above. We cannot legitimately infer very much, I think, from the parodies which have come down to us, and which consist mainly of Biblical texts woven together in the most laughable collocations. " The solemn mockery of the result," write Professors Tout and Johnstone, " is as ingenious as it is profane. . . . Incidentally the parody shows how little basis there is for the popular view that the Middle Ages had but a slight acquaintance with the Bible." [40] But this last sentence, designed to combat an exaggeration which has not really been popular among scholars since S. R.

Maitland exploded it, may well convey to most readers an equal exaggeration in the other direction. To compose such a parody, after all, it needed only a single clerk who knew his Bible as well as the average mid-Victorian Anglican priest ; and, for an appreciative audience, it would suffice that half a dozen colleagues should know only half as much as he, or less. The Vulgate, like the Authorized Version, has a literary flavour that is easily recognizable (when once the mind is directed that way) by any reader, even though he may never have read, or may have subsequently forgotten, that particular text. For instance, there was a parody current among schoolboys of the 'seventies, beginning with Jezebel's fall from the window and ending " last of all the woman died also," which was enjoyed by many of us who could scarcely have named the context of a single sentence. Again, that Virgilian cento which Calverley called his *Carmen Saeculare* was appreciated by some very callow students of Virgil. We knew that each line or phrase, exquisitely ludicrous in its present setting, was drawn from some serious passage in the *Bucolics* or *Georgics* or *Æneid* ; it was a great pleasure to recognize them in detail ; but, in default of that, the poem still had the flavour of an elaborately-composed sauce.[41] A correct analysis of its actual ingredients might indeed be helpful, but was not essential.

CHAPTER IV

REVOLT AND VICTORY OF VERNACULARS

It remains now to trace briefly the revolt against this monopoly. Not that any conscious revolt can be traced from the beginning ; but revolt was implied in the growth of vernacular tongues—commencing as a mere undergrowth beneath the great trees of the Latin forest, but destined by a law of nature to hasten the decay of those forest trees.

Abailard, the man who inherited so much of the old tradition of classical scholarship, and who reached so far into the future that his *Sic et Non* may be counted as the foundation-stone of scholasticism, was also a sweet love-singer, and possibly in the vulgar tongue.[1] During his lifetime, the greatest classical revival before the Renaissance was working strongly, especially at Chartres and Orléans. But those same years were those of the great vernacular impulse in France. It was about 1080, possibly in Abailard's actual birth-year, that the *Chanson de Roland* took its final shape, and at once became a classic ; in 1130 it was translated into German ; and this began a whole century of epics and romances of adventure. Written lyric poetry was exactly contemporaneous ; so that, towards the end of the twelfth century, while John of Salisbury was lamenting the decay of such Latin studies as had formed his own scholarship at Chartres, vernacular poetry was going on from strength to strength, and even prose was coming to its own, as we may see in the French translations of St. Bernard's sermons. For, when once the vernacular enjoyed something like an equal chance, the struggle was practically decided in the field of literature proper. Among Latin poems posterior to 1250, there are very few comparable to the works of the Troubadours, Trouvères, and Minnesänger. If, in prose, the Latin dominance lasted longer, this was partly because many generations are needed to form a good prose tradition, and partly by reason of that truth which Dante emphasizes : Latin had an enormous business (as apart from literary) advantage. The chroniclers were still predominantly monastic ; more so, in fact, than they had been in the twelfth century ; and the average monk, with all his literary imperfections, knew more Latin than the average cleric : it was most natural that he should write in the language of his liturgy and of nearly all his endowments and charters. Yet, when once the Crusades inspired Villehardouin and Robert de Clari and Joinville in the thirteenth century, the beginning of the end came even in prose. Dante's Italian *Vita Nuova* is far better written than his Latin *De Monarchia*. That which killed Latin literature in the later Middle Ages was not the extraneous cause which is sometimes cited—the decree of the Council of Rouen in 1231 [2]— but the plain fact that, for a century past, some men had written better in the vernacular than their fellows could in the learned tongue. Nobody now reads Petrarch's or Boccaccio's or Gower's Latin writings except for their historical interest. Dante marks the complete victory of the mother-tongue, not only in that *Commedia* which has scarcely a rival even in Latin antiquity, but in his own deliberate choice of language, and in the explicit reasons he gives for this. He, like many predecessors, was faced to begin with by academic and snobbish prejudice. Professor Chambers has brought out admirably the earlier phases of this struggle.[3] " When a Teutonic tribe settled within the Roman Empire, there were Latin or Greek clerks ready to write letters for its chieftains, or to record its laws or its history ; so that the traditions, for example of the Gothic and Longobardic conquerors were written down, not in their own language, but in Latin. Native prose was choked, before it could spring up, by Latin competition." In England, after the Conquest, " the effect of the Norman-French clerks, allowing nothing but Latin, and entrenched in the monastery schools and the king's court, was bound to be felt as time went on. After the eleventh century, such English official documents are of the rarest occurrence till the time when, three centuries later, English begins to be used, very charily, in the latter part of the reign of Richard II." So, although English vernacular prose before the Conquest was perhaps the most developed in Europe, and though the *English Chronicle* will bear comparison with the best Latin of its time, and early English translations do not shame even such great originals as St. Bernard and Hugh of St.-Victor, yet English prose ran almost underground, in treatises of mystical piety and translations, until it emerged with Malory and More. The pundits, as a rule, despised it : their verdict was that " the vernacular has no savour of sweetness in the nostrils of the clergy "—*Lingua Romana coram clericis saporem suavitatis non habet.*[4] For, whereas Latin was called *Romana* during the earlier centuries while it still lived in Gaul as a vernacular, in all the later medieval centuries it is used for the common speech of the "Latin" countries, just as scholars speak now of "the Romance languages." To quote Professor Chambers again (page 113) : "The trouble during so much of the Thirteenth and Fourteenth Centuries was, that whilst English nationality had asserted itself, custom still demanded that Latin or French should be used, even by people for whom Latin or French was not the natural means of expression, and who can only use these languages with difficulty, *au meuz ke jeo say*, as Peter of Peckham put it. Prose in England begins to have a great future when, early in the Fifteenth Century, English begins to be used, in place of Latin or French, for the affairs of every day ; as in grievances of London citizens."

Dante's master, Brunetto Latini, was an excellent Latinist ; yet it was in French that he wrote his popular encyclopædia, the *Trésor* [1260]. In his prologue he says : "And if any man ask wherefore this book is written in Romance, according to the language of the French, since I am Italian, then will I answer that this is for two reasons. The first, because I am in France ; and the other, because the [French] speech is more delectable and more common to all men " (b. 1, p. 1, c. 1). Again, Dante's *De Vulgari Eloquentia* and *Convivio* show us even more plainly the Italian side of this struggle. Boccaccio tells a story which is almost equally significant whether it be true or false in detail. Dante (he says) " reflected that if Virgil and the other Latins were almost entirely neglected, he could not expect a better fate for his own work. He therefore made up his mind to suit his poem, at least so far as concerned its outside form, to the understandings of the present generation ; who,

if by chance they wish to see any book, and it happens
to be written in Latin, straightway have it translated into
the vernacular. From which he concluded that if his
poem were written in the vulgar tongue it might meet
with favour ; whereas if it were in Latin it would be
cold-shouldered. So, abandoning his Latin lines, he
wrote the *Commedia* in vernacular rimes, as we see it.
(*Comento*, I., 102-3)." [5] But there were deeper reasons
than this ; Dante knew that he could pour out his whole
soul in Italian as he could not in Latin : he had " the
natural love of my own tongue . . . for both naturally
and incidentally I love it, and have loved. . . . Not only
love, but most perfect love of it abideth in me. . . .
A man's proper vernacular is nearest unto him, inasmuch
as it is most closely united to him ; for it is singly and
alone in his mind before any other." Again : " This
vernacular it was that brought together them who begat
me, for by it they spoke ; even as the fire disposeth the
iron for the smith who is making the knife ; wherefore
it is manifest that it took part in my begetting and so
was a certain cause of my being. Moreover, this my
vernacular led me into the way of knowledge, which
is our specific perfection ; inasmuch as by it I entered
upon Latin, which was explained to me in it ; which
Latin was then my path to further advance ; wherefore,
it is plain, and is acknowledged by me, that it [the
vernacular] hath been my benefactor in the highest
degree." And, yet again, " if friendship grows by
comradeship, as is plain to the sense, then it is manifest
that it hath grown in me to the highest, since I have
passed all my time in company with this same vernacular.
Wherefore it appears that all the causes which can
generate and foster amity have combined for this

friendship ; whence cometh the conclusion that not only love, but most perfect love for it, is that which I ought to have and which I have." [6] Nor is he less emphatic in the *De Vulgari Eloquentia*, in which he may be said to carry the war into the enemy's territory, writing in Latin to explain how Latin is definitely "secondary" to the vernacular. "Vernacular speech is that which we acquire without any rule, by imitating our nurses. . . . The vernacular is the nobler, as being natural to us, whereas the other is rather of an artificial kind." [7]

That this bold counter-attack was timely, we may see in the light of tacit confessions from within the Latin stronghold itself. It transpires from the evidence already given here in the matter of translations ; and it transpires also from the increasing use of the vernacular by ecclesiastics in communication with each other ; sometimes, indeed, by very eminent ecclesiastics.[8] The monasteries begin to record and preserve business documents in the vernacular ; and here I am counting not the many cases in which one party is a layman, which might account for it, but those cases alone where both parties were ecclesiastics. Here is a specimen. At the Premonstratensian abbey of Mondaye, " the first deeds of our chartulary written in French are dated 1290, 1297, and 1303. The first half of the fourteenth century affords numerous examples." [9] Again, the chartulary of Zwyveke in Flanders shows eight (or perhaps ten) charters in the vernacular, though the parties concerned were all nuns or clerics, between 1310 and 1345.[10] Thomas de la Mare, abbot of St. Albans was " learned beyond even the highest clerks ; an excellent writer, preacher and speaker in the English, Latin and French tongues." Yet, in 1381, the business letters between him and his friend Dom William Strete at Rome are all in French. [11]

It is only recently that it has occurred to me to collect these instances of vernacular charters ; further results of this gleaning are in my note.[12] Again, it is surprising how often we find the clergy preferring to write to brother-clerics in English, even where writers and recipients are of great dignity—bishops, abbots, or priors. The *Literae Cantuarienses* (R.S., from St. Augustine's Canterbury) show this from 1325 onwards ; see vol. ii., p. 162 (Prior to Archbishop), vol. iii., pp. 174, 182, 210, 240, 262, 272, 274, 299, 304, 334. Very significant also is the rate of acceleration in the late fourteenth century, when education was spreading. In 1362, it was in French that the prior and convent made an indenture with Thomas Arundel, clerk, the future archbishop.[13] The monastic commissioners who, in 1376, were sent to reform Monte Cassino, the greatest house in Italy, wrote their two reports in Italian, sprinkled here and there with half a dozen words of poor Latin.[14] The last testament of Jean Fleury, Bishop and Abbot of Luçon in 1441, was in French.[15] But perhaps the most striking evidence of all comes from the cathedral priory of Christ Church, Canterbury, which is often quoted as having witnessed a great revival of studies in the fifteenth century in the lifetime of Prior Sellyng, and which does to some real extent deserve this praise. A volume of correspondence from this monastery was published in 1877 by the Camden Society.[16] It contains 85 letters, 37 of which are purely ecclesiastical, either between monk and monk, monk and cleric, or cleric and cleric. One of these (82) is part-English, part-Latin. Of the remaining 36, only 8 are in Latin, and 28 in

English. Prior Sellyng himself writes to Archbishop Morton in English (No. 58, about 1494).

Again, we begin about the same time to find indications that monks preferred the vernacular for reading. It is recorded of Abbot John, elected to S. Martino delle Scale in 1386, that he brought with him a number of books. Among these are seven volumes in the Sicilian vernacular, five of which are theological and one a commentary on Aristotle's *Ethics*. There was already at least one other vernacular book of piety in the same abbey.[17]

Apart from business documents, we have evidence from all sides for the extent to which the monks thought and spoke in the vernacular. The *Anglo-Saxon Chronicle* was kept up at Peterborough abbey, from time to time, until 1155 ; these different writers and their readers evidently felt most at home in the mother-tongue. Again, the only chronicle written at the great monastery of St.-Ouen-de-Rouen, at any rate between 1248 and the Reformation, is in French. Moreover, the author does not seem to exclude the possibility that even important business of the abbey might be transacted in the vernacular ; for, in three places, he finds it worth while to note, apparently by way of distinction, that the archbishop and the abbot-elect and his proctor, at the public consecration, carried out the usual formalities " en paroles latines . . . en latin . . . en paroles latines." [18] About 1270, the minister provincial of the Dominicans assumes that a Dominican prioress and her confidential nun will be able to read his Latin letter only through an interpreter.[19] Meister Eckhart [1320] uses the French definite article for the sake of adding extra clearness to his Latin in certain cases ; this is common among the scholastic philosophers, and would seem to suggest that these writers thought to some extent in French.[20] In 1349, the Franciscan Johann Zum Rosse writes a brief German letter to a brother-friar concerning the Minister-General and the Pope.[21]

There is also considerable evidence for speech in the vernacular, even where in theory it was most strictly forbidden. Chapter 63 of The Council of Aachen (817) prescribes that "learned monks be chosen to speak with monks who come from other monasteries." At Merton College, Oxford, in 1284, only seven years after the Founder's death, "the rule enjoining Latin conversation was habitually broken, and grammarians were despised."[22] From 1290 onwards, the Benedictine Provincial Chapters take formal notice of this defect. In 1325, the Augustinians begin to allow French as an alternative to Latin : if not the language of learning, at least that of upper-class courtesy ! Episcopal visitations show plainly that monks frequently, if not always, gave their evidence in native English.

In 1362, the Carmelite General Chapter legislated against friars who " sang worldly [*seculares*] songs or composed them or taught them or learned them."[23] In 1382, the German " nation " at Orléans university issued two statutes complaining of its own decay during the Papal Schism, and providing for the possibility of being reduced to one single member. Part of the preamble runs : " In truth, nowadays scarce any sound is heard here of the German tongue, the clangour whereof, with its tumultuous clash of sounds, was wont to ring through all the streets, and to smite even into mid-air, so that thou shouldst believe thyself a dweller in thine own Fatherland."[24] The statutes of the English Benedictine Chapter of 1444, cap. XIII., seem to provide for the necessity of preaching in monasteries in the vulgar tongue as well as in Latin.[25]   Such a provision would naturally be all the more necessary in proportion as the brethren had relaxed the original rule of taciturnity. St. Benedict had prescribed (and his early disciples had accepted the prescription) that few words should ever be exchanged, and those almost exclusively on religion or on necessary business.   But when, amid general relaxations, this restriction was neglected, the easy talk among monks would naturally fall into the vernacular. So the Benedictine Provincial Chapter at York, in 1290, complained that monks " accustomed themselves to chattering in English and were often sent to great folk on business of their monastery " ; therefore, " lest they fall into disgrace for default of correct speech [*boni ydiomatis*] we have decreed that all in chapter, when they accuse each other or correct or converse, and in their *parliamentum* or their times of solace or in other places, shall speak French or Latin ; let the transgressor be publicly accused in chapter and punished after his deserts." [26]   Again, in the Augustinian Order, the English Provincial Chapter allowed French as an alternative to Latin as early as 1325 ; and, in 1446 (as noted above), it had to deal with two priors to whom it had committed the visitation of the Welsh houses, and who had left the task undone " because the people and the language of that land was utterly unknown to us visitors." The Chapter rejected this excuse, reminding the priors that " the Latin idiom is presumed to be common both to the visitors and to the monasteries visited." [27]   To return to the Benedictines ; this vernacular question exercised the Provincial Chapter again in 1343.   The abuse of English-speaking in the refectories was solemnly condemned : it was complained that " when the monks are sent abroad on the business of their convent, they frequently fall into shame for lack of the Latin and French speech." It was therefore enacted that, if not in Latin, they should at least talk in French, the language of the upper classes. The abuse was still so prevalent a century later, in 1444, that the Provincial Chapter formally repeated their decree.[28] At the cathedral monastery of Ely, we find Bishop Fordham permitting French as an alternative in 1400.[29] And, half a century earlier still, the statutes even of the Cistercian General Chapter were sometimes recorded in French.[30] Episcopal visitors frequently reproduce the exact words of this or that monastic witness on this or that occasion ; these are so often in English as to suggest that inquiry was generally conducted in that language.[31] One instance may be here given in full for its added personal interest ; it is from the visitation of Walsingham in 1514, within a few months of that pilgrimage of Erasmus which he has immortalized in his *Colloquies*.[32] The Prior was accused of manslaughter, concubinage, malversation, and irreverence at the church services ; but he had done his best to intimidate the witnesses. In spite of this, there were a few who dared to speak up when the Bishop came to visit in person. The third prior reported the Prior for having said publicly at the Chapter meeting, " Doo the best that ye can and complayn what ye woll, it shall be never the better." At another time : " And I wist that my lorde [the Bishop] shulde be against me, I shulde so provide that my lorde shulde doo me litle hurt." And again : " When my lorde is goon I shall rule and aske him noon leave." Dom John Rase reported two other speeches : " When my lorde of Norwiche is goon I shall turne every thing as I woll " ; " if I knew my lorde wolde take part withe you I shall provide otherwise that he shall not hurt me." Dom John Ailesham corroborated, adding that the Prior had said, " I had lever spende the substance of this house [in litigation] then ye shulde have your intente." And again, when one of the monks sat in the town and a layman rebuked him for his behaviour, that the answer was : " As long as I doo noo wors then oure fader priour doithe, he can not rebuke me." Similarly, at Wymondham abbey, when Dom Richard Cambridge threatened to report the prior's misdeeds to the Bishop, the reply was " tell my lord both and my ladie, for I care nott " ; the Bishop himself not having an unspotted reputation.[33]

In literary histories, too little is commonly made of the influence of conversation. There are many small indications to show that the language in which Chaucer wrote had been made ready for him for generations of good vernacular talk, and often studied talk, at the courts of great men ; barons and knights and prelates and rich citizens. In *Sir Gawayne and the Green Knight*, when the lord of that remote castle hears that his new guest is none other than a knight of Arthur's court, the first thought of the other guests is not of war but of speech ; they laugh aloud and rejoice with each other : " Now we shall hear sleights of courtesy, and taintless terms of talking noble ! " Professor Chambers has well brought out the immense influence exerted upon English prose by many generations of quiet mystical treatises and manuals of piety. But we must not forget the spoken word, so far more potent at that time ; men and women who studied to attract their fellows by talk of everyday things, and others who, under political or religious enthusiasm, spoke probably far better than they or any others of their time could write. Side by side with all the Professor's illuminative citations from the orthodox, we must remember also the fashionable sceptic of the Middle Ages, and the rebel Lollard. *Piers Plowman* tells us of the sceptic : " I have heard high men eating at table " and discussing the thorniest theological problems with the utmost freedom : " Thus they drivel at their dais, the Deity to know, and gnaw on God with the gorge, when their gut is full." [34] And, as for the Lollard, William Thorpe's account of his trial for heresy before Archbishop Arundel will bear comparison here and there, both for pithy satire and for exalted religious feeling, even with St. Thomas More of a century later.[35]

But to return to the written word. It has been truly said that " Wycliffe's Latinity is that of a time when scholars were ceasing to *think* in Latin. . . . Often the readiest way of understanding an obscure passage is to translate it into English." [36] In 1391, an accord between St.-Ouen and the Carthusians of Rouen was drawn up in French.[37] The reforming monastery of Windesheim, deriving as it did from the Brethren of Common Life, took a special interest in popular education [1400]. One whole department of its library consisted of *libri Teutonici*, among which were French books also ; and one of the brethren, himself a diligent translator into both languages, was specially deputed as keeper of this department, and as reader to the layfolk at dinner and supper.[38] Autun, with its great civic and ecclesiastical traditions, had an abbey of somewhere near thirty monks even in the lean years of the fifteenth century. Yet in 1438, when a

reforming Abbot drew up fresh statutes for the monastery, these were written in the vulgar tongue. In 1442,
the abbot tried to mend matters by sending two novices
yearly to the city grammar-school.[39] The *Petite Chronique
Limousine* (804 to 1370) seems certainly written by a
monk of St.-Martial.[40] Cullum conjectures, with much
probability, that both bailiff and master were much
handicapped in business by the Latin tradition (as, for
instance, we know the doctor and apothecary to have
been in later times) ; and he quotes appositely from the
will of the Countess of Stafford in 1439 : " I ordeyne
and make my testament in English tonge, for my most
profit, redyng, and understandyng." [41] When we turn
to the Paston Letters, we find that parson Howes, in
1468, writes a very important business letter to Cardinal
Bourchier, not in Latin, but in English.[42] On the other
hand, the more confidential parts of Friar Brackley's
letters to Sir John Paston are always in Latin ; so also
when Brackley is in a preaching mood.[43] Pierre le
Prestre, Abbot of St.-Riquier (1419–80) wrote a chronicle
partly taken from others, partly recording notes of his
own life and experience. His editor remarks, "everything
concurs to prove that he never had the judgment of
posterity in view, nor any ambition of being useful to
future historians. He worked for himself alone ; and,
in his own thought, his manuscript, which was a sick
man's distraction, was not destined to survive him."
This may be somewhat exaggerated ; but no reader can
doubt that the book is an intimate personal document ;
yet it is written in French, though he tells us he spent
fourteen years at school before taking the monastic
vows.[44] The nuns of Ghent called " Riches-Claires,"
about 1500, had indeed a Latin Bible in their library ; but,

to judge from the published extract from their catalogue, the majority of books were in Flemish or French. These include translations of such standard works as a *Vitae Sanctorum*, the *Historia Scholastica*, the *Speculum Historiale*, the *Vitaspatrum*, and the *Lives* of Christ and of St. Clare.[45] In 1519, Cardinal Wolsey drew up a series of statutes for the reform of the Augustinian Order, in which he decreed : " Forasmuch as it profiteth little that a man read a book if he lack the understanding thereof and know not the Latin tongue, or if no learned person be present meanwhile to explain that which is not understood, therefore . . . let those brethren who know how to speak Latin or French by all means use those tongues in speech with each other, in default of good excuse to the contrary, unless some stranger be present, or except it be some more solemn feast-day." [46] At a visitation of Malmesbury in 1527 the Prior " accused the abbot of mismanagement,—of the chapter being held in English, not in the Latin tongue, and other disorders." [47] At Melrose, in 1556, the monks' solemn protest to their abbot was drawn up in English.[48] St. Teresa, writing in 1562, speaks of her troubles in the earlier days of her spiritual progress. Incidentally we learn that she had received almost her first great stimulus from St. Augustine's *Confessions* ; at a later date, she was immensely consoled by finding in some book " which I have reason to believe was put into my hands by God, those words of St. Paul, that God was very faithful, who would never consent that those who loved him should be deceived by the devil." But when the Inquisition condemned the Dominican Luis of Granada with his translations from St. John Climacus, and many other vernacular translations of pious books, then St. Teresa felt it as a great blow. "When they forbade many books in Spanish, that they might not be read, I felt much pain, since some of them gave me refreshment in the reading, and [now] I could no longer read them because they were in Latin."[49]

These instances—and, doubtless, infinitely more might be collected by any one who had time to specialize on the subject—may suggest why the vernaculars grew so steadily in importance, and the Latin withered more and more. Though it lingered on into the seventeenth century and beyond, yet the books that really mattered were more and more frequently written in the vernacular, even among philosophers and theologians. We have seen how the victory of the vernacular had been consciously and methodically planned by some writers from the beginning of the fourteenth century at least. In those early days, we may suppose that most men looked upon the innovators as over-hasty, if not Utopian. There was some reality in the excuse that, even in late fourteenth-century France, the vernacular was not yet sufficiently developed to bear the weight of translation from scientific Latin.

Nicolas Oresme [1380] recognized that it was not always possible to translate Latin "proprement" into French ; and he gave two interesting examples. For *homo est animal*, French could supply nothing nearer than *homme est beste* ; for *mulier est homo*, nothing better than *femme est homme* ; therefore, for the sake of clearness, words like *animal* and *humanus* must be imported from Latin. His contemporary, Pierre Berçuire, felt the same ; each, therefore, supplied his book with a glossary of the new words which he had been obliged to use.[50] But the flood of translations swelled and swelled ; a mere glance at our Early English Text Society list will show what an enormous proportion of surviving fifteenth-century literature was drawn from Latin originals ; therefore Latin words came in more and more, either directly or through the French.[51]

Even great scholars were brought by experience and common sense to abandon the Latin monopoly. The scholar's own Latin was far from perfect ; many of the clearer minds at the universities realized this imperfection, and were glad to escape, if only occasionally, into that open air of vernacular speech in which they could move and breathe more freely. The *Literae Cantuarienses* themselves testify that the men could already write English at least as well as they wrote Latin (*e.g.* Vol. III., pages 274ff., 1474). And Cardinal Pietro Bembo [1520], himself one of the very best Latinists among Renaissance scholars, clearly recognized the victory of the vernacular. He wrote probably in definite recollection of Dante's words ; certainly in harmony with them. He pointed out how " it is nearer unto us, seeing that we live all our lives in the vulgar tongue, while with Latin it is not so." And again : " We must say that the vulgar tongue is not only near unto us, but is something more ; it is native and proper to us, while the Latin tongue is foreign. For, even as the Romans had two tongues, one proper and natural, to wit Latin, and the other foreign, to wit Greek, even so we also possess two fashions of parlance, the one proper and natural and homely, which is the vernacular, and the other foreign and unnatural, which is Latin." [52] Thus Latin, with all its natural advantages, suffered increasingly under the inherent and fatal defect of artificiality. " The Italian scholars, the successors of the Romans, aimed at restoring their literary inheritance by utilizing Latin for all grave and serious purposes. But they were already too late, and by the end of the century it had become evident to their successors that in the vernacular a not unworthy instrument was ready to hand even for the higher purposes of Literature. Poliziano and Bembo used both Latin and Italian indifferently. Thereupon, as an inevitable consequence, Latin became once for all an artificial language, and therefore merely imitative." [53]

Sometimes, in the Middle Ages and beyond, Latin did what no vernacular could possibly have done. Its lapidary force lent itself perfectly to liturgical poetry. St. Thomas Aquinas could have written his best hymns in no modern language. Here and there the scholastic philosophers, like Spinoza after them, expressed themselves with a pointed and impressive brevity which renders translation very difficult. Latin had the enormous advantage of helping international inter-communication, in ages when travel was difficult, and immeasurably more dangerous than to-day. It produced, during the Middle Ages, a little secular poetry which is comparable to the best in the vernacular ; yet very little when we consider the scholarly *élite* and the many generations and the vast territories from which these choice specimens are drawn. But, for many generations before its disappearance as a written language, it had been little more than a stop-gap, holding its ground mainly because no organized and systematic attempt was made to supersede it. It had begun as a support to European learning ; and for centuries it justified that claim ; but before the Reformation it was becoming a hindrance. It would be difficult to find a better historical illustration of Tennyson's line : " Lest one good custom should corrupt the world." The barrier between "literate" and "illiterate" folk, which for so many centuries had rested upon the question of "Latin" or "no-Latin," broke down at last through natural and irresistible causes, and to the advantage of both sides.

APPENDIX

SECTION I

CHAPTER I

[1] See evidence from *The Complaynt of Scotland*, on a later page.

[2] F. M. Powicke. "Aelred of Rievaulx" (reprinted from *Bulletin of the John Rylands Library*, 1921–22), p. 108.

[3] A Schönbach, *Ueber eine Grazer Handschrift*, p. 20 (Graz, 1890).

[4] *Werke*, ed. Melchior Diepenbrock, 3rd Ed., 1854, p. 157. The "Little Book" has been translated into English. (Angelus Company, n.d.)

[5] *Liber de Reformatione*, ed. Grube, 1887, p. 787.

[6] *Ibid.*, p. 215 (*Chronicon Windeshemense*).

[7] *Continuity of English Prose*, Early English Text Society, 1932, p. cxxxii. It has been suggested that the 11th–12th-century bishop of Norwich, Herbert de Lozinga, preached sometimes in the vernacular. (G. R. Owst, *Literature and Pulpit*, 1933, p. 17 *note*.)

[8] H. Durand du Laur, *Erasme*, 1872, p. 674 ; Knight's *Erasmus*, 1726, p. 349.

[9] *Casus S. Galli*, c. 80.

[10] Albers, Vol. III., p. 93.

[11] *Reminiscences of a Maynooth Professor*, 1925, pp. 183–87 ; again, pp. 226, 348, 350, 352, 365, 408. " Schools," in these pages, includes the four years of seminary training after the National University course.

[12] Manitius, Vol. I., pp. 7–8. It is well known that proof-readers in great printing houses sometimes find it no great disadvantage to know little or nothing of the subject of the book upon which they work.

[13] *Ibid.*, p. 3.

[14] Some very striking French examples are quoted at length in Petit de Julleville, *Hist. Litt.*, Vol. II., 1, p. xlix.

[15] Dante, *Vulg. Eloq.*, I., 11.

[16] Julien Havet, *Oeuvres*, Vol. II., 1896, p. 187.

[17] I say, "quasi-monastic," because there seems no reason to believe that the notaries whose charters have often come down to us were at all more ignorant than the monks of the same district. No doubt the ordinary parish priests were; but that is a very different thing.

[18] Manitius, Vol. I., p. 253, where the reference is to Gregory's outspoken contempt of grammatical minutiae.

[19] *Ibid.*, p. 246.

[20] *Ep. ad Egbertum* (Opp. ed. Plummer, Vol. I., p. 408).

[21] Von Arx, Vol. I., p. 191. The translations of the Lord's Prayer, Creed, etc., in that same library (*ibid.*, pp. 203ff) may have been meant only for layfolk, but it is possible that they were intended for the weaker brethren.

[22] The A.-S. Rule was edited by H. Logeman in 1888; for the others, see *Studien und Mittheilungen*, 1914, pp. 525ff. Eight of these, from the twelfth to the fourteenth century, have been published for the Medieval Academy of America by Carl Selmer.

[23] J. M. Clark, *The Abbey of St. Gall*, pp. 249ff.

[24] Gaston Paris, *Esquisse hist. de la litt. française*, 1907, p. 83.

[25] *P.L.*, Vol. 198, c. 184. Abbé Bourgain (*Chaire française*, p. 195, followed by Petit de Julleville in *Hist. litt. française*, II., ii., p. 228) assumes that these bad Latinists must be layfolk; but this is contrary to the whole context. Adam is preaching to his own Religious, and warning them against their own temptations: after exposing the folly of such hypercriticism he goes on to exhort them: "But do not thus, O my brethren."

[26] Innocentius IV., *in V. Libros Decretalium*, (Turin, 1581), f. 173a.

[27] Wadding, *Annales*, Vol. III., p. 382.

[28] *Reg. Visit. O.R.*, p. 647. W. G. Pantin, *Provincial Chapters*, etc., 1931, p. 111.

[29] *Romania*, Vol. XV., p. 302, ll. 273ff.

[30] Denifle-Ehrle, *Archiv.*, Vol. II., p. 644 *note*.

[31] J. du Breul, *Aimoini Monachi*, etc., 1603, pp. 841ff.

[32] *Prémontré*, par Ch. Taiée, (Laon, 1872), p. 95.

[33] *Reg. Pontissara*, pp. 127, 319. For the state into which legal French had fallen long before it was finally abandoned as an official language, see P. H. Winfield, *The Chief Sources of English Legal History* (1925), pp. 9ff.

[34] *Aurillac*, Vol. II., pp. 114, 484, 491.

[35] Remling, Vol. I., p. 329.

[36] Deanesly, *Lollard Bible*, p. 213.

[37] *Clementina*, lib. III., tit. X. ; J. du Breul, *Aimoini Monachi Libri*, etc., 1603, p. 862.

[38] Taiée, p. 104.

[39] Warton, *Hist. Eng. Poet.* (ed. Ward Lock and Co.), p. 390. There were also English and German translations of the Benedictine Rule ; for the latter, see *Studien und Mittheilungen*, 1914, pp. 525ff. Molinier writes (*Obituaires*, p. 52) : " We know one or two monasteries where the Rule of St. Benedict was translated into French ; for instance, in the Obituary-book of Ste.-Colombe at Sens." At one nunnery, the obituary itself is written in French ; *ibid.*, p. 73.

[40] Lyndwood, *Provinciale*, 1679, Appendix, p. 143.

[41] The reference here is to Gratian's *Decretum*, Pars II., c. xvi., q. 1, § 36, where St. Augustine is quoted as saying this in contradiction to " the common folk themselves, who will jest upon us, saying ' a bad monk is a good clerk.' "

[42] *i.e.* all but the Mendicant Orders ; *cf.* Chaucer, *C.T.*, D., 1722.

[43] Thorne, in Twysden *Scriptores Decem*, 2064–65.

[44] Pantin, Vol. II., pp. 84–85, 181, 207, 214.

[45] H. E. Salter, *Aug. Gen. Chap.*, 211.

[46] B. Pez, *Bibliotheca Ascetica*, VIII. (1725), 517.

[47] *Rev. bénédictine*, Vol. 40 (1928), p. 348.

[48] F. Hurter, *Tableau des Institutions*, etc., trad. J. Cohen, Paris, 1843, Vol. II., p. 233.

[49] F. A. Scharpff, I. (1843), 190.

[50] J. Hefele, *Der Cardinal Ximenes* (1851), 165.

[51] *Revue Mabillon*, 1931, 205.

[52] Pantin, Vol. III., 83.

[53] *Vis. Dioc. Nor.*, pp. 73, 193, 253.

[54] Lincoln Record Soc., Vol. 7, pp. 35, 75, 81, 100, 121, 127 ; *cf.* Vol. 14, pp. 86, 139, [171] ; Vol. 21, pp. 237, [260], 319, [371, 373], 393–94, 414. At one of these monasteries (Newnham, 1442) the visitors report how " certain of the Canons of the said priory are so unlettered and almost witless that they barely read, and what they read they do not understand " (p. 237). Even at Norwich Cathedral priory, in 1514, the visitors had to translate their Latin for the monks (*Vis. Dioc. Nor.*, p. 72).

[55] E.E.T.S. Vols. 133, 142.

[56] *Reg. Bothe*, p. 67.

[57] *Continuity of English Prose*, E.E.T.S., 1932, pp. xciii, cxiv, cxxvii, cxxxii.

[58] *Gesta Abbatum*, R.S., Vol. II., p. 402.

[59] *Med. Eng. Nunneries*, pp. 240–55 ; compare Deanesly, pp. 320, 336–40.

[60] Deanesly, 252.

CHAPTER II

[1] Migne *P.L.*, Vol. 148, col. 555.

[2] M. Deanesly, *Lollard Bible*, p. 23.

[3] J. M. Clark, p. 250.

[4] *Universities of Europe*, 1st Ed., Vol. I., p. 27. For the value of Latin see *ibid.*, Vol. II., pp. 602–3 ; but we must discount to some extent the exaggeration which he quotes from Thorold Rogers : " The bailiff of every manor kept his accounts in Latin."

[5] Compare Petit de Julleville, Vol. II., ii., p. 267, where a French translator of [1400] confesses that to translate the Bible literally is " a perilous thing for the ears of layfolk."

[6] " Utcunque " (Celano, *Leg. Prima*, c. 9).

[7] *Chron. XXIV. Gen.*, p. 639 ; *cf.* p. 638.

[8] Bishop Fisher, *English Works* (E.E.T.S., 1876), p. 292.

[9] L. Wadding, *Annales*, an. 1224 (Vol. II., p. 83).

[10] *Chron. Villarense* (Martène, *Thesaurus*, Vol. III., col. 1326). On the other hand, Leopold Delisle argues for a considerable knowledge of Latin the in later thirteenth century, among the French nobility. (Offprint from the *Journal général de l'instruction publique*, 1855 or 1856.)

[11] *Archiv für Kirchen- und Litteraturgeschichte*, Vol. I., p. 227.

[12] A. F. Leach, *Winch. Coll.*, 1899.

[13] Léopold Deslisle corrected exaggerated accusations of ignorance in his address " De l'instruction littéraire de la noblesse française au m-a," printed by the *Journal général de l'instruction publique et des cultes*, in 1855 or 1856 (Camb. Univ. Library, Acton c. 26. 2711). He seems, however, to incline rather too far in the other direction. When, for instance (p. 4), he points out that a very large proportion

of the notaries' posts in different provinces were held by men of noble family, we may easily explain this by the economic considerations which Dante so plainly rehearses.

[14] M. Deanesly, p. 213.

[15] *Dialogus Miraculorum*, Vol. II., p. 255 ; *Alphabet of Tales*, Vol. I., p. 71.

[16] Capitulary of A.D. 787, quoted in Mullinger, *Schools of Charles the Great*, 1877, p. 98. Already, about 782, he had written to revive " the study of letters [*i.e.* of Latin], wellnigh extinguished through the neglect of our ancestors " (*ibid.*, p. 101).

[17] *Capitularia* (ed. Boretius, *M.G.H.*), Vol. I., p. 110.

[18] Ep. XIV. (*P.L.*, Vol. 100, col. 163).

[19] A. F. Leach, *Educational Charters and Documents* (1911), p. 23.

[20] L. Tosti, *Badia di Monte Cassino*, 1842, Vol. I., p. 218.

[21] Guil. Malmesb, *De Gestis Regum*, lib. III. (R.S., p. 304).

[22] *P.L.*, Vol. 149, cols. 727, 762.

[23] Throughout this chapter I shall give exact dates in some cases, but confine myself in others to approximate dates [in *square* brackets].

[24] *Chron. Abingdon*, R.S., Vol. II., p. 404. *Litterae, litteratus,* and even *legere,* have not so wide a sense as in modern English ; they frequently refer to the Latin language only ; but that does not affect the significance of this particular passage.

[25] Herrgott, p. 467. In a Premonstratensian Chapter-document the word is formally glossed ; an abbot's election is voided " si sit ydeota ; hoc est, illiteratus " (*Coll. Anglo-Prem.*, Vol. I., p. 124).

[26] William of Worcester, *Itinerarium*, p. 348.

[27] *Hist. MSS. Com.*, 9th *Report*, p. 91. Compare the case at Christchurch, Canterbury, in 1324, where a candidate is refused by the prior because " he has not yet the use and art of singing and reading " ; let him therefore, while he is still in his youth, learn these things and apply again (*Lit. Cant.*, R.S., Vol. I., p. 126). For contrary instances, see *Sussex Archaeol. Coll.*, Vol. 9, p. 64 (Boxgrove Priory).

[28] *P.L.*, col. 844. The whole of this fascinating autobiography has now been translated by Mr. C. C. S. Bland (Routledge).

[29] *P.L.*, Vol. 156, col. 913.

[30] *Ibid.*, col. 699.

[31] *P.L.*, Vol. 202, col. 13 ; Deanesly, *Lollard Bible*, p. 255.

[32] *P.L.*, Vol. 203, col. 816b.

[33] Bradshaw Soc., Vol. XXIII (1902), pp. 264, 274, 276 ; Vol.

XXVIII. (1904), pp. 225–28. At St. Augustine's, provision is made for the possibility that the lay-brother may not be able to write this Latin formula himself.

[34] *Coll. Top. et Gen.*, Vol. III. (1836), p. 108.

[35] *Dialogus Miraculorum*, Vol. II., p. 5 ; English version in *Alphabet of Tales*, Vol. I.

[36] *Regula Illustrata*, p. 240.

[37] *Opp. Ined.*, R.S., 1859, p. 413.

[38] *The Journey of William Rubruck*, Hakluyt Soc., 1900, p. 158 ; cf. *Contemporaries of Marco Polo*, ed. Manuel Komroff, 1928, p. 120.

[39] *Cont. Impugnant. Rel.*, Cap. IV., § 10.

[40] Mansi, Vol. XXIII., c. 935.

[41] Richard, *Analysis Conciliorum*, I., 226.

[42] *Reg. Pontissara*, p. 237 ; cf. pp. 347, 356, 403–4, 427. Mr. C. R. Cheney tells me that these Constitutions, though dated 1295 in the printed *Register*, date almost certainly from the episcopate of John Gerveys.

[43] J. Peckham, *Reg. Epist.*, R.S., Vol. III. (1885), p. 813.

[44] E. Martene, *Thesaurus*, Vol. IV., col. 1505.

[45] H. Rashdall, *Universities of Europe*, Vol. II., pp. 555, 598. For the state of Latin among the younger Oxford scholars, see Rashdall and Rait, *New College*, 1901, pp. 25–26, and Rashdall, *Universities*, Vol. II., p. 571.

[46] A. F. Leach, *Educational Charters*, etc., p. 402.

[47] *M.G.H. Scriptt*, Vol. XXXII., p. 277.

[48] *Registrum Epistolarum*, R.S., Vol. III., p. 777.

[49] Walsingham, *Gesta Abbatum*, R.S., Vol. II., p. 114.

[50] *Tractatus*, pp. 285 (pars II., tit. XXIX.) and 325–26 (pars III., tit. XLIV.).

[51] *Defensor Pacis*, ed. Previté-Orton, pp. 185, 326, 371 ; cf. 210.

[52] D. Patrick, *Statutes of the Scottish Church*, 1907, p. 68.

[53] Beaurepaire, Vol. I., p. 21.

[54] *Register*, p. 1192 ; fully translated in my *Life in the Middle Ages*, Vol. II., p. 113 ; and by A. F. Leach, *Educational Charters and Documents*, Cambridge, 1911, p. 315.

[55] *Mon. Hist. Carm.*, p. 183. The assembled fathers complained also that the younger friars were sent out to beg when they ought to have been attending lectures.

[56] Twysden, *Scriptores Decem*, col. 2699.

[57] Deanesly, p. 141.

[58] *C.P.L.*, Vol. IV., p. 188.

[59] B-text, passus V., l. 424.

[60] B. passus XV., l. 365 ; C. xviii., 107.

[61] Livre II., c. 266 (*Traitez des droits et libertés de l'Eglise Gallicane*, Vol. II., 1731, p. 125).

[62] A. F. Leach, *Schools of Medieval England*, p. 204.

[63] J. B. Mullinger, *History of Cambridge University*, Vol. I., 1873, p. 303.

[64] A. F. Leach, *Winch. Coll*, 1899, p. 24, from MS. in the possession of the Warden of New College. In this same year, 1387, it is recorded of the abbot of the great monastery of S. Prospero at Reggio that " nesciebat legere nisi male." (C. Affarosi, *Storia di S. P. di R.*, Padua, 1733, Vol. I., p. 311.)

[65] H. E. Salter, *Aug. Chap.*, p. 201.

[66] *Ibid.*, p. 83.

[67] Martène, *Thesaurus*, Vol. IV., coll. 1505, 1583, 1608-9, 1623. In 1472 the visitor found that there was no grammar-master for the young monks at the Cistercian house of Holm Cultram (*V.C.H. Cumberland*, Vol. II., p. 165).

[68] H. E. Salter, *Aug. Chap.*, p. 135.

[69] Bibliothèque Nationale, MS. lat. Nouv. Acq., 1502, f. 127a.

[70] *Chron. Windesheim*, ed. K. Grube, p. 54.

[71] *De Ref. Mon.*, p. 469.

[72] v.d., Hardt, *Mag. Const. Concil*, Vol. I., pars VIII., col. 427.

[73] *De Visitatione Praelatorum* ad fin (*Opera*, 1606, Vol. 2, p. 641).

[74] *Opera*, Vol. XXXVII, pp. 41, 139, 213. This was a favourite story ; *cf. Alphabet of Tales* (E.E.T.S., Vol. 127), p. 508, and a similar tale in S. Gaselee, *Anthology of Med. Latin*.

[75] *A.F.H.*, Vol. XI. (1918), p. 129.

[76] H. E. Salter, *l.c.*, p. 111.

[77] *Loci e Libro Veritatum*, Oxford, 1881, p. 191.

[78] *Reg. Whethamstede*, R.S., Vol. I., p. 24.

[79] *Correspondence* ; R.S., Vol. I., p. 172.

[80] *Calendar of Papal Letters*, Vol. XI., pp. 430, 597.

[81] *Summa Angelica*, s.v. *Clericus*, II., 2.

[82] *Institutio Vitae Sacerdotalis*, cap. IV., in *Opp. Pia*, ed. Busaeus, 1605, p. 775.

[83] J. A. Riegger, *Amoenitates Litterariae* (1775), p. 253.

[84] *Ship of Fools*, 1874, Vol. I., p. 144.

[85] Erasmus, *Opera*, Leyden, 1704, Vol. V., col. 808 ; P. S. Allen, *Selections from Erasumus*, p. 17.

[86] *English Works*, 1557, p. 1222.

[87] *Ibid.*, p. 723, d.

[88] A. Riegger, *Amoenitates*, Fasc. I., p. 126.

[89] P. Labbe, *Concilia*, Vol. XIV. (1672), col. 427.

[90] Leach, *Ed. Charters*, 1911, p. 445.

[91] Canon J. M. Wilson in *Contemporary Review*, April 1923, p. 492.

[92] Riegger, *Amoenitates*, p. 121.

[93] *Cart. St. Frideswide*, Vol. II., p. 374 ; Rymer's *Foedera*, Vol. XIV. (1712), p. 15.

[94] *Norwich Visitations*, ed. Jessopp, p. 198 (Camden Soc.).

[95] *Chronique du Bec*, ed. Porée Soc. Hist., p. 263.

[96] Wadding, *an.* 1224 (Vol. II., p. 83).

[97] *Opera*, Paris, 1606, Vol. IV., p. 962, d.

[98] *Buke of the Monarche*, Bk. I., ll. 608ff.

[99] Bk. I., c. 9 ; Bk. III., c. 11. Compare Rashdall, *Universities*, Vol. II., pp. 707ff.

CHAPTER III

[1] Zach., Ep. VII., Migne, *P.L.*, Vol. 89, col. 949.

[2] H. Florez, *España Sagrada*, Vol. XI. (1753), p. 274 ; *cf.* Helen Waddell, *Wandering Scholars*, p. 69.

[3] *Opera*, R.S., Vol. III., pp. 234, 368. *Cf.* Wilkins, *Concilia*, II., 150. For further evidence, see chapter XII. of my *Medieval Panorama*.

[4] *Ibid.*, Vol. I., p. 90.

[5] *Ibid.*, Vol. II., pp. 341–46. He was, of course, thinking of *equus* and *saltare*.

[6] *Ibid.*, Vol. II., pp. 341ff.

[7] *Thoughts in a Garden*—
> " The mind, that ocean where each kind
>   Doth straight its own resemblance find."

[8] *The Confutation of Tyndale's Answer*, Bk. V., in *English Works* (1557), p. 561 c.

[9] *Regestrum Visitationum Odonis Rigaldi*, ed. Bonnin, pp. 159, **173,**

217, 332, 395, 787. I have translated these in full in my *Medieval Garner*, pp. 273ff, and *Life in the Middle Ages*, Vol. II., pp. 42ff.

[10] Wilkins, Vol. I., p. 589, § 24. It must be remembered that the validity of baptism, and therefore the question of the child's actual chances of heaven, were held to depend on the correct use of this brief Latin formula. In 1237 the Council of London decreed that archdeacons must ensure that the priests " know, and have a wholesome comprehension of, the words of the Canon of the Mass and the baptismal formula" (Wilkins, I., 650, § 3). About the same time Bishop Hugh de Welles of Lincoln prescribed to his archdeacons, as the first among fifty articles of inquiry on their visits, " Are any of the rectors or vicars or priests [in this rural deanery] excessively ignorant of Latin ? " *enormiter illiterati* (Wilkins, Vol. I., p. 627). The Council of Béziers, in 1233, decreed that none should receive the clerical tonsure " who could not read [Latin] and sing " (Canon 7). So again Ravenna, 1311 (Canon 16), Sens, 1320 (Canon 9), Lavaux, 1368 (Canon 20). In 1286 the 11th Canon of the Council of Bourges prescribed that each parish priest must have copies of two recent papal and archiepiscopal decrees, *in the vulgar tongue.*

[11] *Catalogue of the Bishops*, 1615, p. 659. For the original see *Hist. Dunelm Scriptores Tres*, Surtees Soc., p. 118.

[12] Taiée, p. 95.

[13] H. Wharton, *Anglia Sacra*, Vol. I., p. 449 *note.*

[14] *Eiflia Sacra*, Vol. I., pp. 401–7. We find a similar case in the register of Fox, founder of Corpus Christi College, Oxford, when he was bishop of Durham. He undertook to institute John Walys to the rectory to which the patron had presented him, only on condition that he would appear at Midsummer before the bishop's commissary " and shall well and sufficiently read and construe the text and rubrics of the first ten leaves in any copy of the Sarum Missal" (*Reg. Durham*, Surtees Soc., 1932, p. 27).

[15] *Prediche Volgari*, Vol. II., p. 127.

[16] *De Ref. Mon.*, 1887, p. 443.

[17] *Ibid.*, p. 750.

[18] Gabriel Barleta, *Sermones* (Venice, 1571), tom I., f. 114a : *Feria II. tert. hebd. Quadrages.*

[19] *History of the Papacy*, 1903, Vol. IV., p. 57. The author, Paris de Grassis, was in the service of cardinals and popes from about 1474 onwards.

20 *Opera*, Bâle, 1601, Vol. II., p. 887.

21 Pantin, Vol. II., pp. 5–9. The editor writes of one of the best among these MSS., " It has many peculiarities and blunders " (p. 27).

22 *Chartes de l'Abbaye de C.*, ed. A. Bernard and A. Bruel, 1876, Vol. I., p. xlvii.

23 *Hist. Eng. Poetry* (Ward Lock and Tyler's ed.), p. 398 ; *cf.* the footnote on the same page.

24 A. XI. 246. In the B- text (X. 368), though the passage is recast, this error is repeated.

25 *Die Heilige Regel für ein Vollkommenes Leben*, ed. R. Priebsch, Berlin, 1909.

26 E.E.T.S., 1913, p. xxvii.

27 *Lit. Cant.*, R.S., Vol. II., p. 155 (1337).

28 *Registrum*, ed. Caspar, 1920, p. 403 ; Migne, *P.L.*, Vol. 148, col. 801.

29 I told this whole story in a paper read before the Historical Association in 1921 (*History*, July 1921, p. 67).

30 *E.g.* a sentence of Gregory IX., one of the greatest canon lawyers of all the popes, in 1229. While decreeing what in strict law language is *nullity of marriage*, he calls this *sententiam divortii*, and the two parties (King and Queen of Aragon) twice use the same word. (Mansi, *Concilia*, Vol. XXIII., c. 209.)

31 *E.g.* Aquinas, *Sum. Theol.*, Suppt. q., LXXIII. [LXXI.], ad 2 ; T. Bautz, *Die Hölle*, 1882, pp. 198ff.

32 Abbé E. Vacandard, *Vie de St. Bernard*, 2me ed., Vol. II., p. 298, an admirable account of the whole incident:

33 An Italian legist has written a brief and interesting monograph on this subject : E. R. Avondo, *Il Principio Maggioritario* (Turin, 1927). See especially pp. 27ff.

34 Vicomte G. d'Avenel, *La fortune privée*, etc., 1925, p. 42.

35 Johann Busch, liberal as he was for his own day [1450], would not permit nuns to possess breviaries in the vernacular.

36 *Opp. Ined.*, R.S., p. 328.

37 *Reisebuch*, ed. V. Langmantel, Tübingen, 1885, p. 105.

38 This is very strongly brought out by Miss M. Deanesly, *The Lollard Bible* ; see her index s.v. *plenaries*.

39 An excellent example of this is the second letter of Hermann v. Minden in H. Finke, *Dominikanerbriefe*, 1891, p. 125.

40 *State Trials of Ed. I.*, 1906, p. 93. The parody there alluded to is printed also in P. Lehmann, *Parodische Texte*, 1923, p. 23.

[41] A classical scholar supplies me with an illustration from his own school days : " In reading Calverley I relished every word of his parody on Tennyson's *Brook*, knowing the original by heart. But this gave me a great relish also for his parodies on Jean Ingelow, though I had never read a word of her poems : for it enabled me to guess at the originals."

CHAPTER IV

[1] The possibility is suggested by Héloïse's language in her first letter, *etiam illitteratos*, etc., though this may refer only to the air and not to the words (*P.L.*, Vol. 178, c. 185).

[2] This may be found in Mansi, *Concilia*, Vol. XXIII., col. 215, § 8. It runs : " We decree that ribald clerics, especially those who are called of the family of Golias, shall be ordered to be clipped or even shaven by bishops, archdeacons, officials, and rural deans, so that no clerical tonsure be left ; yet let this be done without scandal and peril." Mansi points out that this was decreed in the same words at the provincial council of Tours in the same year, and that both are repeated from a council of Sens about A.D. 920. But it must be noted, first, that these are merely *provincial* decrees, which had no binding force outside, so that they are not directly applicable to some of the districts where Goliardic poetry most flourished (*e.g.* Paris, Rhineland, and N. Italy). Secondly, even in those Rouen and Tours provinces, the prohibition would affect only ribald singers of wine, women, and anticlerical satire ; if there had been any true vitality in medieval Latin poetry, it might have flourished still. Some of the best hymns were written after 1231 : for hymnology Latin is particularly well suited, and here was a living inspiration. If there had been equal inspiration in Latin love-poetry, all the councils in the world could not have killed it.

[3] *Continuity of English Prose*, pp. 59, 82 ; *cf.* 88, 95–96, 106.

[4] Petit de Julleville, *op. cit.*, Vol. II., ii., p. 228.

[5] Paget Toynbee, in *Mod. Lang. Review*, Jan. 1907, p. 115.

[6] *Convivio*, Bk. I., cc. 10–13.

[7] Bk. I., c. 1.

[8] We cannot safely set against this those *libri dictaminis* which contain models for Latin letters even from citizens, their wives, and peasants. These were literary exercises, in which university scholars

made their very meanest characters express themselves in Latin, just as it is the tragic poet's business to make them speak in rhyme.

[9] G. Madelaine, *L'Abbaye de Mondaye*, 1874, p. 124.

[10] *Cartulaire de l'Abbaye de Zwyveke-les-Termonde* (Gand, 1869), pp. 97–132.

[11] *Gesta Abbatum*, R.S., Vol. III., pp. 169, 175, 179, 183.

[12] French Charters in the *Chartulary of Jully*, pp. 147, 149, 283, 316, 327, 331, 430. In that of Bricot-en-Brie, pp. 317, 327 ; St.-Martin-d'Autun, Bulliot, Vol. II., pp. 231, 258, 284 ; St. Mary's York, Fletcher, p. 202. Bury St. Edmund's *Memorials of St. E.*, R.S., Vol. III., p. 215. Moir Bryce, *Scottish Greyfriars*, Vol. II., p. 13. (Indenture in English between Warden of Haddington, Franciscans, and Vicar of Greenlaw, 1478.) Letters of Abbot to Abbot in *Collect. Anglo-Prem.*, Vol. I., p. 236, and Vol. II., p. 44. Indenture between Abbot and Vicar in S. O. Addy, *Beauchief*, p. 130. So again in Italy : see C. Affarosi, Vol. II., pp. 129, 133, 375.

[13] *Lit. Cant.*, II., 506.

[14] Tosti, Vol. III., p. 100.

[15] Luçon, Vol. I., p. 293.

[16] N.S., Vol. XIX., *Christ Church Letters*. Of the English letters, 14 are between monk and monk, 10 between monk and cleric, 4 between cleric and cleric. If, as is probable enough, Sellymg's patron was a cleric (No. 12) and the bedell of Bocking (No. 48), then my total of 37 becomes 39.

[17] Soc. Sic. Storia Patria *Documenti*, Serie IV., Vol. xi. (1913).

[18] *Chronique de St.-Ouen*, pp. 35–36.

[19] H. Finke, *Dominikanerbriefe*, Paderborn, 1891, p. 27n.

[20] See Denifle's note in *A.L.K.G.*, Vol. II. (1886), p. 452.

[21] *Chron. XXIV. Gen.*, p. 638.

[22] Maxwell Lyte, *Hist. Univ. Oxford*, 81 (Abp. Pecham's injunctions).

[23] *Mon. Hist. Carm.*, p. 182.

[24] M. Fournier, *Statuts et privilèges des universités*, etc., Vol. I., p. 145 ; *cf.* Helen Waddell, *Wandering Scholars*, p. 147. We get an earlier indication, though not quite so definite, from a story told of the great goliardic poet Primas, in the palmy days of scholarship at Orléans. Primas was ready, whenever challenged, to cap a Latin verse with French. See L. Deslisle in *Ann. Bull. Soc. Hist. France*, 1869, p. 147.

[25] Reynerus, App. III., p. 136.

[26] W. E. Pantin, *Chapters of the English Black Monks*, Vol. I. (1931), p. 261. The Editor has also occasion to note how full of blunders are some of the monastic copies of these chapter records, sometimes even making nonsense of the text (pp. 62–63).

[27] H. E. Salter, *Chapters of Aug. Canons*, 1922, pp. 14, 111.

[28] Wilkins, Vol. II., p. 722b. Reynerus, App., p. 129.

[29] Stewart's *Ely*, p. 208.

[30] F. Winter, *Cist. d. N. O. Deutschlands*, Vol. III., pp. 322ff.

[31] It is just possible, of course, that the main body of the testimony was given in Latin, with only occasional quotations from the vernacular. But at least this would corroborate the authorities' complaints of English-speaking in cloister.

[32] *Peregrinatio Religionis Ergo.* The visitation is in *Vis. Dioc. Nor.*, pp. 113ff.

[33] *Vis. Dioc. Nor.*, p. 99 ; F. Godwin, Catalogue of the Bishops (1615, p. 431) s.v. *Richard Nyx* : " he hath the report of a vicious and dissolute liver."

[34] B. passus X., ll. 52ff.

[35] *Fifteenth Century Prose and Verse*, ed. A. W. Pollard, 1903 ; *e.g.* pp. 140, 167.

[36] R. L. Poole, *Wycliffe and the Movements for Reform*, 1889, p. 85. Compare Petit de Julleville on the style of the later friar-preachers : " ce latin barbare, dont les mots, les tournures et la construction sont français " (*His. Litt.*, Vol. II., ii., p. 227).

[37] Pommeraye, p. 445.

[38] Busch, pp. 125, 192.

[39] J. G. Bulliot, *L'Abbaye de St.-Martin d'Autun*, 1849, pp. 309, 313 ; *cf.* p. 287.

[40] *St.-Martial*, p. 149.

[41] *History of Hawsted*, by Sir John Cullum, Lond., 1784, p. 192. Cullum believed, and Thorold Rogers popularized the idea, that the manorial accounts were written by the bailiffs and stewards who rendered those accounts. But Mr. H. S. Bennett, who is studying this and similar subjects intensively, assures me that the evidence to the contrary is very strong indeed : that the accounts were written commonly, if not almost always, by one of those multitudinous clerics in lower Orders whom we know to have lived by odd jobs of this kind. He quotes me one case where the " clericus faciens compotum " charges for 3 manors ; another, for 5 or 6. He notes that, in most cases, the scribe got $3^s/4^d$, $4^s/-$, or $6^s/8^d$ for his

EUROPE'S APPRENTICESHIP

work. At the same time, it must be confessed that any attempt to simplify or abridge this rather complicated question involves risk of exaggeration on one side or the other.

42 Paston Letters, ed. Gairdner, 1900, no. 589.

43 Ibid., nos. 289, 331, 341, 349, 355–56, 364, 996–99, and suppt. nos. XXV., XLII., XLIV.–V., XLVIII.

44 Prestre, pp. 3–8.

45 J. de St.-Genois, in Messager des Sciences historiques for 1837, p. 482.

46 Dugdale-Caley, Vol. VI., p. 854.

47 Cal. State Papers Henry VII., Vol. IV., pt. ii., p. 1649.

48 Melrose Regality Records, Vol. III., 1917, p. 218.

49 Vida, cc. XXIII., XXVI. ; ed. Nelson, pp. 157, 179 ; cf. Ch. Weiss, L'Espagne depuis le règne de Philippe II., 1844, Vol. II., p. 322.

50 Petit de Julleville, Hist. Litt., Vol. II., ii., pp. 261–63 ; cf. 474ff.

51 For the obstacles to this movement, see Petit de Julleville, II., ii., pp. 228, 276 ; for the victory of the translator, and his contributions to the Renaissance, Gaston Paris, Esquisse historique, p. 256.

52 Opere, Milan, 1810, Vol. X., pp. 23–24 (Della Volgar Lingua).

53 W. H. Woodward, Vittorino da Feltre, 2nd Ed., p. 11.

SECTION II
MEDIEVAL SCHOLARSHIP

CHAPTER I

THE MEDIEVAL SCHOOL

I AM not able to explain myself better, here at the beginning, than by repeating the details briefly given in chapter xxxi. of my *Medieval Panorama*. In this field admirable pioneer work was done by the late A. F. Leach, who wrote truly :

"In England, from the first, education was the creature of religion ; the school was an adjunct of the Church, and the schoolmaster was an ecclesiastical officer. For close on eleven hundred years, from 598 to 1670, all educational institutions were under exclusively ecclesiastical control. The law of education was a branch of the Canon Law. The Church courts had exclusive jurisdiction over schools and universities and colleges, and until 1540 all schoolmasters and scholars were clerks, or clerics or clergy, and in Orders, though not necessarily holy Orders."

All this is true not only in England but everywhere north of the Alps. In Italy, indeed, a good many Roman grammar schools probably survived from imperial times. Consequently, education was there much more of a lay matter. In England, the first Church decree on the subject is that of the Council of Cloveshoe in 747, which aimed at the establishment of an elementary school in every parish. Eugenius II. (826) decreed something of the same kind for all Europe. About 994, an English synod prescribed " that priests shall keep schools in the villages and teach small boys without fee : priests ought always to keep schools of schoolmasters in their houses, and if any of the faithful is willing to give his little ones to be educated he ought to receive them willingly and teach them kindly." That decree, however, is only slightly varied from one of Theodulph, Bishop of Orléans, in 797, which itself repeated a decree of 682 at Constantinople—that is, among people of ancient culture, untouched by the barbarian invasions. " Applied either to France in the days of Charlemagne or England in the days of Etheldred, these can have been little more than a pious aspiration." (Leach.)

Again, all the records of the period show the miserable quality of texts and reference books. In pre-Conquest England there were schools nominally at each episcopal see, where the clergy were centred, and generally in practice at most of them. But King Alfred complains of the immense ignorance of his time ; and, though we must not exaggerate the contrast introduced by the Normans, we have little record of schools until we come to the Conquest. From that time forward we may sometimes find elementary schools in parishes, with occasional monastic and episcopal schools. But the elementary school depended on the energy and goodwill of the particular priest. The grammar schools seem at first to have been generally offshoots of the episcopal schools, which, at their best, taught a certain amount of philosophy and theology, but in which a large proportion of scholars would get no further than the grammar. Very seldom do we find a monk teaching in any grammar school, nor were such, as a rule, founded by monks ; although the community of the adjacent monastery was very commonly made into governors of the school, and entrusted with its finances. The monks, contrary to a venerable superstition, were not the ordinary schoolmasters of the Middle Ages. This truth has been emphasized as definitely by Professor Mandonnet, late Rector of the Roman Catholic University of Fribourg, as by any one else. It transpires clearly from St. Benedict's Rule that he contemplates monastic education only for the " oblates " : that is, children offered to the monastery and destined to take the vows when they grew up and never to leave the precincts until their death. Pictures from these " oblate " schools will be found in Section III. : but here is another example from Dom Berlière's article in the *Bulletin de l'Académie Royale de Belgique* (Classe des Lettres, 1921). A parent committed a boy to the abbey of Mozat in these terms : " I entrust him to you to be well taught and severely chastised, and to live according to the [Benedictine] Rule, and to be ordained only at the advice of his parents."

Under early missionary conditions, in the Dark Ages, the monks did fairly often teach outside pupils. But, in the Middle Ages proper, the only " external " schools were the song and almonry schools. The former was mainly a choir school, of comparatively late growth. When, early in the thirteenth century, every great church built its Lady Chapel and had its supplementary services of Our Lady, it was natural that the monks should commit the singing there to hired boys ; and, again, that they should not leave those boys entirely without education. But these song schools were very small—from half a dozen to a dozen pupils. The almonry school, again, like the song school, we scarcely find except in the larger monasteries. The almoner gradually began to accept it as one of his duties to board and feed a certain number of young clerics who were anxious to pursue their education ; and the monks hired a schoolmaster to teach them : it is rare to find the monks themselves teaching either in the choir or in the almonry school.

The general tendency in our own day is to exaggerate the number and the efficiency of medieval schools. For this there is a double reason. We live under a strong reaction, generous and healthy in the main, against old-fashioned Protestants and Free-thinkers who despised medieval society as they despised Gothic architecture. Again, few readers have studied enough originals for themselves, even in translations, to escape from ana-chronistic modern impressions. They do not realize the full force of environment to change human instincts. Education, real or so-called, is such an inevitable feature of modern life, that they attribute proportionate im-portance to it in the past. Or, to speak more exactly, they attribute exaggerated importance to book-learning. They know that large numbers of books were destroyed at the Reformation, yet do not realize that the majority of these were only service-books or others which had already found their way into print before the Dissolu-tion of the Monasteries. They take no account of the reli-gious " specialist's " frequent jealousy of such education as threatened to break down the immemorial division of classes between priest, warrior, and wage-earner. In 1391, the House of Commons petitioned that serfs should not be permitted to send their boys to school. This, fortunately, was rejected : yet at the same time even such a broad churchman as the author of *Piers*

Plowman was scandalized at the idea of humbly-born bishops. The monks, who had far more opportunities for creating a real national system than any others, not only hung back, but sometimes exercised as jealously as any others the veto which their legal monopoly granted them. The right to keep school was then a privilege as exclusive, and sometimes almost as lucrative, as the landlord's right to keep a mill or an oven. In many cases, though the Bishop or Abbot had not founded a school, he had been appointed by the Founder as trustee : and he was not infrequently tempted to a jealous maintenance of this privilege. We have frequent indications of a state of things similar to that which Leach illustrates on page 285 of his *Schools of Medieval England*. " On 23 December, 1423, Sir John Bernard and William Brynge, chaplains, were summoned before John Hatfield, abbot of Walden, to show why and on what authority they practised the exercise of teaching small boys of Walden, and instructing them in the alphabet, the graces and other higher books, without asking or obtaining leave from the abbot, though they had previously been reproved for their presumption in doing this, and though according to the statutes and customs of the monastery the faculty of granting and conferring schools on grammar masters in the town of Walden and preferring masters to such schools belonged wholly and solely to the abbot and convent. The two chaplains confessed their offence and submitted themselves to the abbot, who interdicted them from teaching any boys of Walden in the alphabet or graces or other higher books. But eventually on the instance of the approved and more substantial men of Walden then present who wished their boys to be taught the alphabet, the chaplains were allowed to teach one boy of each inhabitant the alphabet and graces but no higher books. The ' graces ' in question were the graces before and after meat, usually included with the alphabet in primers and horn-books."

Education came originally from the Church : for a thousand years she was practically the only educator in book-learning. Then, at last, her monopoly became mischievous : she too often took away the key of knowledge and hindered those that were entering therein.

We see this in the conservatism of the grammar curriculum : grammar, of course, in its extended meaning of Latin scholarship. The grammar school summed up Secondary Education in the Middle Ages : above it were only the few cathedral schools in Theology, and the still fewer universities. Below it was such elementary education as the priest or his clerk sometimes undertook, or the song school which can be met occasionally in the towns. In this, as Chaucer's *Prioress's Tale* shows us, even the senior boys might not be able to construe the Latin of the hymns they sang.

The medieval classroom is still misty to us ; for documents are scanty, and few scholars have delved with determination into the deeper and less accessible veins of information. It is encouraging, however, to know that the task is now being undertaken in earnest by Professor Carl Young of Yale ; he is attempting an exhaustive evaluation of the MS. sources ; and we may hope shortly for fresh light from him and his pupils. Meanwhile, a brief summary must be given here of what is already available elsewhere.

Our earliest glimpse of the English classroom is in

the *Colloquy* of Aelfric, Abbot of Eynsham, about A.D. 1005. Two extracts will be found at a later page in this present volume. An excellent edition of this, in Latin and Anglo-Saxon, has recently been published by Mr. Garmonsway in Methuen's *Old English Library*. We must, of course, make wide allowance for the didactic object of this little conversational manual, especially where the young monk (who may be called head-pupil) names among his schoolfellows the members of twelve other callings. Yet we have many indications that these rare schools, at that wild time, were sometimes of a kind seldom dreamt of in our philosophy ; and, though inconsistencies may be found in the *Colloquy*, there is nothing outrageously impossible.

In an ordinary way, pupils began by memorizing a little Latin with the help of a word-list in the vernacular or, more frequently, by viva voce teaching. The first reading book was often the Psalter : *Psalterium docere* or *discere* are often used of elementary school teaching. For grammar, there were the late Latin Priscian and Donatus, but far more frequently, the *Doctrinale* of Alexander de Villa Dei (1199) metrically written to assist the memory. Only in later times was the pupil likely to have a book of his own. The beginner might have a " horn-book " : a slab of wood where a scrap of parchment, protected by a thin slice of horn, contained the alphabet, the Lord's Prayer, and little else. The master himself had seldom a dictionary, and it was a great innovation in [1260] to compose an alphabetical word-list. This became the standard dictionary, *Catholicon* ; but it is far from universal in the catalogues even of good libraries. Beyond the Psalter, early Christian authors were most often read, with the *Fables* of Æsop and the moral saws of Cato. Of the great classics, Virgil was most frequent ; but even advanced pupils were more familiar with books of extracts than with any author as a whole. It was enough if the learner picked up sufficient Latin to follow lectures at Oxford or Cambridge or some cathedral school. But only a small proportion, even of the priests, went on to such higher education as that. There were no theological seminaries in the modern sense. The majority of priests evidently learned their job by practical apprenticeship. The grammar school, or tuition in the boy's own village, fitted a promising pupil for the " benefice " of Parish Clerk. There, by reciting the responses, or even the full Hours, in Church during his priest's absence, he would learn enough of the ceremonies to pass an examination which was evidently not always searching, even when the prescribed routine was actually obeyed.

The last two centuries before the Reformation showed a great change, if not in the quality at least in the quantity of education. In 1357, an energetic bishop of Exeter was much disturbed at the parrot-teaching which he found to be usual in his diocese ; his circular is printed by A. F. Leach (*Educational Charters, etc.*, p. 314). But by that time there had begun a considerable increase in numbers. Benefactors were ceasing to endow the monasteries. The desire to secure Masses for their souls and those of their kinsfolk was more securely satisfied by founding separate chantries than by leaving fresh legacies to the monks, who were too often embarrassed, by this time, to fulfil their obligations already incurred. Therefore we now find numberless cases in which the legacy is destined to create an independent foundation ; it supplies a living wage for a priest who, with his successors, is to say a daily Mass to the world's end. Presently, we find these benefactors adding a clause that the pay must cease if the Masses are no longer said. A similar impulse drove them one step further : the priest must not only say his daily Mass—in other words, be kept in almost complete idleness on a bare living wage—but keep school also for such boys as may apply. At first, these were " free " schools : but by a process which was far from ceasing at the Reformation, these " free " scholars found themselves practically compelled to pay fees. To choose a trivial but familiar parallel from our own day, the process was that of hotels where we pay ten per cent. for " service " and as much again, perhaps, under severe moral pressure from the waiter. These Chantry schools became very numerous, but often, in those more difficult economic conditions of the Middle Ages, very decayed. Whether the benefactor appointed clerics or layfolk to administer his benefaction, there was still the insistent problem, *Quis custodiet ipsos custodes?* quite apart from the general insecurity of social and commercial conditions. Another page from Leach (p. 402) paints in detail the decay of such schools, and the remedial foundation of Christ's College at Cambridge. Under Edward VI., the Government disendowed nearly all these schools, on the pretext that the main object of the endowment was the superstitious Mass : this was one of the most unjust and foolish excesses of the Reformation. The schools which Edward VI. refounded on a securer foundation were few indeed compared with those which he thus destroyed : about thirty to about four hundred. But though this meant, as Leach pointed out, that Medieval England had more grammar schools than modern England had until the memory of living

man, yet this contrast must not be extended, as it sometimes is, to schools in general. When we count elementary as well as secondary, and girls as well as boys,
we have now twenty or thirty times more scholars, in
proportion to population, than in the Middle Ages.

It was another great step forward when a few of these
Chantry schools were founded on a sufficiently liberal
scale to allow a considerable class of boarders. Winchester (1382) was the first of these, founded by the
enormously wealthy William of Wykeham as a preparatory establishment to his New College at Oxford.
His later successor in the see of Winchester, Waynflete,
founded in 1459 two similar schools for his new college
of Magdalen. Meanwhile (1440) Henry VI. endowed
" the King's College of Our Ladye of Eton besyde
Wyndesore " for ten priests, four singing clerks, six
choir-boys, " and twenty-five poor and needy boys to
learn grammar there ... and twenty-five poor and disabled
men to pray for the souls " of his father and mother and
all his forefathers and all the faithful departed, with " a
Master or Informator in Grammar to teach the said
needy scholars and all others from any part of England
coming there, *gratis*, without exaction of money or
anything else." In connection with this he founded
King's College at Cambridge.

Incautious writers have often been misled by the
emphasis laid on the word *poor*, in these and similar
foundation deeds. Leach sums up what Rashdall and
others have shown to be the true explanation. By
Canon Law, all Church property was most strictly earmarked for the Church, either directly or to be expended
" in pious uses." No bishop or abbot, for instance, could
legally free his serf except for his full market-price :

otherwise he was wasting the goods of the Church. But nearly all school or college endowments were in the form of Church goods : rectories, or small dissolved priories, or revenues of that kind. It was therefore a necessary legal form to emphasize the charitable nature of these institutions in favour of which so much Church property had been alienated. As a matter of fact, Wykeham, though one of the wealthiest men in England, expressly gave priority at Winchester to his own kin. His scholars had to swear that they had not income of their own to the extent of more than five marks a year, in days when there were many vicarages whose whole revenues amounted to less. Their food and lodging were on middle-class scale, rather upper than lower ; and Leach has traced many of the earliest scholars to county families. As he sums up : " The notion that the endowments of Winchester or any other school before Christ's Hospital, which was for foundlings and the gutter pauper, have been perverted from the patrimony of the poor into an appanage of the rich, will not bear investigation " (*Schools of Medieval England*, p. 208). Christ's Hospital was founded from part of the endowments of the Grey Friars, dissolved in 1552, for " about 400 poor fatherless children."

In these new boarding schools the old monastic tradition was still showing. The boys were not allowed to stray from the precincts, and there were no regular vacations, though, of course, the red-letter days of the Church were holidays in the same sense that Sunday was. Sports were rather discouraged than otherwise ; it was only on December 6 (St. Nicholas' Day) that the boys had free—not to say riotous—licence. Otherwise games were under suspicion, partly as ministering to body rather than spirit, and partly because of their frequent violence in days when umpires or referees had not yet been invented. Football, naturally enough, was under special disapprobation ; here again I am able to supply an illustrative extract from the *Miracles of Henry VI.* (ed. Knox and Leslie, p. 91). We shall see in the next chapter that schoolboy discipline was, to a great extent, carried on into the universities also. On the Continent there was even university flogging, though very rarely in England.

It is sometimes argued that, though our remote ancestors may have left room for improvement in book-learning, yet that is only a small part of education proper : character matters more than learning. We may accept this last sentence as profoundly true, yet refuse assent, in face of the actual records, to the first. Though oral teaching predominated in the Middle Ages, and close personal contact gives the most direct opportunities of influencing character, and the spiritual side of true education far outweighs the material, yet, for all these things, we may be glad that the world has changed since the Middle Ages. What is more, we may find evidence to convince us that our medieval ancestors themselves, if they could be recalled to-day, would be the first to welcome the sum total of those changes, however critical they might be of details.

I have dealt with the religious education of our pre-Reformation ancestors in the seventh of my *Ten Medieval Studies.* A good deal, again, may be inferred from the earlier chapters of this present volume.

In 1281 Archbishop Pecham stigmatized, at the Synod of Lambeth, the " damnable negligences " of the clergy, their irreverence, and their ignorance. His decrees begin :

" The ignorance of the priests hurls the people into the ditch of error, and the folly or ignorance of the clergy, who are commanded to teach the Catholic Faith to the faithful, sometimes profits more to error than to sound learning." Therefore he enjoins that all parish priests should, four times a year, expound in English to their congregations the Apostolic Creed, the Ten Commandments, the Duty to God and to one's neighbour, the seven Works of Mercy, the seven deadly Sins, with their offshoots, the seven principal Virtues, and the seven Sacraments. " And lest any excuse himself on the plea of ignorance (although all ministers of the church are bound to know these things) we here give a brief and hasty summary thereof." This summary occupies only two folio pages, and shows how elementary was the minimum which the Archbishop attempted with such emphasis to enforce.

A whole series of similar decrees may be found in David Wilkins's great collection, down to the Reformation. Pecham's exact words, *Ignorantia Sacerdotum*, etc., form the opening sentence of a Provincial Council for York in 1466, and of Wolsey's decree for educational reform in 1518. In each case the decree rehearses the inefficacy of its predecessors, and appends the same childishly simple manual for the instruction of ignorant priests. Dean Colet, the friend of Erasmus and St. Thomas More, pleaded in his famous convocation sermon of 1511 that none should be ordained without "a moderate knowledge of Holy Scriptures," but in vain. For, in fact, the Church was regularly starved by the system of " appropriation." Where we find nowadays a vicarage, this nearly always means that two-thirds of the income of the original rectory had been appropriated by some monastery and cathedral, leaving the actual minister of the parish sometimes only the barest living wage or less. The vicar was thus handicapped not only in money but in respect. He could not exercise the hospitality which Canon Law required of him. He was often driven to eke out his subsistence by invidious exactions from his parishioners, not even legal. He might, again, be hired in the cheapest market. Therefore, quite apart from the satirists, nearly all our records point to a state of things far below the lofty theories of the Church, and there is no trace of anything even resembling a Sunday-school system.

Yet we must beware of laying more stress upon the shortcomings in practice than upon the aspiring ideal. We must bear in mind those long centuries when the Church, for better or worse, was practically the only friend education had ; the centuries during which her monopoly grew up naturally and was exercised to the great advantage of civilization. As the world widened, and as the Church's children grew up, this monopoly became mischievous. One movement which went far to break it down—not consciously and not of set purpose, but indirectly—was that of the Brethren of Common Life, in the Low Countries, under Gerard Groote (1340–84) and Florent Radewyns (1350–1400). This was an institution intermediate between monastic and lay life : men who organized themselves in groups, without indelible life-vows, and maintained themselves by copying books and by teaching. These men practically revolutionized education, partly by opening schools of their own, partly by taking over and giving fresh life to existing schools, partly by forming a sort of normal school from which teachers went out as missionaries.

By the time of Erasmus, the institution had begun to petrify ; but its work had been to place the Netherlands higher in general education than any country but North and Central Italy. Its teachers and pupils were, of course, churchmen, but not great dignitaries ; and in fact the Friars declared themselves as enemies of the movement.

In other directions, the new ground gained was much more definitely to the advantage of the laity. Even in England, a comparatively backward country, the founder of Sevenoaks Grammar School, in 1432, prescribed that his master must not be in Holy Orders ; he himself was a London grocer. More and more frequently, lay-folk were constituted as governors of some town school. Dean Colet's public and emphatic preference for the Mercers' company over the Chapter of St. Paul's is well known. In Italy, and in busy trade districts like Rhineland, the Baltic, and the Low Countries, this was even more marked. Henry VIII. lived up, far better than most sovereigns, to his reputation for learning and intelligence, and his reign marks a real advance : for even when the monasteries were dissolved the most conspicuous of their moderately populous schools were continued under different control. This is too little known ; yet Leach proves it with a wealth of details in his last chapter. We may accept with very little discount his final words (p. 331) : " The advancement of science and learning comes from a cultured middle class. No such class could be formed when the cultured individual established no family to be a centre of culture, and left no sons behind him to inherit his ability and widen the circle of culture, by founding more educated families to hand on the lamp of life. The success in life of the child of the parsonage and the manse has become proverbial. While monasticism prevailed, that source of national energy was cut off. The extension of education to the laity, in the prince, the noble, and the merchant, which was the distinguishing mark of the Renaissance, produced great results, and Henry VIII. himself was not the least of them. . . . The expansion of Elizabethan England, which took the world by surprise, not only in navigation, in commerce, in colonization, but in poetry and the drama, in philosophy and science, was due to the immense extension of lay initiative and effort in every department of national life ; and not least in the sphere of education and the schools."

CHAPTER II

THE HIGH SCHOOLS

IN the field of higher education, there were those great revivals during our period, centring round the dates A.D. 800, 1000, and 1200.

Charles the Great, in one of his greatest legislative enactments, set himself resolutely to restore learning in Europe, " at present well-nigh extinguished by the neglect of our forefathers." Alcuin of York became practically his Minister of Education ; he supplied the stimulus and compiled the textbooks, apart from his other writings which were creditable for the age but lost their interest as time went on. During the comparative anarchy into which Europe lapsed under Charles's weak successors, nothing was completely lost of that which had been gained in Alcuin's time. The most definite failure was in the attempt to utilize the monasteries as places of higher education for secular clerics. This measure was definitely rescinded by Charles's successor, since it was found that it disturbed the monks without corresponding gain to the Church in general.

The next revival began, roughly, about the year 1000. All through the Middle Ages there were alarmist expectations of the Second Advent of Christ, waxing and waning in proportion to men's discouragement by war, famine, plague, comets, or other mystical suggestions. The year 1000 was naturally strikingly suggestive from a numerical point of view, and our ancestors gave immense importance to the symbolism of numbers. Thus, at the very beginning of our period, St. Jerome counts 1 as the perfect number (there is one God) and all even numbers as evil (the unclean beasts went into the Ark by twos and twos). Three, again, is most excellent, for it is odd, and there are three Persons in the Trinity. Thus to Dante the square of three has immense significance. He and Beatrice first beheld each other when each was nine years old; and of her he writes: "This lady was a 9, that is, a miracle, whose root is no other than the marvellous Trinity." He adds modestly, "it may be that some more subtle person can find in this a more subtle reason"; and indeed we may sometimes find page after page expounding the significance of numbers, after the Pythagorean principles passed on by Plato. Seven was the number sacred to the Catholic Church compounded of Doctrinal Perfection (3 for the Trinity), *plus* Universality (the 4 quarters of the earth).

Nicholas Cusanus, who may perhaps be called the last original thinker of the Middle Ages, recurs again and again to the philosophical significance of numbers: one has only to glance at the index to the Basel edition of his works. Numbers are "a symbolic exemplar of things," "a certain natural and sprouting germ of the fabric of Reason": "the main track which leads us to wisdom." Coming to detail, in one of his sermons in which he expounds the parable of the hundred sheep in the wilderness, he lays stress on the significance of ten, as a "perfect" number, of a hundred as its square, and of a thousand as the cube of ten (p. 542). In his

Conjectures on the Day of Judgement, he makes great play with the number seven. He is writing in 1452. God made the world in six days, and rested on the seventh. Seven times seven makes forty-nine ; add to this a year of rest, and you have the "jubilee" period of fifty years. Christ's death was in his twenty-ninth year, and twenty-nine jubilees bring us to 1450. Appealing to the prophecies of Daniel and Ezekiel, by mathematical processes difficult for the ordinary reader to follow, he attributes specially fateful significance to the years from A.D. 1700 to 1750. This result is very remarkable ; for medieval writers, even about that date, were too obsessed with the thought of imminent judgment to grant the world any probability of so many years yet to come. But, however remarkable this result, the method is quite medieval, and it would have been strange if the year 1000 had not aroused more than usual apprehensions, followed by a more than usual reaction of relief when these were belied. We must remember also how constantly the number 1,000 recurs in the Apocalypse, that book upon which the Middle Ages pored with perpetual terror. Moreover, many circumstances coincided about that time to give fresh hope to Europe ; for instance, the cessation of large-scale barbarian invasions and the gradual formation of something like stable national boundaries. Synchronous with these was a revival marked outwardly by that "White Robe of Churches" described by the chronicler Glaber ; and more deeply by a more extensive and intensive intellectual life. Then came a period of great migratory leaders, missionaries of culture, of whom the best known to British readers are Lanfranc and Anselm and Abailard (d. 1142). As these multiplied, and collected by natural gravitation at certain important centres—Paris, Bologna, Orléans, etc.—it was almost inevitable that they should form themselves into gilds ; the masters in most cases, but the students in many others, combining for mutual protection and orderly regulation of their studies, to be finally ratified by the hall-mark of a formal " degree." This aimed at supplying definite assurance of capacity, wherever the teacher might go ; a right to teach wherever he could find a school ; the *jus ubique docendi*.

The two first universities were at Bologna and Paris : neither can clearly show precedence. The word *universitas* has not, as was long popularly supposed, anything to do with any ideal of universal learning. Bologna, in fact, had no Faculty of theology ; others had none of medicine ; not one had a professorship of mathematics or physical science or history. *Universitas*, both in classical and in medieval Latin, is applied to a corporation of any kind. The medieval universities, therefore, were modelled on the lines of trade or craft gilds. The full course for a degree, theoretically at least, was seven years. At the end of four years, as the apprentice saddler became a " journeyman," and might earn a little money while he went on learning, so the apprentice student became a " bachelor," or pupil-teacher. Three years more might bring him to the coveted mastership ; but only a small proportion held out so long. At Leipzig, where statistics have survived, even on the verge of the Reformation only about one-third of the students arrived at B.A., and about one-twentieth at M.A. Scholars were expected, before leaving the grammar school, to have completed their *Trivium* (hence the adjective *trivial*). This consisted of Grammar, Logic, and Rhetoric. But many came up so ill prepared in

Latin that grammar schools were set up in university towns. The full degree course included the *Quadrivium*—Arithmetic, Geometry, Astronomy, and Music. All those, however, were elementary : the real gist of the course was in logic, continued from the *Trivium* and applied to the study of Aristotelian philosophy. That was the " Arts " course, in the sense of " liberal " or " humane," as distinguished from the " mechanical " art of handiworkers, from the painter or sculptor down to the cobbler. Its Aristotelian content gave it an equal right to be called " philosophical " ; hence the man whom France or England called a Master of Arts was in Germany Doctor of Philosophy—*Ph.D.*—since " Master," " Doctor," " Professor " were synonymous almost everywhere during nearly all the Middle Ages. For all three denoted the same thing ; a man who had earned the *jus docendi* from some recognized corporation. If the Master wished to pass on from his Arts to Theology or Law or Medicine, that meant seven years more. There was no written examination at any point : all was oral discussion. It is not surprising that there should be evidence for considerable relaxations or evasions, though Rashdall is doubtless right in saying that the medieval degree never became so inconsiderable as it was with a pass-man at Oxford or Cambridge within the memory of living men.

The students originally lived in private lodgings, as in most universities to-day. They were far less numerous than legend represents : the story of 30,000 at Oxford is irreconcilable with known facts : it is doubtful whether it ever had more than 1,500, or at the end of the Middle Ages more than 1,000. Gradually " Halls " or " Hostels " grew up, kept by masters as a private speculation. Then came the era of colleges. The first of these were the settlements of the Mendicant Friars early in the thirteenth century. The monks imitated them much later, and on a far smaller scale. Meanwhile, other benefactors had begun to endow colleges, modestly at first and then, with Wykeham's foundation of New College at Oxford, on a grand scale, reminiscent of the liberality with which men had endowed monasteries in earlier days. Dr. H. E. Salter, whose knowledge of the Oxford documents is unrivalled, writes : " I estimate that the six [secular] colleges which existed in 1360 would contain about 10 undergraduates, 23 bachelors, and 40 masters. The founding of New College nearly doubled these figures, but if all the colleges had been dissolved in 1400 it would not have been a crushing blow to the University." Moreover, contrary to common belief, no early college was primarily founded for undergraduates, but for graduates who studied for further degrees. In other words, all were " Fellows " in the modern sense, a " Scholarship " and a " Fellowship " were as exactly synonymous as a " Master " and a " Doctor." Only gradually did the distinction arise ; and it was still later that the colleges were freely opened to those who merited neither title, but were simply " Pensioners "—paying guests. The students of earlier university days sometimes went through heroic difficulties, far greater than in the later centuries. One conspicuous example was St. Edmund Rich, afterwards Archbishop of Canterbury (*d.* 1240) and St. Richard Wych, Bishop of Chichester (*d.* 1253), whose story will be found briefly told in my third section. Both were of gentle birth, and both fought their way through such obstacles as have sometimes confronted the poorest Continental or Scottish peasants. At the other end of the scale were wealthy churchmen (or, much more rarely, the sons of nobles) who brought their own servants with them. Such an attendant was often glad to pick up crumbs of learning in the lecture-room, as of bread from his master's table ; in post-medieval times they developed into a recognized class—of " servitors " or " sizars."

Life was strenuous and often rough here, as everywhere at the time. The student rose for lecture at 6 a.m. in summer ; artificial light was very costly, and we must describe a typical schedule for the summer half. He washed at a trough in the college hall or the open court. Breakfast was a much less regular institution in the Middle Ages than to-day. The hardy man would go without it, as he went without afternoon tea until this last generation of ours. Dinner was commonly at 10, an hour which survived at Oxford even into the eighteenth century. After this, and a natural interval of rest, work would go on again from 12 or 1 to 5, the hour of supper. When supper was over (to quote from the statutes of King's, Cambridge) " after grace duly said . . . for that which hath been received . . . then, without further delay, when the loving-cup hath been administered to all who wish to drink, and after the potations in Hall at the hour of curfew, let all the seniors, of whatsoever condition or degree, betake themselves to their studies or to other places, nor let them suffer the juniors to tarry longer in Hall, save only on the principal holy-days, or when College Councils are to be held in Hall after the meal, or other arduous business touching the said Royal College ; or again when, in honour of God or of His Mother or of some other saint, the fellows are indulged with a fire in Hall at wintertide. Then it shall be lawful for the scholars and fellows, after dinner or supper, to make a decent tarrying in Hall for recreation's sake, with songs and other honest pastimes, and to treat, in no spirit of levity, of poems, chronicles of realms, and wonders of this world, and other things which are consistent with clerical propriety." Chess was considered specially inconsistent; for it was regularly played for money, and we find it frequently forbidden to the medieval clergy. Field sports of all kinds received general discouragement, even when they were not prohibited.

There was very commonly an evening repetition of what had been learned in the day's lectures; but the student would be in bed by 8 or 9. If this seems incredibly strenuous, it must be remembered that the Holy-Days were also holidays, about fifty in the year; so that the average working week was of five days only. Moreover, we have abundant evidence, especially in complaints from disciplinarian writers or other authorities, that it was common enough for the medieval student, like the modern, to treat his university time as one of enjoyment rather than labour.

The Principal alone had a separate room to himself, either in a Hall or in a College. At New College and King's the living rooms were subdivided for two or more students by wooden partitions; and it is characteristic of those foundations that students are specially relieved by statute from the necessity of sleeping two in a bed. After all, perhaps the worst disadvantage to a modern man would be the cold. The lecture halls would often be, especially in earlier days, mere sheds, unceiled, unfloored, and unglazed. The cold in winter must have been far worse than even that of ordinary medieval indoor life.

In book-production, the universities took a great step forward. Monastic copying was far less than is commonly supposed ; where we have the statistic evidence of catalogues, it points to no more done than could be produced by one monk in fifty, working at half-time in the intervals of his services. Even monastic reading, too, averaged only one volume per annum in theory, and the practice was evidently often far less than this. The universities could not satisfy themselves with this, for between 1200 and 1250 they brought a rush of fresh life into the Republic of Letters. The Dominican, Thomas Cantimpratanus, recounts with strong party animus, but with fundamental truth, the contrast between the conservative secular teachers and these mendicants whose competition became at once so successful and therefore so provocative (see extract in section III). There was much truth in the Franciscan, Roger Bacon, who wrote of the mendicants as " the Student Orders " in contradistinction to the brethren of the great Benedictine and other abbeys. These active new-comers not only gave great stimulus to the teaching—their first two generations coincided with the golden age of Scholastic Philosophy—but created indirectly a new industry of systematic book-production. After more than eight centuries of book-hunger, the universities brought Europe again into a position remotely comparable to the days of Imperial Rome, and leading logically, within five or six generations, to the invention of printing. Take Bologna for an instance. The whole copying trade was supervised by a university committee, who appointed official booksellers, *stationarii*, and controlled their work on strict gild principles. There were severe fines for incorrect work, for refusing to lend volumes to be copied—even by private owners—and for exceeding the statutory price per *pecia* : *i.e.* for the standard unit of sixteen pages. Scholars were forbidden to speculate ; if the bookseller knowingly sold to any man who meant to sell again, he was fined five pounds, one of which went to the informer. Similar restrictions were imposed upon all " merchants " who were rich enough to deal in second-hand books. It was within this network of minute regulations that the professional copyists, illuminators, correctors, and binders worked. The *stationarius* was bound to keep pure and legible texts ; he must lend out the books or the *peciae* at a tariff fixed by the university. As the cost of living went up from generation to generation, there was a temptation to diminish the size of the *pecia* : but this could not long go on undiscovered ; for the same committee which had fixed the original tariff recorded also the number of *peciae* in each *exemplar*.

This advance of book-production, so far beyond anything attempted during the previous eight centuries of monastic writing, must be put definitely to the credit of the medieval universities. So also must we give them all credit for their sharpening of the tools of thought. Those generations which struggled for a working synthesis of the unerrant Bible and the almost unerrant Aristotle did not only quicken men's curiosity to a very high degree, but fashioned instruments for further thought ; many of our commonest abstract terms were either fashioned altogether or first popularized by these schoolmen. When we hear from the lips of an ordinary labourer such a sentence as " it ain't the quantity of the food I object to, but the *quality*," that man is drawing a necessary distinction more easily and familiarly than many educated Romans could have done in Cicero's day. Yet, while all this mental exercise taught men much, it ingrained also in their minds many things from which the world, both orthodox and unorthodox, has freed itself very slowly and painfully.

It is very difficult to strike an exact balance in our estimate of medieval education. Certainly it fell very far below what might have been expected from the lofty ideals, and the sweeping disciplinary claims, of the Church which monopolized it. On the other hand, no judgment can be fair which, in effect, penalizes people for nourishing high ideals. The Church did far less than she professed : yet, for many centuries at least, she did far better than the laity were likely to have done if they had taken the matter out of her hands. Only towards the end can we blame the clergy for not making a far better use of their exclusive privileges ; and, then, the cities did in fact begin to take the place of the ecclesiastical corporations. Of the universities at the height of their influence Rashdall writes very truly :

" When all allowances have been made for medieval exaggeration, it is probable that a larger proportion of the population received a university education at the close of the Middle Ages than is now the case in modern countries. Certainly that was the case as regards England. Doubtless these crowds of students included thousands whose proper place would have been at a secondary school, but it must be remembered that in those days men went to the universities later as well as earlier than now. High ecclesiastical dignitaries of mature years were found seated on the benches of the schools side by side with mere boys. When all allowances are made for the mixed motives which drew men to the universities, when we have allowed for the coarseness and brutality of the life that was lived in them, when we have admitted to the fullest extent the intellectual deficiencies of their most brilliant products, the very existence of the universities is evidence of a side of the Middle Ages to which scant justice has often been done—their enormous intellectual enthusiasm."—(*Camb. Med. Hist.*, vi., p. 601).

Certainly this enthusiasm cooled a great deal in the later centuries, and the rapid advance of thought from (say) 1200 to 1350 contrasts with its crystallization in the fifteenth century. Like Christianity itself, Christian philosophy had begun as a revolutionary force and settled down into conservatism. Yet, a generation or two before that religious revolution which we call the Reformation, the increasing secularization of the European universities had begun to produce new fruit. Professor G. R. Potter puts this pointedly and truly : " The new teaching, secular in spirit, practical and scientific in its methods, even if restrained in scope by reverence for the writings of antiquity, was certain to triumph in the new conditions of Europe, even in those countries in which the religious innovations were most decisively rejected."—(*Camb. Med. Hist.*, viii., p. 716).

Chapter III

CONTRASTS BETWEEN MEDIEVAL AND CLASSICAL LATIN

For a much fuller analysis, readers should consult the Introduction to Professor C. H. Beeson's *Primer of Medieval Latin*, to which this present brief sketch is much indebted.

The order of words in M.L. approaches much more nearly to that of modern vernacular speech.

Vocabulary.—Words are used far more loosely in M.L. than in C.L. : *e.g.* se and sibi as personal pronouns ; tanti=tot. Many change their meaning, passing especially into ecclesiastical senses, as cardinalis, communio. Words that were vulgar in C.L. become usual. Thus the soldier's slang drives out the C. word : equus becomes caballus (cheval) ; os becomes bucca (bouche) ; caput becomes testa (tête). The diminutive often replaces the C.L. form : *e.g.* vasculum (vaisseau) from vas. Simpler words are replaced by superfluous formations, aetas becomes aetaticum (âge). Satis, perhaps more frequently than not, means very (Ital. assai). Infra is used for intra : fore or existere for esse.

Spelling changes considerably. Ae and oe often become e ; -tio becomes -cio ; h is added or omitted ; thus we get hostium for door, or ortus for garden. In less strictly literary language (legal documents, account-rolls, etc.), c before e or i often becomes s, as servisia for cerevisia.

Gender often changes; especially neuter plurals become feminines singular (biblia, chronica, etc.).

Cases are often used with great irregularity : *e.g.* dative for motion, instead of ad with accusative ; ablative for duration of time ; in manibus instead of in manus, or vice versa. De is sometimes used almost as in modern French or Italian : as digitus de manu, consilia de meis amicis.

Pronouns.—se, sibi, suus, lose their reflexive restriction, as in Fr. son. Hic, iste, ipse, ille, are used interchangeably: often they are used as a definite article, as unus is used for the indefinite. For alter . . . alter we get unus . . . alter.

Tenses are used far more loosely than in C.L. ; especially perfect and imperfect are interchanged, or changed to pluperfect, even in the same sentence. Compound tenses are formed, as in modern vernaculars, with debeo, habeo, facio, sum.

Infinitive is used almost as in the modern vernaculars, especially with facio, or to express purpose. The C.L. accusative and infinitive construction is constantly replaced by a substantive clause introduced with ut, quod, quia, quoniam. Sometimes quod, etc., are mere marks of quotation, leaving the construction of the sentence unaffected.

Subjunctive is used with great looseness. It may be said to follow, roughly, the line which has evolved into the modern French usage.

Adverbs are often combined with prepositions : *cf.* ab ante (avant), a modo.

Conjunctions.—Et is often superfluous. Many conjunctions have become so weakened as to be often un-translatable ; they often serve merely as particles of transition, *e.g.* at, autem, enim, etenim, nam, namque, sed, siquidem, tamen, vero.

Comparison.—The comparative is commonly used as a superlative, as melior for optimus (le meilleur).

A SCHOLAR IN MEDITATION

From A. Alciati's *Book of Emblems*
(Paris, Wechel, 1542).

SECTION III
EXAMPLES

I. BIBLIA VULGATA

This Psalm CXIII. (*A.V.* Ps. CXIV. and CXV.) is chosen to begin with, not only on account of its intrinsic literary merit, but also for Dante's sake (*Purgatorio*, II. 46). His souls, freed at last from all fear of hell, " sang it all together with one voice " as " the celestial pilot " carried them to the mount of Purgatory.

PSALM CXIII

In exitu Ifrael de Ægypto, domus Jacob de populo barbaro, facta eft Judæa fanctificatio ejus, Ifrael poteftas ejus. Mare vidit, & fugit : Jordanis converfus eft retrorfum. Montes exultaverunt ut arietes : & colles ficut agni ovium. Quid eft tibi mare quòd fugifti : & tu Jordanis, quia converfus es retrorfum ? Montes exultaftis ficut arietes, & colles ficut agni ovium. A facie Domini mota eft terra, a facie Dei Jacob, Qui convertit petram in ftagna aquarum, & rupem in fontes aquarum. NON NOBIS DOMINE, NON NOBIS ; fed nomini tuo da gloriam. Super mifericordia tua, & veritate tua : nequando dicant Gentes : Ubi

When Israel went out of Egypt, the house of Jacob from a barbarous people, Judea was made his sanctuary, Israel his dominion. The sea saw and fled : Jordan was turned back. The mountains skipped like rams, and the hills like the lambs of the flock. What ailed thee, O thou sea, that thou didst flee : and thou, O Jordan, that thou wast turned back ? Ye mountains, that ye skipped like rams, and ye hills, like lambs of the flock ? At the presence of the Lord the earth was moved, at the presence of the God of Jacob, who turned the rock into pools of water, and the stony hill into fountains of waters. Not to us, O Lord, not to us ; but to thy name give glory. For thy mercy, and for thy truth's sake : lest the Gen-

est Deus eorum ? Deus autem noster in coelo : omnia quæcumque voluit, fecit. Simulachra gentium argentum & aurum, opera manuum hominum. Os habent, & non loquentur : oculos habent, & non videbunt. Aures habent, & non audient : nares habent, & non odorabunt. Manus habent, & non palpabunt : pedes habent, & non ambulabunt : non clamabunt in gutture suo. Similes illis fiant qui faciunt ea : & omnes qui confidunt in eis. Domus Israel speravit in Domino: adjutor eorum & protector eorum¹ est. Qui timent Dominum, speraverunt in Domino : adjutor eorum & protector eorum est. Dominus memor fuit nostri : & benedixit nobis. Benedixit domui Israel : benedixit domui Aaron. Benedixit omnibus, qui timent Dominum, pusillis cum majoribus. Adjiciat Dominus super vos ; super vos, & super filios vestros. Benedicti vos a Domino, qui fecit coelum & terram. Coelum coeli Domino : terram autem dedit filiis hominum. Non mortui laudabunt te Domine, neque omnes qui descendunt in infernum. Sed nos qui vivimus, benedicimus

tiles should say : Where is their God ? But our God is in heaven : he hath done all things whatsoever he would. The idols of the Gentiles are silver and gold, the works of the hands of men. They have mouths and speak not ¹ : they have eyes and see not. They have ears and hear not : they have noses and smell not. They have hands and feel not : they have feet and walk not : neither shall they cry out through their throat. Let them that make them become like unto them : and all such as trust in them. The house of Israel hath hoped in the Lord : he is their helper and their protector. The house of Aaron hath hoped in the Lord : he is their helper and their protector. The Lord hath been mindful of us, and hath blessed us. He hath blessed the house of Israel : he hath blessed the house of Aaron. He hath blessed all that fear the Lord, both little and great. May the Lord add blessings upon you : upon you, and upon your children. Blessed be you of the Lord, who made heaven and earth. The heaven of heaven is the Lord's but the earth he has given to the children of men. The dead shall not praise thee, O Lord : nor any of them that go down to hell. But we that

---

¹ This Douay Version has turned the futures into presents.

Domino, ex hoc nunc & usque in sæculum.

live bless the Lord from this time now and for ever.

Psalm CXXV

In convertendo Dominus captivitatem Sion, facti sumus ficut confolati. Tunc repletum eft gaudio os noftrum : & lingua noftra exultatione. Tunc dicent inter gentes : Magnificavit Dominus facere cum eis. Magnificavit Dominus facere nobifcum : facti sumus laetantes. Converte Domine captivitatem noftram, ficut torrens in Auftro. Qui feminant in lacrymis, in exultatione metent. Euntes ibant & flebant, mittentes femina fua, venientes autem venient cum exultatione, portantes manipulos fuos.

When the Lord brought back the captivity of Sion, we became like men comforted. Then was our mouth filled with gladness ; and our tongue with joy. Then shall they say among the Gentiles, The Lord hath done great things for them. The Lord hath done great things for us ; we are become joyful. Turn again our captivity, O Lord, as a stream in the south. They that sow in tears shall reap in joy. Going they went and wept, casting their seeds. But coming they shall come with joyfulness, carrying their sheaves.

Isaiah LV

Omnes fitientes venite ad aquas : & qui non habetis argentum, properate, emite, & comedite : venite, emite abfque argento, & abfque ulla commutatione vinum & lac. Quare appenditis argentum non in panibus, & laborem veftrum non in faturitate ? Audite audientes me, & comedite bonum, & delectabitur in craffitudine anima veftra. Inclinate aurem veftram,

All ye that thirst, come to the waters : and you that have no money, make haste, buy, and eat : come ye, buy wine and milk without money, and without any exchange. Why do ye spend money for that which is not bread, and your labour for that which doth not satisfy ye ? Hearken diligently to me, and eat that which is good, and your soul shall be delighted in fatness. Incline your ear, and come to

& venite ad me : audite, & vivet anima vestra, & feriam vobiscum pactum sempiternum, misericordias David fideles. Ecce testem populis dedi eum, ducem ac praeceptorem Gentibus. Ecce gentem, quam nesciebas, vocabis : & Gentes, quae te non cognoverunt, ad te current, propter Dominum Deum tuum, & sanctum Israel, quia glorificavit te. Quaerite Dominum, dum inveniri potest : invocate eum, dum prope efi. Derelinquat impius viam suam, & vir iniquus cogitationes suas, & revertatur ad Dominum, & miserebitur ejus, & ad Deum nostrum, quoniam multus est ad ignoscendum. Non enim cogitationes meae, cogitationes vestrae : neque viae vestrae, viae meae, dicit Dominus. Quia sicut exaltantur caeli a terra, sic exaltatæ sunt viae meae a viis vestris, & cogitationes meae a cogitationibus vestris. Et quomodo descendit imber, & nix de cælo, & illuc ultra non revertitur, sed inebriat terram, & infundit eam, & germinare eam facit, & dat semen serenti, & panem comedenti, sic erit verbum meum, quod egredietur de ore meo : non revertetur ad me vacuum, sed faciet quaecumque volui, & prosperabitur in his ad quæ misi illud. Quia in lætitia

me : hear and your soul shall live, and I will make an everlasting covenant with you, the faithful mercies of David. Behold I have given him for a witness to the people, for a leader and a master to the Gentiles. Behold thou shalt call a nation, which thou knewest not : and the nations that knew not thee shall run to thee, because of the Lord thy God, and for the holy One of Israel, for he hath glorified thee. Seek ye the Lord, while he may be found : call upon him, while he is near. Let the wicked forsake his way, and the unjust man his thoughts, and let him return to the Lord, and he will have mercy on him ; and to our God for he is bountiful to forgive. For my thoughts are not your thoughts nor your ways my ways, saith the Lord. For as the heavens are exalted above the earth, so are my ways exalted above your ways, and my thoughts above your thoughts. And as the rain and the snow come down from heaven, and return no more thither, but soak the earth, and water it, and make it to spring, and give seed to the sower, and bread to the eater : so shall my word be, which shall go forth from my mouth : it shall not return to me void, but it shall do whatsoever I please, and shall prosper in the things for which I sent it. For

egrediemini, & in pace deducemini : montes & colles cantabunt coram vobis laudem, & omnia ligna regionis plaudent manu. Pro faliunca afcendet abies, & pro urtica crefcet myrtus : & erit Dominus nominatus in fignum æternum, quod non auferetur.

ye shall go out with joy, and be led forth with peace : the mountains and the hills shall sing praise before you, and all the trees of the country shall clap their hands. Instead of the shrub shall come up the fir-tree, and instead of the nettle, shall come up the myrtle-tree : and the Lord shall be named for an everlasting sign, that shall not be taken away.

ROMANS VIII. 5

Qui enim fecundum carnem funt, quæ carnis funt fapiunt ; qui verò fecundùm fpiritum funt : quæ funt fpiritus fentiunt. Nam prudentia carnis, mors eft : prudentia autem fpiritus, vita & pax, quoniam fapientia carnis inimica eft Deo : legi enim Dei non eft fubjecta : nec enim poteft. Qui autem in carne funt, Deo placere non poffunt. Vos autem in carne non eftis, fed in fpiritu : fi tamen fpiritus Dei habitat in vobis. Si quis autem Spiritum Chrifti non habet, hic non eft ejus. Si autem Chriftus in vobis eft, corpus quidem mortuum eft propter peccatum, fpiritus verò vivit propter juftificationem. Quodfi Spiritus ejus, qui fufcitavit Jefum a mortuis, habitat in vobis, qui fufcitavit Jefum

They that are according to the flesh, mind the things that are of the flesh ; but they that are according to the spirit, mind the things that are of the spirit. For the wisdom of the flesh is death : but the wisdom of the spirit is life and peace. Because the wisdom of the flesh is an enemy to God : for it is not subject to the law of God, neither can it be. And they who are in the flesh, cannot please God. But you are not in the flesh, but in the spirit, if so be that the Spirit of God dwell in you. Now if any man have not the Spirit of Christ, he is none of his. And if Christ be in you, the body indeed is dead because of sin, but the spirit liveth because of justification. And if the Spirit of him that raised up Jesus from the dead, dwell in you, he that raised up

Chriſtum a mortuis, vivificabit & mortalia corpora veſtra, propter inhabitantem Spiritum ejus in vobis. Ergo fratres debitores ſumus non carni, ut ſecundum carnem vivamus. Si enim ſecundum carne vixeritis, moriemini : ſi autem ſpiritu faſta carnis mortificaveritis, vivetis. Quicumque enim ſpiritu Dei aguntur, ii ſunt filii Dei. Non enim accepiſtis ſpiritum ſervitutis iterum in timore, ſed accepiſtis ſpiritum adoptionis filiorum, in quo clamamus : Abba (Pater.) Ipſe enim Spiritus teſtimonium reddit ſpiritui noſtro, quod ſumus filii Dei. Si autem filii, & heredes : heredes quidem Dei, coheredes autem Chriſti : ſi tamen compatimur, ut & conglorificemur. Exiſtimo enim, quòd non ſunt condignae paſſiones hujus temporis ad futuram gloriam, quæ revelabitur in nobis. Nam expeſtatio creaturæ revelationem filiorum Dei expeſtat. Vanitati enim creatura ſubjeſta eſt non volens, ſed propter eum, qui ſubjecit eam in ſpe : quia & ipſa creatura liberabitur a ſervitute corruptionis, in libertatem gloriae filiorum Dei. Scimus enim quòd omnis creatura

Jesus Christ from the dead shall quicken also your mortal bodies, because of his Spirit that dwelleth in you. Therefore, brethren, we are debtors, not to the flesh, to live according to the flesh. For if ye live according to the flesh, ye shall die. But if by the spirit ye mortify the deeds of the flesh, ye shall live. For whosoever are led by the Spirit of God, they are the sons of God. For ye have not received the spirit of bondage again in fear ; but ye have received the spirit of adoption of sons, whereby we cry : Abba (Father). For the Spirit himself giveth testimony to our spirit, that we are the sons of God. And if sons, heirs also : heirs indeed of God, and joint heirs with Christ : yet so if we suffer with him, that we may be also glorified with him. For I reckon, that the sufferings of this time are not worthy to be compared with the glory to come, that shall be revealed in us. For the expectation of the creature waiteth for the revelation of the sons of God. For the creature was made subject to vanity, not willingly, but by reason of him that made it subject, in hope : Because the creature also itself shall be delivered from the servitude of corruption, into the liberty of the glory of the children of God. For we know that every creature groaneth, and

ingemiſcit, & parturit uſque adhuc. Non ſolum autem illa, ſed & nos ipſi primitias ſpiritus habentes, & ipſi intra nos gemimus, adoptionem filiorum Dei expectantes, redemptionem corporis noſtri. Spe enim ſalvi facti ſumus. Spes autem quae videtur, non eſt ſpes : nam quod videt quis, quid ſperat ? Si autem quod non videmus ſperamus, per patientiam expectamus. . . . . Scimus autem quoniam diligentibus Deum omnia cooperantur in bonum, iis, qui ſecundum propoſitum vocati ſunt ſancti. Nam quos præſcivit, & praedeſtinavit conformes fieri imaginis Filii ſui, ut ſit ipſe primogenitus in multis fratribus. Quos autem praedeſtinavit, hos & vocavit : & quos vocavit, hos & juſtificavit : quos autem juſtificavit, illos & glorificavit. Quid ergo dicemus ad haec ? ſi Deus pro nobis, quis contra nos ? Qui etiam proprio Filio ſuo non pepercit, ſed pro nobis omnibus tradidit illum : quomodo non etiam cum illo omnia nobis donavit ? Quis accuſabit adverſus electos Dei ? Deus qui juſtificat, quis eſt qui condemnet ? Chriſtus Jeſus, qui mortuus eſt, immo qui & reſurrexit, qui eſt ad dexteram Dei, qui etiam interpellat pro nobis. Quis ergo nos

travaileth in pain even till now. And not only it, but ourselves also, who have the first fruits of the spirit, even we ourselves groan within ourselves, waiting for the adoption of the sons of God, the redemption of our body. . . . For we are saved by hope : but hope that is seen is not hope : for what a man seeth, why doth he hope for. But if we hope for that we see not, we with patience await it. . . . And we know that to them who love God all things work together for good, to them who are called saints according to his purpose. For whom he foreknew, he also predestinated to conform to the image of his Son, that he might be the first-born among many brothers. Moreover whom he predestinated, he also called ; and whom he called, he also justified ; and whom he justified, he also glorified. What shall we then say to these things ? If God be for us, who is against us ? He that spared not even his own son but delivered him up for us all, how hath he not also, with him, given us all things ? Who shall accuse against the elect of God ? God that justifieth. Who is he that shall condemn ? [It is] Christ Jesus that died, yea that is risen also again, who is at the right hand of God, who also maketh intercession for us. Who then shall

ſeparabit a charitate Chriſti? tribulatio? an anguſtia? an fames? an nuditas? an periculum? an perſecutio? an gladius? (ſicut ſcriptum eſt: Quia propter te mortificamur tota die: aeſtimati ſumus ſicut oves occiſionis.) Sed in his omnibus ſuperamus, propter eum qui dilexit nos. Certus ſum enim, quia neque mors, neque vita, neque angeli, neque principatus, neque virtutes, neque inſtantia, neque futura, neque fortitudo, neque altitudo, neque profundum, neque creatura alia poterit nos ſeparare a charitate Dei, quæ eſt in Chriſto Jeſu Domino noſtro.

separate us from the love of Christ? shall tribulation? or distress? or famine? or nakedness? or danger? or persecution? or the sword? As it is written: *For thy sake we are put to death all the day long. We are accounted as sheep for the slaughter.* But in all these things we overcome because of him that hath loved us. For I am sure that neither death, nor life, nor Angels, nor principalities, nor powers, nor things present, nor things to come, nor might, nor height, nor depth, nor any other creature shall be able to separate us from the love of God, which is in Christ Jesus our Lord.

Revelation XXI

Et vidi caelum novum, & terram novam. Primum enim caelum, & prima terra abiit, & mare jam non eſt. Et ego Joannes vidi ſanctam civitatem Jeruſalem novam deſcendentem de caelo a Deo, paratam, ſicut ſponſam ornatam viro ſuo. Et audivi vocem magnam de throno dicentem: Ecce tabernaculum Dei cum hominibus, & habitabit cum eis. Et ipſi populus ejus

And I saw a new heaven and a new earth. For the first heaven and the first earth was gone, and the sea is now no more. And I John saw the holy city the new Jerusalem coming down out of heaven from God, prepared as a bride adorned for her husband. And I heard a great voice from the throne, saying: Behold the tabernacle of God is with men, and he will dwell with them. And they

erunt, & ipſe Deus cum eis erit eorum Deus : & abſterget Deus omnem lacrymam ab oculis eorum : & mors ultra non erit, neque luctus, neque clamor, neque dolor erit ultra, quia prima abierunt. Et dixit qui ſedebat in throno : Ecce nova facio omnia. Et dixit mihi : Scribe, quia hæc verba fideliſſima ſunt, & vera. Et dixit mihi : Factum eſt. Ego ſum A, & Ω : initium, & finis. Ego fitienti dabo de fonte aquæ vitae, gratis. Qui vicerit, poſſidebit haec, & ero illi Deus, & ille erit mihi filius. Timidis autem, & incredulis, & execratis, & homicidis, & fornicatoribus, & veneficis, & idolatris, & omnibus mendacibus, pars illorum erit in ſtagno ardenti igne & ſulphure : quod eſt mors fecunda. Et venit unus de ſeptem Angelis habentibus phialas plenas ſeptem plagis noviſſimis, & locutus eſt mecum, dicens : Veni, & oſtendam tibi ſponſam, uxorem Agni. Et fuſtulit me in ſpiritu in montem magnum & altum, & oſtendit mihi civitatem ſanctam Jeruſalem deſcendentem de cælo à Deo, habentem claritatem Dei : &

shall be his people : and God himself with them shall be their God. And God shall wipe away all tears from their eyes : and death shall be no more, nor mourning ; nor crying, nor sorrow shall be any more, for the former things are passed away. And he that sat on the throne, said : Behold, I make all things new. And he said to me : Write, for these words are most faithful and true. And he said to me : It is done. I am Alpha and Omega : the beginning and the end. To him that thirsteth I will give of the fountain of the water of life, freely. He that shall overcome shall possess these things, and I will be his God : and he shall be my son. But the fearful, and unbelieving, and the abominable, and murderers, and whoremongers, and sorcerers, and idolaters, and all liars, they shall have their portion in the pool burning with fire and brimstone, which is the second death. And there came one of the seven angels, who had the vials full of the seven last plagues, and spoke with me, saying : Come, and I will shew thee the bride, the wife of the Lamb. And he took me up in spirit to a great and high mountain : and he shewed me the holy city Jerusalem coming down out of heaven from God, having the glory of God ; and the light

lumen ejus fimile lapidi pretiofo tamquam lapidi jafpidis, ficut cryftallum. Et habebat murum magnum & altum, habentem portas duodecim : & in portis angelos duodecim, & nomina infcripta, quae funt nomina duodecim tribuum filiorum Ifrael. . . . Et templum non vidi in ea, Dominus enim Deus omnipotens templum illius eft, & Agnus. Et civitas non eget fole, neque luna, ut luceant in ea ; nam claritas Dei illuminavit eam, & lucerna ejus eft Agnus. Et ambulabunt gentes in lumine ejus : & reges terrae afferent gloriam fuam & honorem in illam. Et portae ejus non claudentur per diem : nox enim non erit illic. Et afferent gloriam & honorem gentium in illam. Non intrabit in eam aliquod coinquinatum, aut abominationem faciens & mendacium, nifi qui fcripti funt in libro vitae Agni.

thereof was like to a precious stone, as to the jasper-stone, even as crystal. And it had a wall great and high, having twelve gates, and in the gates twelve angels, and names written thereon, which are the names of the twelve tribes of the children of Israel. . . . And I saw no temple therein. For the Lord God Almighty is the temple thereof, and the Lamb. And the city hath no need of the sun, nor of the moon, to shine in it. For the glory of God hath enlightened it, and the Lamb is the lamp thereof. And the nations shall walk in the light of it : and the kings of the earth shall bring their glory and honour into it. And the gates thereof shall not be shut by day : for there shall be no night there. And they shall bring the glory and honour of the nations into it. There shall not enter into it anything defiled, or that worketh abomination or maketh a lie, but they that are written in the book of life of the Lamb.

II. THE MISSAL

The Canon of the Mass—its central and essential portion—dates from A.D. 300 at latest ; the list of Popes and Saints commemorated testifies to high antiquity. St. Leo the Great made one small addition [460] ; St.

Gregory the Great another [600]; since that it has remained unaltered to the present day. Apart from its great religious value, it has here the interest of casting significant sidelights upon that clerical examination which is recounted in my first section.

Te igitur, clementissime Pater, per Jesum Christum Filium tuum Dominum nostrum, supplices rogamus ac petimus uti accepta habeas et benedicas haec † dona, haec † munera, haec † sancta sacrificia illibata, in primis, quae tibi offerimus pro Ecclesia tua sancta Catholica : quam pacificare, custodire, adunare, et regere digneris toto orbe terrarum, una cum famulo tuo Papa nostro N., et Antistite nostro N., et omnibus orthodoxis, atque Catholicae et Apostolicae Fidei cultoribus.

Memento, Domine, famulorum famularumque tuarum, N. et N. Et omnium circumstantium, quorum tibi fides cognita est, et nota devotio : pro quibus tibi offerimus, vel qui tibi offerunt hoc sacrificium laudis, pro se, suisque omnibus, pro redemptione animarum suarum, pro spe salutis et incolumitatis suae : tibique reddunt vota sua, aeterno Deo, vivo et vero. Communicantes, et memoriam venerantes, imprimis

We therefore humbly pray and beseech thee, most merciful Father, through Jesus Christ thy Son, our Lord, that thou wouldst vouchsafe to accept and bless these † gifts, these † presents, these † holy unspotted sacrifices, which, in the first place, we offer thee for thy holy Catholic Church, to which vouchsafe to grant peace ; as also to protect, unite, and govern it throughout the world, together with thy servant N. our Pope, N. our Bishop, as also all orthodox believers and professors of the Catholic and Apostolic Faith.

Be mindful, O Lord, of thy servants, men and women, N. and N. And of all here present, whose faith and devotion are known unto thee ; for whom we offer or who offer up to thee this sacrifice of praise for themselves, their families and friends, for the redemption of their souls, for the hope of their safety and salvation, and who pay their vows to thee, the eternal, living, and true God. Communicating with, and honouring in the first place the memory of the glorious

gloriosae semper Virginis Mariae, Genitricis Dei et Domini nostri Jesu Christi : sed et beatorum Apostolorum ac Martyrum tuorum, Petri et Pauli, Andreae, Jacobi, Joannis, Thomae, Jacobi, Philippi, Bartholomaei, Matthaei, Simonis et Thaddaei ; Lini, Cleti, Clementis, Xysti, Cornelii, Cypriani, Laurentii, Chrysogoni, Joannis et Pauli, Cosmae et Damiani, et omnium Sanctorum tuorum ; quorum meritis precibusque concedas, ut in omnibus protectionis tuae muniamur auxilio. Per eundem Christum Dominum nostrum. Amen.

and ever Virgin Mary, Mother of our Lord and God Jesus Christ ; as also of the blessed Apostles and Martyrs, Peter and Paul, Andrew, James, John, Thomas, James, Philip, Bartholomew, Matthew, Simon and Thaddeus ; Linus, Cletus, Clement, Xystus, Cornelius, Cyprian, Lawrence, Chrysogonus, John and Paul, Cosmas and Damian, and of all thy Saints ; by whose merits and prayers grant that we may be always defended by the help of thy protection. Through the same Christ our Lord. Amen.

III. ST. AUGUSTINE

St. Augustine (354–430), like St. Jerome, comes only on the confines of the Middle Ages ; but this book would be incomplete without them, since their influence was enormous. The African, St. Augustine, born of a heathen father and Christian mother, fought his way slowly to Christianity and asceticism through early irregularities and Manichaean heresy, mainly by the influence of his mother and of St. Ambrose, Bishop of Milan. In this first extract he relates the *sortes biblicae* which he regarded as decisive for his conversion.

Confessions, VIII. 12.

C. XII.   Ubi vero a fundo arcano alta consideratio contraxit et congessit totam mise-

But when deep reflection had drawn and heaped together, from the secret depths, all my

riam meam in conspectum cordis mei, oborta est procella ingens ferens ingentem imbrem lacrimarum. Et ut totum effunderem cum vocibus suis, surrexi ab Alypio. Solitudo mihi ad negotium flendi aptior subgerebatur. Et secessi remotius, quam ut posset mihi onerosa esse etiam eius praesentia. Sic tunc eram, et ille sensit : nescio quid enim puto dixeram, in quo adparebat sonus vocis meae iam fletu gravidus ; et sic surrexeram. Mansit ergo ille ubi sedebamus nimie stupens. Ego sub quadam fici arbore stravi me, nescio quomodo, et dimisi habenas lacrimis, et proruperunt flumina oculorum meorum, acceptabile sacrificium tuum. Et non quidem his verbis, sed in hac sententia multa dixi tibi : Et tu, Domine, usque quo ? Usque quo, Domine, irasceris in finem ? Ne memor fueris iniquitatum nostrarum antiquarum. Sentiebam enim eis me teneri. Jactabam voces miserabiles : Quam diu ? quam diu ? Cras et cras ? Quare non modo ? quare non hac hora finis turpitudinis meae ? Dicebam haec, et flebam amarissima contritione cordis mei. Et ecce audio vocem

wretchedness in the sight of mine own heart, there arose a mighty tempest, bearing with it a mighty shower of tears. And, in order to pour it all out with its [accompanying] cries, I rose up from Alypius. Solitude was suggested to me as better fitted for this business of weeping. So I went far apart, farther than even his presence could be burdensome to me. Thus was it then with me, and he perceived it ; for I think I had said I know not what, wherein the sound of my voice appeared already heavy with weeping ; and thus I had risen. He therefore remained, in great amazement, where we sat. I cast myself down, I know not how, under a fig tree, and gave a loose rein to my tears, and the floods of mine eyes brake forth, an acceptable offering to Thee. So I said much unto Thee, not indeed in these words, but to this effect : " And Thou, O Lord, how long ? How long, O Lord, wilt thou be angry for ever ? O remember not our ancient iniquities " ; for I felt myself held by these. I uttered lamentable cries : " How long, how long ? To-morrow and to-morrow ? Why not now ? why not in this hour an end to my baseness ? " Thus I spake, and wept in bitterest contrition of my heart. And lo ! from a

de vicina domo cum cantu dicentis et crebro repetentis, quasi pueri, an puellae nescio : Tolle, lege ; tolle, lege. Statimque mutato vultu intentissimus cogitare coepi, utrumnam solerent pueri in aliquo genere ludendi cantitare tale aliquid : nec occurrebat omnino audivisse me uspiam. Repressoque impetu lacrimarum surrexi, nihil aliud interpretans, nisi divinitus mihi iuberi, ut aperirem codicem, et legerem, quod primum caput invenissem. Audieram enim de Antonio, quod ex evangelica lectione, cui forte supervenerat, admonitus fuerit, tamquam sibi diceretur quod legebatur : *Vade, vende omnia, quae habes, et da pauperibus, et habebis thesaurum in coelis; et veni, sequere me* (Matth. 19, 21.) ; et tali oraculo confestim ad te esse conversum. Itaque concitus redii ad eum locum, ubi sedebat Alypius ; ibi enim posueram codicem Apostoli, cum inde surrexeram. Adripui, aperui, et legi in silentio capitulum, quo primum coniecti sunt oculi mei : *Non in comessationibus et ebrietatibus, non in cubilibus et impudicitiis, non in contentione et aemulatione ; sed*

house hard by I heard a voice as of a boy or a girl, I know not which, saying in chant and frequently repeating, " Take and read, take and read ! " Forthwith, with change of countenance, I began to think most intently whether children were wont, in any kind of play, to sing anything of that sort ; nor did it come to my mind that I had ever heard it anywhere. So I restrained the rush of my tears and arose, interpreting it no otherwise than that God commanded me to open a book and read the first chapter I might find. For I had heard of [St.] Antony [the first hermit] that, by a reading of the Gospel into which he had come in by chance, he had taken warning as though the words that were read were addressed to himself : " Go, sell all that thou hast and give to the poor, and thou shalt have treasure in heaven : and come and follow me ; " and that by such an oracle he had been converted straightway unto Thee. Thus I returned in all haste to that place where Alypius sat ; for there I had laid a volume of the Apostle when I arose from thence. I seized, opened, and read in silence the chapter upon which mine eyes were first cast : " Not in rioting and drunkenness, not in chambering and wantonness, not in strife and envying ; but

induite Dominum Iesum Christum, et carnis providentiam ne feceritis in concupiscentiis. (Rom. 13, 13. 14.) Nec ultra volui legere, nec opus erat. Statim quippe cum fine huiusce sententiae, quasi luce securitatis infusa cordi meo, omnes dubitationis tenebrae diffugerunt. Tum interiecto aut digito, aut nescio quo alio signo, codicem clausi, et tranquillo iam vultu indicavi Alypio. At ille, quid in se ageretur, quod ego nesciebam, sic indicavit : petit videre, quid legissem. Ostendi ; et adtendit etiam ultra quam ego legeram, et ignorabam, quid sequeretur. Sequebatur vero : *Infirmum autem in fide recipite.* (Rom. 14, 1.) Quod ille ad se retulit, mihique aperuit. Sed tali admonitione firmatus est ; placitoque ac proposito bono, et congruentissimo suis moribus, quibus a me in melius iam olim valde longeque distabat, sine ulla turbulenta cunctatione coniunctus est. Inde ad matrem ingredimur. Indicamus : gaudet. Narramus, quemadmodum gestum sit : exsultat et triumphat ; et benedicebat tibi, qui potens es ultra quam petimus aut in-

put ye on the Lord Jesus Christ, and make not provision for the flesh to fulfil the lusts thereof." Nor would I read further, nor was there need. In truth, instantly with the end of this sentence, as though the light of certainty had flooded my heart, all my doubts of darkness fled away. Then I shut the book, either putting my finger between [the leaves] or with I know not what other sign, and, with a calm countenance, made it known to Alypius. But he thus indicated what was wrought in him, unknown to me ; he asked to see that which I had read. I showed it, and he looked even further than I had read ; for I knew not what followed. There followed in fact : " Him that is weak in the faith, receive." This he took to himself, and disclosed it to me. So by this admonition he was strengthened, and by a good resolution and purpose, most accordant to his manners, wherein from long time past he always differed greatly and widely from me for the better, he joined me without any agitated delay. Thence we went in unto my mother ; we told her, and she rejoiced. We recounted how it had come to pass ; she exulted and triumphed and blessed Thee, who art able to do above that which we ask or think ; for she saw that Thou

telligimus facere, quia tanto amplius sibi a te concessum de me videbat, quam petere solebat miserabilibus flebilibusque gemitibus. Convertisti enim me ad te, ut nec uxorem quaererem, nec aliquam spem saeculi huius, stans in ea regula fidei, in qua me ante tot annos ei revelaveras. [Cf. 3, 11.] Et convertisti luctum eius in gaudium multo uberius quam voluerat, et multo carius atque castius, quam de nepotibus carnis meae requirebat.

hadst granted her more concerning me than she had been wont to ask with wretched and lamentable groans. For thou hadst converted me to Thee so that I sought neither a wife nor any hope in this world, standing in that rule of faith wherein Thou hadst revealed me to her [in vision] so many years before. So didst Thou turn her mourning into joy, far more richly than she had desired, and far dearer and more chastely than she was wont to require from grandchildren, [born] of my flesh.

Augustine and his mother purposed to return to Africa ; but she died before they could embark at Ostia Compare Matthew Arnold's poem, " Monica's Prayer."

Confessions, X. 23.

C. X. Impendente autem die, quo ex hac vita erat exitura, quem diem tu noveras ignorantibus nobis, provenerat (ut credo) procurante te occultis tuis modis, ut ego et ipsa soli staremus incumbentes ad quamdam fenestram, unde hortus intra domum quae nos habebat prospectabatur, illic apud Ostia Tiberina, ubi remoti a turbis, post longi itineris

Now, as the day now approaching whereon she was to depart this life (which day Thou well knewest, but we knew not), it came to pass, (Thyself, as I believe by Thy secret ways so ordering it), that she and I stood alone, leaning at a certain window, which looked into the garden of the house which then sheltered us, there, at Ostia on the Tiber : for here, removed from the din of men after the fatigues of a long journey, we

laborem, instaurabamus nos navigationi. Colloquebamur ergo soli valde dulciter, et praeterita obliviscentes, in ea quae ante sunt extenti, quaerebamus inter nos apud praesentem veritatem, quod tu es, qualis futura esset vita aeterna sanctorum, quam nec oculus vidit, nec auris audivit, nec in cor hominis adscendit. Sed inhiabamus ore cordis in superna fluenta fontis tui, fontis vitae, qui est apud te, ut inde pro captu nostro adspersi quoquo modo rem tantam cogitaremus. Cumque ad eum finem sermo perduceretur, ut carnalium sensuum delectatio quantalibet, in quantalibet luce corporea, prae illius vitae iocunditate non comparatione, sed ne commemoratione quidem digna videretur; erigentes nos ardentiore adfectu in id ipsum, perambulavimus gradatim cuncta corporalia, et ipsum coelum, unde sol et luna et stellae lucent super terram. Et adhuc adscendebamus interius cogitando et loquendo, et mirando opera tua, et venimus in mentes nostras, et transcendimus

were preparing for the voyage. We were discoursing then together, alone, very sweetly; and *forgetting those things which are behind, and reaching forth unto those things which are before,* we were inquiring between ourselves in the presence of the Truth, which Thou art, of what sort the eternal life of the saints was to be, *which eye hath not seen, nor ear heard, nor hath it entered into the heart of man.* But yet, with the mouth of our heart, we gasped after those heavenly streams of Thy fountain, *the fountain of life,* which is *with Thee;* that, being bedewed thence according to our capacity, we might in some sort meditate upon so high a mystery. And when our discourse was brought to that point, that the very highest delight of the earthly senses, in the very purest material light, in respect of the sweetness of that life, was not only not worthy of comparison, but not even of mention; we, raising up ourselves with a more glowing affection towards the "Self-same," did by degrees pass through all bodily things, even the very heaven, whence sun and moon and stars shine upon the earth. And we were soaring higher yet, by inward musing and discourse and admiring of Thy works; and we came to our own minds, and

eas, ut adtingeremus regionem
ubertatis indeficientis, ubi pascis
Israel in aeternum veritatis pa-
bulo, et ubi vita sapientia est.
Dicebam talia, etsi non isto
modo et his verbis. Tamen, Domine, tu scis, quod illo die cum
talia loqueremur, et mundus iste
nobis inter verba vilesceret cum
omnibus delectationibus suis,
tunc ait illa : " Fili, quantum ad
me adtinet, nulla iam re delector
in hac vita. Quid hic faciam
adhuc, et cur hic sim nescio, iam
consumta spe huius saeculi.
Unum erat, propter quod in hac
vita aliquantum immorari cupie-
bam, ut te Christianum Catholi-
cum viderem, priusquam mo-
rerer. Cumulatius hoc mihi
Deus meus praestitit, ut te etiam
contemta felicitate terrena ser-
vum eius videam. Quid hic
facio ? " Ad haec ei quid res-
ponderim, non satis recolo :
cum interea vix intra quinque
dies, aut non multo amplius,
decubuit febribus. Et cum
aegrotaret quodam die, defectum
animae passa est, et paululum
subtracta a praesentibus. Nos
concurrimus, sed cito reddita est
sensui, et adspexit adstantes, me

went beyond them, that we
might arrive at that region of
never-failing plenty, where *Thou
feedest Israel* for ever with the
food of truth, and where life is
Wisdom. . . . Such things was
I speaking, and even if not in
this very manner, and these same
words, yet, Lord, Thou knowest,
that in that day when we were
speaking of these things, and
this world with all its delights
became, as we spake, con-
temptible to us, then she said,
" Son, for mine own part I have
no further delight in any thing
in this life. What I do here any
longer, and to what end I am
here, I know not, now that my
hopes in this world are consum-
mated. One thing there was,
for which I desired to linger for
a while in this life, that I might
see thee a Catholic Christian
before I died. My God hath
granted me this more abundantly, that I should now see thee,
despising earthly happiness, become His servant also. What
do I here ? " What answer I
made her unto these things, I
remember not clearly. For
meanwhile, within five days, or
not much more, she fell sick of a
fever ; and in that sickness one
day she fell into a swoon, and
was for a while withdrawn from
these present things. We hast-
ened round her ; but she was
soon brought back to her senses ;

et fratrem meum, et ait nobis quasi quaerenti similis : " Ubi eram ? " Deinde nos intuens moerore adtonitos : " Ponetis hic, inquit, matrem vestram ? " Ego silebam, et fletum frenabam. Frater autem meus quiddam locutus est, quo eam non peregre, sed in patria defungi tamquam felicius optaret. Quo audito, illa vultu anxio reverberans eum oculis, quod talia saperet, atque inde me intuens : " Vide, ait, quid dicit." Et mox ambobus : " Ponite, inquit, hoc corpus ubi-cumque, nihil vos eius cura con-turbet : tantum illud vos rogo, ut ad Domini altare memineritis mei, ubi fueritis." Cumque hanc sententiam verbis quibus pote-rat explicasset, conticuit, et in-gravescente morbo exercebatur.

Ego vero cogitans dona tua, Deus invisibilis, quae immittis in corda fidelium tuorum, et pro-veniunt inde fruges admirabiles, gaudebam et gratias agebam tibi, recolens quod noveram, quanta cura semper aestuasset de sepul-cro, quod sibi providerat et prae-

and looking on me and my brother standing by her, said to us as one inquiring : " Where was I ? " And then looking fixedly on us, who were aghast with grief, " Here," saith she, " shall you lay your mother." I held my peace and restrained my tears ; but my brother spake something, to the effect that he wished for her, as the happier lot, that she might die, not in a strange place, but in her own land. Hearing this, scanning him with her eyes, and with an anxious look, for that he still *savoured such things*, and then looking upon me ; " Behold," saith she, " what he saith." And soon after to us both : " Lay," she saith, " this body any where ; let not the care for that any way disquiet you : this only I request, that at the Lord's altar you would remember me, wher-soever you may be ! " And having delivered this sentiment in what words she could, she held her peace, and struggled with her growing sickness.

But I, considering Thy gifts, Thou unseen God, which Thou instillest into the hearts of Thy faithful ones, whence wondrous fruits do spring, did rejoice and give thanks to Thee, recalling what I knew, with what care she had ever burned concerning her place of burial, which she had provided and prepared for her-

paraverat iuxta corpus viri sui. Quia enim valde concorditer vixerant, id etiam volebat, ut est animus humanus minus capax divinorum, adiungi ad illam felicitatem, et commemorari ab hominibus, concessum sibi esse post transmarinam peregrinationem, ut coniuncta terra amborum coniugum terra tegeretur. Quando autem ista inanitas plenitudine bonitatis tuae coeperat in eius corde non esse, nesciebam, et laetabar admirans, quod sic mihi aperuisset ; quamquam et in illo sermone nostro ad fenestram, cum dixit : " iam quid hic facio ? " non adparuit desiderare in patria mori. Audivi etiam postea, quod iam cum Ostiis essemus, cum quibusdam amicis meis materna fiducia colloquebatur quodam die de contemtu vitae huius et bono mortis, ubi ipse non aderam : illisque stupentibus virtutem feminae, quam tu dederas ei, quaerentibusque utrum non formidaret tam longe a sua civitate corpus relinquere : " Nihil, inquit, longe est Deo, neque timendum est, ne ille non agnoscat in fine saeculi, unde me resuscitet."

self beside the body of her husband. For because they had lived in great harmony, she also wished (so little can the human mind embrace things divine) to have this addition to that happiness, and to have it remembered among men, that after her pilgrimage beyond the seas, what was earthly of this united pair had been permitted to be covered by the same earth. But when this emptiness had through the fulness of Thy goodness begun to cease in her heart, I knew not, and rejoiced admiring what she had so disclosed to me ; though even in that our discourse at the window, when she said, " What do I here any longer ? " there appeared no desire of dying in her own country. I heard afterwards also, that when we were now at Ostia, she with a mother's confidence, when I was absent, one day discoursed with certain of my friends about the contempt of this life, and the blessing of death : and when they were amazed at the woman's courage, which Thou hadst given to her, and asked, " Whether she were not afraid to leave her body so far from her own city ? " she replied, " Nothing is far to God ; nor was it to be feared lest at the end of the world He should not recognize whence He were to raise me up." So on the

Ergo die nono aegritudinis suae, quinquagesimo et sexto anno aetatis suae, trigesimo et tertio aetatis meae, anima illa religiosa et pia corpore soluta est.	ninth day of her sickness, and the fifty-sixth year of her age, and the three and thirtieth of mine, was that religious and holy soul freed from the body.

IV. ST. JEROME

St. Jerome (331 ?–420) was the most learned of all Fathers of the Western Church. His translation of the Bible, based upon earlier Latin versions, testifies to his Hebrew and Greek scholarship. It became the official (Vulgata) version, and practically superseded, during the Middle Ages, the original text. In the Roman Church it still enjoys this official and practically exclusive recognition. Jerome was not only a profound scholar but a most energetic and impressive stylist ; in satirical power he is scarcely inferior to Juvenal. He and his surroundings are admirably characterized by Professor S. Dill (*Roman Society in the Last Century of the Western Empire*, pages 104ff.). He retired from Rome to ascetic solitude at Bethlehem, whence he commented from afar on the invasions which ravaged Europe. One of his most remarkable letters, quoted as classical throughout the Middle Ages, is No. CXXIII., to a wealthy widow at Rome who contemplated a second marriage. The passage printed here is equally famous : eloquent as to the struggle between strict Christianity and the beauties of Pagan literature.

Quae enim communicatio luci ad tenebras ? Qui consensus Christo cum Belial ? Quid facit	For what communication hath light with darkness, and what concord hath Christ with Belial ?

173

cum Psalterio Horatius ? cum
Evangeliis Maro ? cum Apostolo
Cicero ? Nonne scandalizatur
frater, si te viderit in idolio
recumbentem ? Et licet omnia
munda mundis et nihil rejicien-
dum quod cum gratiarum actione
percipitur, tamen simul bibere
non debemus calicem Christi, et
calicem daemoniorum. Re-
feram tibi meae infelicitatis his-
toriam. Cum ante annos pluri-
mos domo, parentibus, sorore,
cognatis, et (quod his difficilius
est) consuetudine lautioris cibi,
propter coelorum me regna cas-
trassem, et Jerosolymam mili-
taturus pergerem, bibiotheca,
quam mihi Romae summo studio ac labore confeceram, carere
omnino non poteram. Itaque
miser ego lecturus Tullium
jejunabam. Post noctium cre-
bras vigilias, post lacrymas, quas
mihi praeteritorum recordatio
peccatorum ex imis visceribus
eruebat, Plautus sumebatur in
manus. Si quando in meme-
tipsum reversus, Prophetas legere
coepissem, sermo horrebat in-
cultus ; et quia lumen caecis
oculis non videbam, non oculorum putabam culpam esse, sed

What doth Horace with the
Psalter, Virgil with the Gospels,
Cicero with St. Paul ? [1] Is not a
brother scandalized if he see
thee sit at meat in the idol's
temple ? And, though all things
be pure to the pure, and nothing
should be rejected which is
received with thanksgiving, yet
we ought not to drink at the
same time the cup of Christ and
the cup of devils. I will tell thee
the story of mine own unhappiness. When, many years ago,
for the Kingdom of Heaven's
sake, I had made myself eunuch
of house and parents, sister and
kinsfolk, and (a harder task) of
the use of choicer food ; and
when I was on my way to
Jerusalem to fight [in such a
cause], I could not entirely do
without the library which I had
made for myself at Rome with
utmost zeal and labour. Therefore, wretch as I was, I fasted
for the reading of Cicero. After
frequent night-watches, after the
tears which were wrung from
my heart-strings by the memory
of my past sins, Plautus was
taken in hand. Whenever I
returned to myself and began to
read the Prophets, their rugged
speech repelled me : and, because with my purblind eyes I
saw no light, I fancied the fault
to be not mine own but the

[1] *Apostolus* by itself, in medieval divinity, is always Paul, the Apostle *par excellence*.

174

solis. Dum ita me antiquus serpens illuderet, in media ferme quadragesima medullis infusa febris corpus invasit exhaustum : et sine ulla requie (quod dictu quoque incredibile sit) sic infelicia membra depasta est, ut ossibus vix haererem. Interim parantur exequiae ; et vitalis animae calor, toto frigescente jam corpore, in solo tantum tepente pectusculo palpitabat : cum subito, raptus in spiritu, ad tribunal judicis pertrahor ; ubi tantum luminis, et tantum erat ex circumstantium claritate fulgoris, ut projectus in terram sursum aspicere non auderem. Interrogatus de conditione, Christianum me esse respondi. Et ille qui praesidebat : Mentiris, ait, Ciceronianus es, non Christianus : ubi enim thesaurus tuus, ibi et cor tuum. Illico obmutui, et inter verbera (nam caedi me jusserat) conscientiae magis igne torquebar, illum mecum versiculum reputans : " In inferno autem quis confitebitur tibi ? " Clamare tamen coepi, et ejulans dicere : Miserere mei, Domine, miserere mei ! Haec vox inter flagella resonabat.

sun's. While the Ancient Serpent thus deluded me, in about mid-Lent, a fever crept into my marrow and invaded my exhausted frame, and without any rest (a thing incredible even to relate) it preyed so upon my wretched limbs that I scarce clave to my bones. Meanwhile the funeral rites were prepared, and, while my whole body was already cold, the heat of vital soul did but palpitate in my poor lukewarm breast alone. Then suddenly I was rapt in spirit and dragged to the Judge's tribunal, where there was such light, and such effulgence from the glory of those who stood around, that I fell to earth and dared not to look upwards. Asked concerning my condition, I answered that I was a Christian ; and He who presided said, " Thou liest : thou art a Ciceronian and no Christian : for where thy treasure is, there is thy heart also." Forthwith I was dumb ; and between my stripes (for he had ordered that I should be beaten) I was more tortured by the fire of conscience, thinking over in myself that verse : " In hell who shall confess unto thee ? " [1] Yet I began to cry aloud, and to lament and say, " Have mercy upon me, O Lord ; have mercy upon me ! " This cry resounded

---

[1] Ps. vi. 6, *Vulg.* In the *A.V.*, vi. 5 : " in the grave who shall give thee thanks ? "

Tandem ad praesidentis genua provoluti qui astabant, precabantur, ut veniam tribueret adolescentiae, et errori locum poenitentiae commodaret, exacturus deinde cruciatum, si Gentilium litterarum libros aliquando legissem. Ego qui, in tanto constrictus articulo, vellem etiam majora promittere, dejerare coepi, et nomen ejus obtestans dicere, Domine, si unquam habuero codices saeculares, si legero, te negavi. In haec sacramenti verba dimissus, revertor ad superos, et, mirantibus cunctis, oculos aperio tanto lacrymarum imbre perfusos, ut etiam incredulis fidem facerem ex dolore. Nec vero sopor ille fuerat, aut vana somnia quibus saepe deludimur. Testis est tribunal illud, ante quod jacui, testis judicium triste, quod timui : ita mihi nunquam contingat in talem incidere quaestionem. Liventes fateor habuisse me scapulas, plagas sensisse post somnum, et among my stripes. At length the bystanders cast themselves at the Judge's feet and besought Him to grant pardon to my youth and to grant a place of repentance for my error, on condition of inflicting torment upon me if ever I read the books of pagan literature. I (who, pinched within this narrow pass, would have been willing to promise even greater things) began to swear, and to call upon His name and say, " Lord, if ever again I possess worldly books, or if I read them, I shall have denied Thee." On the strength of the words of that oath I was dismissed and returned to the upper world ; and, to the amazement of all men, I opened my eyes that swam in such a shower of tears as to convince even the unbelieving through my pain. Nor indeed had that been sleep, or those vain dreams whereby we are often deluded : witness that judgment-seat before which I lay, witness the dismal sentence which I feared : so may it never befall me to fall into such a trial ! I protest that I had my shoulders bruised, that I felt the stripes after my sleep, and that, from thenceforth, I read godly books

tanto dehinc studio divina legisse quanto non ante mortalia legeram.	with such eagerness as I had never before read those that are mortal.[1]

V. THE ABBESS AETHERIA

The Pilgrimage of Aetheria, formerly entitled in error *Peregrinatio Silviae*, is in all probability the earliest of its kind, dating from the last quarter of the fourth century A.D. The lady was abbess of a convent, probably in N.W. Spain, and her style exemplifies the Latin used by educated folk, not writers by profession, in their familiar correspondence. These two extracts are from the edition of W. Heraeus (Heidelberg, 1908), pages 14, 30. An excellent translation and introduction, by M. L. McClure and C. L. Feltoe, is published by the S.P.C.K.

Mount Nebo

Tunc autem qui erant loci notores, id est presbyteri uel monachi sancti, dixerunt nobis : " Si uultis uidere loca, quae scripta sunt in libris Moysi, accedite foras hostium ecclesiae et de summitate ipsa, ex parte tamen ut possunt hinc parere,	So then those who were vouchers for the place (that is, the priests or holy monks) said unto us, " If ye will see the places which are written in the books of Moses, come out from the door of the church, and mark and see from the very summit, yet in the direction that they may be able to appear from

---

[1] In early times, and even in the later Middle Ages, it was as unusual to read silently to oneself as it is now to find a man sufficiently musical to enjoy the silent reading of a score. See the case of Philip and the Eunuch (Acts viii. 34) and St. Augustine's own *Confessions*, Bk. VI. c. 3, where he comments on St. Ambrose's strange habit of silent reading. For the exceptionally expert (and therefore silent) reader, see Chaucer, *House of Fame*, l. 656.

attendite et uidete, et dicimus uobis singula, quae sunt loca haec, quae parent." Tunc nos gauisi satis statim egressi sumus foras. Nam de hostio ipsius ecclesiae uidimus locum, ubi intrat Jordanis in mare mortuum, qui locus subter nos, quemadmodum stabamus, parebat. Vidimus etiam de contra non solum Libiadam, quae citra Jordanem erat, sed et Jericho, que trans Jordanem : tantum eminebat excelsus locus, ubi stabamus, id est ante hostium ecclesiae. Maxima etiam pars Palestinae, quae est terra repromissionis, inde uidebatur, nec non et omnis terra Jordanis, in quantum tamen poterat oculis conspici. In sinistra autem parte uidimus terras Sodomitum omnes nec non et Segor, quae tamen Segor sola de illis quinque in hodie constat. Nam et memoriale ibi est, de ceteris autem illis ciuitatibus nichil aliud apparet nisi subuersio ruinarum, quemadmodum in cinerem conuerse sunt. Locus etiam, ubi fuit titubus uxoris Loth, ostensus est nobis, qui locus etiam in scripturis legitur. Sed mihi credite, domine uenerabiles, quia columna ipsa iam non paret, locus autem ipse tantum ostenditur : columna autem ipsa

hence, and we [will] tell you each, what are these places that appear." Then were we glad, and went out very[1] immediately. For from the door of the church itself we saw the place where Jordan entereth into the Dead Sea ; a place which appeared beneath us as we stood. We saw also, opposite, not only Livias, which was on this side Jordan, but also Jericho which is beyond Jordan : such was the eminence of the lofty place where we stood, that is, before the church door. For the greatest part also of Palestine which is the Land of Promise, was seen from thence ; moreover, the whole land of Jordan, at least in so far as it could be beholden with eyes. But on the left side we saw all the lands of the men of Sodom, and also Zoar, which Zoar standeth alone of those five. For there is a memorial also : but of those other cities nought else appeareth but subversion of ruins, even as they were reduced to ashes. That place also was shown unto us where was the memorial of Lot's wife ; which place is also read of in Scripture. But, believe me, venerable ladies, that the pillar itself appeareth not now ; but only the place itself is shown, but the pillar itself is

---

[1] " Satis," perhaps more often than not, has this force in medieval Latin. Compare the force of Italian " assai."

dicitur mari mortuo fuisse quo-
operta. Certe locum cum uidere-
mus, columnam nullam uidimus,
et ideo fallere uos super hanc rem
non possum. Nam episcopus
loci ipsius, id est de Segor, dixit
nobis, quoniam iam aliquot anni
essent, a quo non pareret columna illa. Nam de Segor forsit-
an sexto miliario ipse locus est,
ubi stetit columna illa, quod
nunc totum cooperit aqua.

said to have been covered by the
Dead Sea. Certainly when we
saw the place we saw no pillar,
and therefore I cannot deceive
you with regard to this thing.
For the Bishop of the place itself,
that is, of Zoar, said unto us that
now were a good many years
that that pillar had not appeared.
For that place (which is now
altogether covered with water)
where that pillar stood, is perchance six miles distant from
Zoar.

The Holy Sepulchre at Jerusalem

Septima autem die, id est
dominica die, ante pullorum
cantum colliget se omnis multitudo, quecumque esse potest in
eo loco, ac si per pascha in basilica, quae est loco iuxta Anastasim, foras tamen, ubi luminaria pro hoc ipsud pendent.
Dum enim uerentur, ne ad pullorum cantum non occurrant,
antecessus ueniunt et ibi sedent.
Et dicuntur ymni nec non an-
tiphonae, et fiunt orationes cata
singulos ymnos uel antiphonas.
Nam et presbyteri et diacones
semper parati sunt in eo loco ad
uigilias propter multitudinem,

Now on the seventh day, that
is, on Sunday,[1] before cock-
crow,[2] the whole multitude
assembleth itself, whatsoever
[multitude] can exist in that
place, as though for Easter, in
the basilica which is in place
beside the Holy Sepulchre, yet
outside, where the lights hang
for this very purpose. For, since
they fear that they will not
come thither at cock-crow, they
come forestalling and sit there.
And hymns are rehearsed, and
anthems also : and prayers are
made after[3] each hymn or
anthem. For both priests and
deacons are always present in
that place for vigils, by reason of
the multitude which gathereth

---

[1] Aetheria begins her account of the ceremonies with Monday : thus
Sunday comes seventh.   [2] Lit. " chicken-crow."   [3] *i.e.* the Greek κατά.

quae se colliget. Consuetudo enim talis est, ut ante pullorum cantum loca sancta non aperiantur. Mox autem primus pullus cantquerit, statim descendet episcopus et intrat intro speluncam ad Anastasim. Aperiuntur hostia omnia et intrat omnis multitudo ad Anastasim, ubi iam luminaria infinita lucent, et quemadmodum ingressus fuerit populus, dicet psalmum quicumque de presbyteris et respondent omnes ; post hoc fit oratio. Item dicit psalmum quicumque de diaconibus, similiter fit oratio, dicitur et tertius psalmus a quocumque clerico, fit et tertio oratio et commemoratio omnium. Dictis ergo his tribus psalmis et factis orationibus tribus ecce etiam thiamataria inferuntur intro spelunca Anastasis, ut tota basilica Anastasis repleatur odoribus. Et tunc ibi stat episcopus intro cancellos, prendet evangelium et accedet ad hostium et leget resurrectionem Domini episcopus ipse. Quod cum coeperit legi, tantus rugitus et mugitus fit omnium hominum et tantae lacrimae, ut quamuis durissimus possit moueri in lacrimis

together there. For the custom is such that the holy places are not opened before cock-crow. So, as soon as the first cock hath crowed, forthwith the Bishop cometh down and entereth into the cave at the Sepulchre. All the doors are opened, and the whole multitude entereth into the Sepulchre, where now numberless lights are shining ; and, even as the people hath entered, some one of the priests rehearseth a psalm and all make response : after this a prayer is made. Again, one of the deacons rehearses a psalm ; likewise prayer made and a third psalm is rehearsed by some cleric, and prayer is made for the third time, and the commemoration of all. So after these three psalms have been rehearsed, and prayers made, lo ! censers are brought into the cave of the Sepulchre, so that the whole basilica of the Sepulchre is filled with odours.[1] And then the Bishop stands there within the altar-rails, takes the Gospel-book, and comes to the door, and the Bishop himself reads the Lord's Resurrection. When he beginneth to read this, there is such a roaring and bellowing of all men, and such tears, that [any man] though, hardest of heart, might be moved to tears that the Lord

---

[1] Possibly the first mention in literature of incense used for public worship in a Christian church.

Dominum pro nobis tanta sustinuisse. Lecto ergo euangelio exit episcopus et ducitur cum ymnis ad Crucem, et omnis populus cum illo. Ibi denuo dicitur unus psalmus et fit oratio. Item benedicit fideles et fit missa. Et exeunte episcopo omnes ad manum accedunt.

had suffered so much for us. So, when the Gospel hath been read, the Bishop goeth forth and is led with hymns to the Cross, and all the people with him. There again a psalm is said and prayer is made. Again, he blesseth the faithful and dismissal is made. And, as the Bishop goeth forth, all come to his hand [for a blessing].

VI. ST. BENEDICT'S RULE

Composed about A.D. 529, this became by far the most influential monastic Rule in Western Christendom. For this extract, see Chaucer, *Prologue*, lines 179ff.

Chapter LX. Ad portam monasterii ponatur senex sapiens, qui sciat accipere responsum et reddere ; cuius maturitas eum non sinat vagari. Qui portarius cellam debet habere iuxta portam, ut venientes semper praesentem inveniant, a quo responsum accipiant. Et mox ut aliquis pulsaverit aut pauper clamaverit, "*Deo gratias*" respondeat, aut benedicat ; et cum omni mansuetudine timoris Dei reddat responsum festinanter, cum fervore charitatis. Qui portarius, si indiget solatio,

Let a wise elder be set at the monastery door, who knoweth how to take and return an answer ; one whose ripe age permitteth him not to wander abroad. This Porter ought to have a cell beside the gate, in order that comers may always find him there, and may take their answer from him. And, as soon as any man hath knocked, or a poor man cried aloud, let him answer, " Thanks be to God," or bless him ; and with all godfearing gentleness let him give his answer hastily, with fervour of charity. If this Porter be in need of comfort, let him

iuniorem fratrem accipiat. Monasterium autem (si fieri potest) ita debet construi, ut omnia necessaria, id est, aqua, molendinum, hortus, pistrinum, vel artes diversae intra monasterium exerceantur, ut non sit necessitas monachis vagandi foras ; quia omnino non expedit animabus eorum. Hanc autem Regulam saepius volumus in congregatione legi, ne quis fratrum de ignorantia se excuset.

take a younger brother. Now the monastery, if it may be, should so be built that all necessaries—to wit, water, mill, garden, bakery, or various handiworks—may be exercised within the precincts, so that there be no need for the monks to wander abroad : for that is altogether inexpedient to their souls. Now we will that this Rule be often read in the congregation, lest any of the brethren excuse himself of ignorance.

[Probably the original Rule ended here, so that the command of frequent reading had not then the very special emphasis upon this ch. lx. which it has as it stands.]

VII. GREGORY OF TOURS

Gregory, Bishop of Tours, wrote his *History of the Franks* at intervals between 576 and 591. His frequent grammatical errors, probably exaggerated to some extent by early copyists, take nothing away from the brilliance of his pictures. One of his most striking figures is Clovis I. (Chlodovech), the ever-successful arch-ruffian who stands head and shoulders above the minor ruffians around him. The extracts are from Omont's edition.

Preface (p. 1).

Decedente atque immo potius pereunte in urbibus Gallicanis

As the cultivation of liberal letters decayed, or rather per-

liberalium cultura litterarum, cum nonnullae res gererentur vel recte vel inprobe, ac feretas gentium desaeviret, regum furor acueretur, aeclesiae inpugnarentur ab hereticis, a catholicis tegerentur, ferveret Christi fides in plurimis, tepisceret in nonnullis, ipsae quoque aeclesiae vel ditarentur a devotis vel nudarentur a perfidis, nec repperire possit quisquam peritus dialectica in arte grammaticus, qui haec aut stilo prosaico aut metrico depingeret versu : ingemiscebant saepius plerique, dicentes : "Vae diebus nostris, quia periit studium litterarum a nobis, nec repperiritur in populis, qui gesta praesencia promulgare possit in paginis." Ista etenim atque et his similia iugiter intuens dixi, pro commemoracione praeteritorum, ut noticiam adtingerent venientum, etsi inculto effatu, nequevi tamen obtegere vel cert-[amen]a flagiciosorum recte viventium ; et praesertim his inlicitus stimulis, quod a nostris fari plerumque miratus sum, quia philosophantem rhetorem intellegunt pauci, loquentem rusticum multi.

ished, in the cities of Gaul, since some matters were carried on either rightly or wrongly, and the wildness of peoples raged, the fury of kings was sharpened, churches were attacked by heretics, and were protected by Catholics, Christ's faith was fervent in very many and grew cold in some, and the churches themselves were either enriched by the devout or stripped by the faithless, nor could any skilled grammarian be found in the art of dialectics, who should depict these things either in prose style or in metrical verse, many men often sighed, saying : " Woe unto our days, for the study of letters hath perished from us, nor is there found among the peoples any man who could publish in his pages the things which are done at present." So I, constantly beholding these and similar things, have said them for the commemoration of things past, in order that they may attain to the notice of men to come, even though with untutored utterance, yet I could not cloak even the conflicts of the wicked [with] those who lived uprightly ; and especially by these unlawful impulses ; for I have often admired that which is said by our [fellow-citizens], that few men understand a rhetorician speaking philosophically, while many understand the rustic in his talk.

The Vase of Soissons.

Eo tempore multae ecclesiae a Chlodovecho exercitu depraedatae sunt, quia erat ille adhuc fanaticis erroribus involutus. Igitur de quadam ecclesia urceum mirae magnitudinis ac pulchritudinis hostes abstulerant, cum reliqua ecclesiastici ministeria ornamenta. Episcopus autem ecclesiae illius missos ad regem diriget, poscens, ut si aliud de sacris vasis recepere non meretur, saltim vel urceum ecclesia sua receperet. Haec audiens rex, ait nuncio : " Sequere nos usque Sexonas, quia ibi cuncta quae adquisita sunt dividenda erunt, cumque mihi vas illud sors dederit, quae papa poscit, adimpleam." Dehinc adveniens Sexonas, cunctum munus praedae in medio positum, ait rex : " Rogo vos, o fortissimi praeliatores, ut saltim mihi vas istud, hoc est de urceo supra memorato dicebat, extra partem concedere non abnuatis." Haec regi dicenti, illi quorum mens sanior erat aiunt : " Omnia, gloriosae rex, quae cernimus, tua sunt, sed

At that time [of Clovis's victory at Soissons, 486] many churches were plundered by Clovis with his army ; for as yet he was wrapped up in fanatical errors. So from one church the enemy had abstracted an urn of marvellous greatness and beauty, with the rest of the ornaments of church ministry. So the bishop of that church sent messengers to the king, beseeching that, if he deserved not to recover any other of the holy vessels, his church might at least recover this urn. When the king heard this he said unto the messenger : " Follow us to Soissons, for there all things which have been taken will be divided ; and, when the lot has given me that urn for which the holy father [1] asketh, I will fulfil it." Then, coming to Soissons, when the whole mass of spoil was set in the midst, the king said : " I ask you, O most valiant warriors, that ye refuse not to grant me this vessel (this he said of the above-mentioned urn) beyond my share." When the king said this, those who were of sounder mind said : " O glorious king, all these things that we see are thine : moreover, we ourselves also are

---

[1] *Papa* was sometimes used in early times for any eminent ecclesiastic.

et nos ipsi tuo sumus dominio subiugati. Nunc quod tibi bene placitum videtur facito ; nullus enim potestate tuae resistere valet." Cum haec ita dixissent, unus levis, invidus ac facilis, cum voce magna elevatam bipinnem urceo inpulit, dicens : " Nihil hinc accipies, nisi quae tibi sors vera largitur." Ad haec obstupefactis omnibus, rex iniuriam suam patientiae lenitate coercuit, acceptumque urceum nuncio ecclesiastico reddidit, servans abditum sub pectore vulnus. Transacto vero anno, iussit omnem cum armorum apparatu advenire falangam, ostensuram in campo Martio horum armorum nitorem. Verum ubi cunctos circuire deliberat, venit ad urcei percussorem ; cui ait : " Nullus tam inculta ut tu detulit arma ; nam neque tibi hasta neque gladius neque securis est utilis." Et adpraehensam securem eius terrae deiecit. At illi cum paulolum inclinatus fuisset ad collegendum, rex, elevatis manibus, securem suam capite eius defixit. " Sic, inquit, tu Sexonas in urceo illo fecisti." Quo mortuo reliquos abscedere iubet, magnum sibi per hanc causam timorem statuens. Multa bella victuriasque fecit.

subject to thy dominion. Do now as seemeth well-pleasing to thee ; for none can resist thy power." When they had said this, one light fellow, envious and thoughtless, with a loud voice smote his uplifted axe upon the urn, saying : " Thou shalt receive nothing from hence, but such as the true lot granteth thee." While all were amazed at this, the king restrained his injury with the mildness of patience ; he took the urn and restored it to the church messenger, keeping the wound hidden in his breast. But, when a year had passed, he commanded his whole host to come in full armour and display the lustre of these arms in the Champ de Mars. So, when he went deliberately round all the men, he came to this urn-smiter, to whom he said : " No man hath brought such disorderly arms as thou ; for neither thy spear nor thy sword nor thine axe is serviceable " ; and he seized his axe and cast it to the earth. So, when the man stooped somewhat to take it up, the king raised his hands and drove his own axe into his head. " Thus," said he, " didst thou at Soissons in the matter of that urn." When the man was dead, he bade the rest depart, setting up a great fear for himself through this thing. He made many wars and victories.

VIII. A QUEEN'S REVENGE

Alboin, the Lombard conqueror of Northern Italy, had conquered and slain the king of a rival tribe (Gepidae) and taken his daughter to wife. Here is the story of his own death in 572 or 573. (Paulus Diaconus, *Hist. Longobardorum*, Book II., page 104, written about 750.)

Qui rex postquam in Italia tres annos et sex menses regnavit, insidiis suae coniugis interemptus est. Causa autem interfectionis eius fuit. Cum in convivio ultra quam oportuerat aput Veronam laetus resederet, cum poculo quod de capite Cunimundi regis sui soceris fecerat reginae ad bibendum vinum dari praeceptit atque eam ut cum patre suo laetanter biberet invitavit. Hoc ne cui videatur inpossibile, veritatem in Christo loquor : ego hoc poculum vidi in quodam die festo Ratchis principem ut illut convivis suis ostentaret manu tenentem. Igitur Rosemunda ubi rem animadvertit, altum concipiens in corde dolorem, quem conpescere non valens, mox in mariti necem patris funus vindicatura exarsit, consiliumque mox cum Hel-

After this king had reigned three years and six months in Italy, he was slain by the treachery of his spouse. Now this was the cause of his murder. As he sat at banquet in Verona, more merry than he should have been, he bade that they should give the queen to drink from the goblet which he had fashioned from the skull of Cunimund his father-in-law ; and he invited her to drink merrily with her father. Lest any man deem this impossible, I speak the truth in Christ : I myself have seen Prince Ratchis, on a certain feast-day, holding that goblet in his hand to show it to his guests. Rosamund, therefore, when she perceived this thing, conceived deep grief in her heart ; and, unable to repress it, she blazed up forthwith for the death of her husband in vengeance for her father's decease. So she presently plotted with Helmechis,

mechis, qui regis scilpor, hoc est armiger, et conlactaneus erat, ut regem interficeret, iniit, qui reginae persuasit, ut ipsa Peredeo, qui erat vir fortissimus, in hoc consilium adsciret. Peredeo cum reginae suadenti tanti nefas consensum adhibere nollet, illa se noctu in lectulo suae vestiariae, cum qua Peredeo stupri consuetudinem habebat, supposuit; ubi Peredeo rem nescius veniens, cum regina concubuit. Cumque illa patrato iam scelere ab eo quaereret, quam se esse existimaret, et ipse nomen suae amicae, quam esse putabat, nominasset, regina subiunxit: "Nequaquam ut putas, sed ego Rosemunda sum," inquit. "Certe nunc talem rem, Peredeo, perpetratam habes, ut aut tu Alboin interficies, aut ipse te suo gladio extinguet." Tunc ille intellexit malum quod fecit, et qui sponte noluerat, tali modo in regis necem coactus adsensit. Tunc Rosemunda, dum se Alboin in meridie sopori dedisset, magnum in palatio silentium fieri praecipiens, omnia alia arma subtrahens, spatham illius ad lectuli caput, ne tolli aut evaginari possit, fortiter conligavit, et iuxta consilium Peredeo Hel-

(who was the king's *scilpor*, that is, esquire, and his foster-brother) to slay the king. He persuaded the queen to bring into this design Peredeo, who was a most valiant man. Since Peredeo would not consent unto the queen's persuasion to so great a crime, she substituted herself by night in the bed of her own chamberwoman, with whom Peredeo habitually intrigued; and Peredeo, coming in ignorance of the matter, lay with the queen. Then, when the crime had been committed, the queen asked him whom he thought her to be, and he named his leman, whom he took her to be; then the queen replied: "It is by no means as thou thinkest; but I am Rosamund. Now, Peredeo, thou hast surely done such a deed that either thou must slay Alboin or he shall make an end of thee with his sword. Then he perceived the evil that he had done; and, whereas of his own accord he had been unwilling, he thus assented by compulsion to the king's death. Then Rosamund, when Alboin had lain down to sleep at noon, commanded that deep silence should be made in the palace, and, withdrawing all other arms, bound his sword fast to the bed's head lest it should be taken up or unsheathed; and, more cruel than any beast, by counsel of Peredeo, intro-

mechis interfectorem omni bestia crudelior introduxit. Alboin subito de sopore experrectus, malum quod imminebat intellegens, manum citius ad spatham porrexit ; quam strictius religatam abstrahere non valens, adprehenso tamen scabello subpedaneo, se cum eo per aliquod spatium defendit. Sed heu pro dolor ! vir bellicosissimus et summae audaciae nihil contra hostem praevalens, quasi unus de inertibus interfectus est, uniusque mulierculae consilio periit, qui per tot hostium strages bello famosissimus extitit. Cuius corpus cum maximo Langobardorum fletu et lamentis sub cuiusdam scalae ascensu, quae palatio erat contigua, sepultum est. Fuit autem statura procerus et ad bella peragenda toto corpore coaptatus. Huius tumulum nostris in diebus Giselpert, qui dux Veronensium fuerat, aperiens, spatham eius et si quid in ornatu ipsius inventum fuerat astulit. Qui se ob hanc causam vanitate solita aput indoctos homines Alboin vidisse iactabat.

Igitur Helmechis, extincto Alboin, regnum eius invadere conatus est. Sed minime potuit, quia Langobardi, nimium de morte illius dolentes, eum moliebantur extinguere. Statimque Rosemunda Longino praefecto

duced Helmechis the murderer.[1] Alboin, suddenly aroused from sleep, and perceiving the imminent evil, promptly stretched his hand to his sword ; but, unable to draw the fast-bound weapon, yet he seized a footstool and defended himself for some time. But, alack and alas ! this man, most warlike and exceeding in courage, availed nought against the enemy, but was slain as one of the weaklings ; and, he who, through so many slaughters of his enemies, had been most renowned in war, perished by the counsel of one mere woman. His body was buried, with bitterest tears and lamentations, under the steps of a stair which adjoined the palace. The man was tall of stature, and his whole body fitted for deeds of war. In our own days Giselpert, Duke of Verona, opened his tomb and carried away his sword and all his ornaments that were found ; and for this cause, with his wonted vanity, he would boast himself before ignorant folk as one who had seen Alboin.

Helmechis therefore, on Alboin's death, attempted to seize his power : but he was utterly unable ; for the Lombards, greatly grieved at his death, sought to slay him. So Rosamund commanded Longinus, the

---

[1] The story is here somewhat confused : one would expect Peredeo to be the principal murderer.

Ravennae mandavit, ut citius navem dirigeret, quae eos suscipere possit. Longinus tali nuntio laetus effectus, festinanter navem direxit, in qua Helmechis cum Rosemunda, sua iam coniuge, noctu fugientes ingressi sunt. Auferentesque secum Absuindam, regis filiam, et omnem Langobardorum thesaurum, velocius Ravennam pervenerunt. Tunc Longinus praefectus suadere coepit Rosemundae, ut Helmechis interficeret et eius se nuptiis copularet. Illa ut erat ad omnem nequitiam facilis, dum optat Ravennatium domina fieri, ad tantum perpetrandum facinus adsensum dedit ; atque dum Helmechis se in balneo ablueret, egredienti ei de lavacro veneni poculum, quod salutis esse adseverabat, propinavit. Ille ubi sensit se mortis poculum bibisse, Rosemundam, evaginato super eam gladio, quod reliquum erat bibere coegit. Sicque Dei omnipotentis iudicio interfectores iniquissimi uno momento perirunt.

Prefect of Ravenna, to send with all speed a ship which might receive them. Longinus, rejoicing at this message, sent a ship with all haste, whereunto Helmechis and Rosamund, who was now his wife, fled and embarked by night. So, carrying away with them Absuinda, the king's daughter, and all the treasures of the Lombards, they came swiftly to Ravenna. Then the Prefect Longinus began to persuade Rosamund that she should slay Helmechis and join him in marriage. She, who was prone to all wickedness, hoping to become Queen of Ravenna, gave assent to the perpetration of that great crime ; and when Helmechis was washing in the bath, she gave him as he came forth from the basin a cup of poison, which she vouched to him as salutary. He, perceiving that he had drunk a cup of death, compelled Rosamund to drain the rest, unsheathing his sword over her head. Thus, by the judgment of Almighty God, did these most wicked murderers die at the same moment.

IX. DIVORCE AND REMARRIAGE

Marculf, a monk of the ninth century, compiled a book of legal formulae which is of extreme historical value both to philologists and to students of social history. This present formula for divorce in the ordinary modern sense is one of several proofs that the Church had not yet arrived at its present attitude of absolute prohibition; it renders credible the other uncertainties which still beset marriage law in the days of Henry VIII. I may here refer to my pamphlet on Divorce, as listed at the end of this volume. This extract is from *M.G.H. Leges*, Vol. V. Bk. II. c. 30.

Libellum Repudii

Dum et inter illo et coniuge sua illa non caritas secundum Deum, sed discordia regnat, et ob hoc pariter conversare minime possunt, placuit utrisque voluntas, ut se a consortio [coniugali] separare deberent; quod ita et fecerunt. Propterea has epistolas inter se [duas] uno tenore conscribtas fieri et adfirmare decreverunt, ut unusquisque ex ipsis, sive ad servitium Dei in monasterio aut copolam matrimonii sociare voluerit, licentiam habeat, et nulla requisitione ex hoc de parte proximi sui habere non debeat. Si quis vero aliqua pars ex ipsis hoc emutare aut contra pare suo repetere voluerit, inferat pari suo auri libra una, et, ut decreverunt,

Deed of Repudiation

Seeing that, between Such and his wife Such there reigneth not love according to God, but discord, and for that cause they are altogether unable to associate on even terms, both are agreed upon the will that they should separate themselves from conjugal companionship; which also they have so done. Wherefore these two letters between each other, written to the same effect, they have decided to have made and to confirm, that each of them, whether he [or she] wishes to associate to God's service in a monastery or to matrimonial conjunction, may have permission, and should not have any demand [made upon him or her], on that account, on the part of his [or her] nearest of kin. If however either party of these two will change this or go to law against his [or her] partner, let him [or her] pay to his [or her] partner one pound of gold;

a proprio consortio sequestrati in eam quam elegerint parte permaneant.

and, as they have decided, let them be separated from lawful companionship and remain on that side which they have chosen.

Facta epistola ibi, sub die illo, anno illo regnante [gloriosissimo domno] illo.

This letter is drawn up at Such place, on Such a day, in Such year, during the reign of Such, the most glorious Lord.

X. WALTHER OF AQUITAINE

The poem of *Waltharius* is interesting as one of the very few epic attempts in medieval Latin. It was written by Ekkehard I. (*d.* 973) while he was yet in the cloister school of St. Gallen, and before the devotional poetry of his later years which helped to make that abbey famous. It was patched up a couple of generations later by another St. Gallen monk, Ekkehard IV., at the bidding of Aribo, bishop of Mainz (1021–31). It is founded on old German legends, and the plot is sadly confused. The following passage describes the escape of Walther, son of the Duke of Aquitaine, whom his father had given as hostage to the conquering Attila. There he betrothed himself with Hiltegund, daughter of the Burgundian king and his fellow-hostage. The rest of the story is a medley of swift flight and single combats, not only with pursuing Huns but also with fellow-Germans. Whole sentences are sometimes borrowed from the classical Latin epics.

Centenos simul accubitus iniere sodales,
Diversasque dapes libans conviva resudat :

Forthwith the companions came in to their hundred couches [at the table], and the guest sweats in supplying various

His et sublatis aliae referuntur
   edendae,
Atque exquisitum fervebat migma per auram.
Aurea bissina tantum stant gau-
   sape vasa,
Et pigmentatus crateres Bachus
   adornat.
Illicit ad haustum species dulce-
   doque potus,
Waltharius cunctos ad vinum
   hortatur et escam.
Postquam epulis depulsa fames
   sublataque mensa,
Heros iam dictus dominum
   laetanter adorsus
Inquit : " in hoc, rogito, clare-
   scat gratia vestra,
Ut vos imprimis, reliquos tunc
   laetificetis."
Et simul in verbo nappam dedit
   arte peractam
Ordine sculpturae referentem
   gesta priorum,
Quam rex accipiens haustu va-
   cuaverat uno,
Confestimque iubet reliquos
   imitarier omnes.
Ocius accurrunt pincernae mox-
   que recurrunt,
Pocula plena dabant et inania
   suscipiebant,
Hospitis ac regis certant hortati-
   bus omnes.
Ebrietas fervens tota dominatur
   in aula,

dishes : even when these have
been removed, others are brought
in to be eaten, and the savoury
mixture [1] steamed through the
delicious air. Golden vessels
alone stand upon the cloth of
fine linen, and spiced [2] wine
crowns the goblets. Spices, and
the sweetness of the drink, entice
men to drain [the cup] ;
Walther exhorts all to wine and
to food. After that hunger had
been banished by feasting, and
the table removed, then the hero
aforesaid addressed the lord with
gladsome mien and said :
" Herein, I beseech you, let your
clemency shine forth, that you,
first and foremost, should glad-
den the rest ; " and therewith as
he spoke he offered the goblet
fashioned with art, which with
the range of its chiselled work
recalled the deeds of his forefathers. The king took it, and
had drained it at a single draught,
and hastily he commanded all
the rest to imitate him. Busily
the cupbearers ran up and
quickly ran again ; they gave
full cups and received the empty ;
all strove in rivalry at the exhor-
tations of the host and king.
Drunkenness boils up and reigns
over the whole hall ; fluency is

---

[1] Probably borrowed from Isaiah xxx. 24, *commixtum migma*, which the
Douay version renders " mingled provender." [2] Compare Chaucer's *piment*.

Balbutit madido facundia fusa
    palato,
Heroas validos plantis titubare
    uideres.
Taliter in seram produxit bachica
    noctem
Munera Walthárius retrahitque
    redire volentes,
Donec vi potus pressi somnoque
    gravati
Passim porticibus sternuntur
    humotenus omnes,
Et licet ignicremis vellet dare
    moenia flammis,
Nullus qui causam potuisset scire
    remansit.
Tandem dilectam vocat ad semet
    mulierem,
Praecipiens causas citius deferre
    paratas.
Ipseque de stabulis victorem
    duxit equorum,
Ob virtutem quem vocitaverat
    ille Leonem.
Stat sonipes ac frena ferox spu-
    mantia mandit.

relaxed, and stammers with drunken mouth ; thou shouldst see stout warriors stagger upon their feet. Thus did Walther prolong his Bacchic gifts until late at night, and drew back those who would have returned ; until, weighed down by the power of the drink, and heavy with sleep, all were strewn at random upon the earth at the gates, and, even though he should wish to set the walls to burning flame, none remained who could have known the matter.[1] Now at length he called to him the beloved maiden, bidding her quickly bring the things that were prepared. He himself brought from the stables the prince of horses, whom he had called Lion for his puissance. There stood the steed, and fiercely champed his foaming bit.

XI. MASTER AND BOYS

Aelfric's *Colloquy* was written as a class-book for conversational Latin. The author, a monk of Eynsham, wrote about A.D. 1005, and must not be confused with Archbishop Aelfric who died in that year. No doubt the *Colloquy* takes certain liberties with facts for the sake of bringing in as many useful words as possible ; but it may be taken as a trustworthy picture in the main.

---

[1] Long before this, *causa* had acquired its French meaning of *chose*.

I quote here from the excellent recent edition by G. N. Garmonsway, pp. 18ff.

Puer. Nos pueri rogamus te, magister, ut doceas nos loqui latialiter recte, quia idiote sumus et corrupte loquimur. *Magister.* Quid uultis loqui? *P.* Quid curamus quid loquamur nisi recta locutio sit et utilis, non anilis aut turpis. *M.* Uultis flagellari in discendo? *P.* Carius est nobis flagellari pro doctrina quam nescire. Sed scimus te mansuetum esse et nolle inferre plagas nobis, nisi cogaris a nobis. *M.* Interrogo te, quid mihi loqueris? Quid habes operis? *P.* Professus sum monachus, et psallam omni die septem sinaxes cum fratribus, et occupatus sum lectionibus et cantu, sed tamen uellem interim discere sermocinari latina lingua. *M.* Quid sciunt isti tui socii? *P.* Alii sunt aratores, alii opiliones, quidam bubulci, quidam etiam uenatores, alii piscatores, alii aucupes, quidam mercatores, quidam sutores, quidam salinatores, quidam pistores, coci . . . *M.* O, pueri, quomodo uobis placet ista locutio? *P.* Bene quidem placet nobis, sed ualde profunde loqueris et ultra etatem nostram protrahis sermonem: sed loquere nobis iuxta nostrum intellectum, ut possimus intelligere que loqueris. *M.* Interrogo uos cur tam diligenter discitis? *P.* Quia nolumus esse sicut bruta

Pupil. We boys beg thee, master, to teach us to speak rightly in Latin; for we are untaught, and we speak corruptly. *Master.* Whereof will ye speak? *P.* What reck we whereof we speak, but if it be right speech, and not in old-wives' fashion or base. *M.* Will ye be beaten in your learning? *P.* It is dearer to us to be beaten for learning than to be ignorant. But we know that thou art kindly, and that thou wilt not inflict stripes upon us unless thou art compelled by us. [*Later, the master adds a little sermon, adding:*] Boys, how doth this speech please you? *P.* It doth indeed please us; yet thou speakest very profoundly. and extendest thy speech beyond our age: but speak unto us according to our understanding, that we may be able to comprehend that which thou sayest. *M.* I ask you, wherefore do ye learn so diligently? *P.* Because we would not be as the brute

animalia, que nihil sciunt, nisi herbam et aquam. *M.* Et quid uultis vos ? *P.* Uolumus esse sapientes. *M.* Qua sapientia ? Uultis esse uersipelles aut mille-formes in mendaciis, astuti in loquelis, astuti, uersuti, bene loquentes et male cogitantes, dulcibus uerbis dediti, dolum intus alentes, sicut sepulchrum depicto mausoleo, intus plenum fetore ? *P.* Nolumus sic esse sapientes, quia non est sapiens, qui simulatione semet ipsum decipit. *M.* Sed quomodo uul-tis ? *P.* Uolumus esse simplices sine hipochrisi, et sapientes ut declinemus a malo et faciamus bona. Adhuc tamen profundius nobiscum disputas, quam etas nostra capere possit ; sed loquere nobis nostro more, non tam profunde. *M.* Et ego faciam sicut rogatis. Tu, puer, quid fecisti hodie ? . . . *M.* Quando vultis cantare uesperam aut com-pletorium ? *P.* Quando tempus erit. *M.* Fuisti hodie uerbera-tus ? *P.* Non fui, quia caute me tenui. *M.* Et quomodo tui socii ? *P.* Quid me interrogas de hoc ? Non audeo pandere tibi secreta nostra. Unusquis-que scit si flagellatus erat an non. . . . *M.* Ubi dormis ? *P.* In dormitorio cum fratribus. *M.* Quis excitat te ad nocturnos ? *P.* Aliquando audio signum et surgo ; aliquando magister meus excitat me duriter cum uirga.

beasts, which know of nought but grass and water. *M.* And what will ye ? *P.* We would fain be wise. *M.* With what wisdom ? Would ye be shifty or thousand-formed in lies, astute in speech, astute, insidious, speaking well and thinking ill, given to honeyed words, nour-ishing treachery within, even as a sepulchre with painted tomb, filled inwardly with filth ? *P.* We would not be wise after that fashion ; for he is not wise who deceiveth himself with dis-sembling. *M.* But how would ye ? *P.* We would be simple without hypocrisy, and wise, that we may turn aside from evil and do good. But hitherto thou reasonest with us more pro-foundly than our age can grasp : but speak unto us after our own fashion, not so profoundly. *M.* I also will do as ye ask. Thou, boy, what hast thou done to-day ?

[*The monk then enumerates his daily choir-services up to the present hour of None.*]

XII. SAINT TO POPE

St. Bernard, by fairly common consent, stands with St. Francis as the greatest Saint of the later Middle Ages. No man did more than those two, and no Pope so much, for the reform of the Church. Bernard wrote his *De Consideratione* at the request of his own pupil, Pope Eugenius III. The main theme of the whole book is that a Pope himself must save his own soul; that he must find time for spiritual contemplation even amid the dizzy whirl of judicial and similar business which holds the Bishop of Bishops in its vortex. None of his writings brings out more strongly two of his greatest qualities: deep affection and absolute fearlessness.

PROLOGUS. — Subit animum dictare aliquid, quod te, Papa beatissime Eugeni, vel aedificet, vel delectet, vel consoletur. Sed nescio quomodo vult, et non vult exire laeta quidem, sed lenta oratio : dum certatim illi contraria imperare contendunt majestas atque amor. Nempe urget ille, inhibet illa. Sed intervenit tua dignatio, qua hoc ipsum non praecipis, sed petis, cum praecipere magis te deceat. Majestate igitur tam dignanter ce-

PROLOGUE.—It cometh into my mind, most blessed Pope Eugenius, to write [1] somewhat that may either edify thee, or please, or comfort. Yet, I know not how, my discourse will and will not come forth, glad indeed, yet slow, while those two contraries strive hard to sway me, majesty and love. In truth the latter impelleth, the former restraineth. Yet in cometh thy condescension, whereby thou dost not command this, but beseech. Therefore, when majesty doth so condescendingly give way, why should not shame

---

[1] *Dictare* is used of all composition, prose or poetry ; it survives in our *ditty* and the German *dichten*. It has sometimes, but comparatively seldom, the restricted sense of *dictate* in modern English.

dente, quidni cedat pudor? Quid enim si cathedram ascendisti? Nec si ambules super pennas ventorum, subduceris affectui. Amor dominum nescit, agnoscit filium et in infulis. Per se satis subjectus est, obsequitur sponte, gratis obtemperat, libere reveretur. Non sic aliqui, non sic: sed aut timore ad ista impelluntur, aut cupiditate. Hi sunt qui in facie benedicunt, mala autem in cordibus eorum; blandiuntur coram, in necessitate deficiunt. At caritas numquam excidit. Ego, ut verum fatear, matris sum liberatus officio, sed non deprædatus affectu. Olim mihi invisceratus es, non tam facile erueris. Ascende in coelos, descende in abyssos: non recedes a me, sequar te quocumque ieris. Amavi pauperem, amabo pauperum et divitum patrem. Non enim, si bene te novi, quia pater pauperum factus, ideo non pauper spiritu es. In te hanc mutationem factam esse confido, non de te; nec priori statui tuo successisse promotionem, sed accessisse. Monebo te proinde, non ut magister, sed ut mater:

yield? For what though thou hast mounted the throne [of Peter]? Though thou shouldest walk on the wings of the wind, thou shalt not be withdrawn from my affection. Love knoweth no master; it recognizeth its child even in pontifical robes.[1] In itself it is submissive enough, obeyeth willingly, complieth unbidden, revereth freely. Not so are some, not so; but they are impelled to those things either by fear or by covetousness. These are they who bless to our face, yet there is evil in their hearts: they fawn in our presence, and fail in our necessity. But love never faileth. I, to say truth, am freed from the mother's duty, yet not robbed of the mother's affection. Thou wert once part of my very bowels; not so easily shalt thou be torn from me. I loved thee poor, I shall love the Father of both rich and poor. For, if I know thee well, since thou art become Father of the poor thou art not on that account no longer poor in spirit. I am confident that this change hath been made in thee, not of thee, and that promotion hath not come in succession to thy former state, but as an accession thereunto. Therefore I will admonish thee not as a master but as a mother:

---

[1] *Infula*, ordinarily only the *mitre*, is sometimes used by extension for all episcopal insignia.

plane ut amans. Amens magis videar, sed ei qui non amat, ei qui vim non sentit amoris.

altogether, as one that loveth. I may seem rather beside myself, but to him that loveth not and who feeleth not the power of love.

St. Bernard reminds the Pope of a great and recent effort for Church reform. He quotes the first three textually, and then proceeds.

Bk. III., c. 5 (P.L., pp. 182, 770).

Nonne os tuum in Remensi Concilio subjecta capitula promulgavit ? Quis ea tenet ? Quis tenuit ? Falleris si teneri putas. Si non putas, ipse peccasti, aut statuens quae non tenerentur, aut quod non tenentur dissimulans. . . . Verba tua haec : tu sanxisti. Quid effectui mancipatum ? Adhuc adolescentes, adhuc qui infra sacros Ordines sunt, in Ecclesia promoventur. Quod ad primum capitulum pertinet ; luxus vestium interdictus, sed non restrictus, poena dictata, sed minime secuta est. Jam quartus annus est, ex quo datum mandatum audivimus ; et neminem adhuc clericorum privatum beneficio, neminem Episcoporum suspensum ab officio luximus.

Hath not thine own mouth decreed the following statutes at the Council of Reims ? Who keeps them, or who hath kept ? Thou art deceived if thou thinkest them to be kept. If thou thinkest not, thou thyself hast sinned, either by decreeing that which would not be kept, or by dissembling the fact that they are not kept. . . . . These are thine own words : thou hast decreed. What has been put into effect ? Still are youths promoted in the Church, and still men below Holy Orders. As regards the first chapter [of your decrees], luxury of garments is forbidden, but it is not restrained ; a penalty is decreed, but not in the least is it followed out. It is now four years since we have heard the command given, and as yet we have mourned for none of the clergy deprived of his benefice, nor for any one of the Bishops suspended

At luctu amarissimo dignum quod secutum est. Quod hoc ? Impunitas incuriae soboles, insolentiae mater, radix impudentiae, transgressionum nutrix. Et beatus, si omni satagas cura malorum omnium primam parentem cavere incuriam. Sed ad hoc tu operam dabis. Et nunc leva oculos tuos, et vide si non aeque, ut prius, pellicula discolor sacrum Ordinem decolorat ; si non aeque, ut prius, fissura enormis pene inguina nudat. Solent dicere : Num de vestibus cura est Deo et non magis de moribus ? At forma haec vestium, deformitatis mentium et morum indicium est. Quid sibi vult quod clerici aliud esse, aliud videri volunt ? Id quidem minus castum minusque sincerum. Nempe habitu milites, quaestu clericos, actu neutrum exhibent. Nam neque pugnant ut milites, neque ut clerici evangelizant. Cujus ordinis sunt ? Cum utriusque esse cupiunt utrumque deserunt, utrumque confundunt.

from his office. Yet that which hath followed is worthy of the bitterest mourning. What is that ? Impunity, offspring of carelessness and mother of indiscipline, root of shamelessness and nurse of transgressions. And blessed art thou if thou strivest with all thy care to beware of carelessness, first parent of every evil : yet to this thou wilt apply thyself. And then lift up thine eyes and see whether the motley film doth not discolour the sacred Order [of priesthood] even as before,[1] and the cloven garment lay bare almost to the groin. They are wont to say : " Doth God care for garments, and not far more for manners ? " Yet this form of garments is a sign of deformity in mind and in manners. What meaneth this, that clerics would fain be one thing, and seem another ? That is not fully chaste, nor fully sincere. In truth, they are knights in their dress, and clerics in their gain, and indeed they show forth neither quality. For they neither fight as knights, nor preach the gospel as clerics. Of what order are they ? While they desire to belong to both, they desert both, they confound both. It is written concerning the resurrection from the dead,

---

[1] Church law repeatedly forbade to the clergy all parti-coloured garments. Their outer garment was to be like the modern cassock, fastened in front as far as below the knees.

Unusquisque, inquit, *in suo ordine resurget*. Isti in quo ? An qui sine ordine peccaverunt, sine ordine peribunt ? Aut si summe sapiens Deus veraciter creditur, a summo usque deorsum nihil inordinatum relinquere, vereor istos non alibi ordinandos, quam ubi nullus ordo, sed sempiternus horror inhabitat.

" Every man in his own order " ; in what order, then, shall these men rise ? Will they who have sinned in disorder perish in disorder ? Or, if we truly believe the all-wise God to leave nothing disorderly, from top to bottom, I fear lest they find themselves, on that day, ordained to no other place than that where no order dwelleth, but everlasting horror. [Job x. 22.]

XIII. REDEMPTION THROUGH CHRIST

Peter Abailard (1079–1142), unjustly condemned for heresy, was in fact a pious though liberal Catholic. He was certainly the most spectacular of medieval philosophers, and, it has sometimes been contended, the most original. He destroyed for ever the old ultra-legal idea that the doctrine of Redemption could be brought under the formulae of the law-courts, as a ransom paid to the Devil for man's soul, which Adam's sin had brought into possession of the evil one. For text, see *Opera*, ed. Cousin, II. p. 206, or *P.L.* pp. 178, 835.

Quomodo etiam nos justificari vel reconciliari Deo per mortem Filii sui dicit Apostolus, qui tanto amplius adversus hominem irasci debuit, quanto amplius homines in crucifigendo Filium suum deliquerunt, quam in transgrediendo primum ejus in para-

How also saith the Apostle [Paul] that we are justified, or reconciled to God, through the death of His Son, seeing that He should have been the more angry towards man, in proportion as men transgressed more by crucifying His Son than by transgressing His first command in

diso praeceptum unius pomi gustu ? Quo enim amplius multiplicata sunt per homines peccata, irasci Deum hominibus amplius justum fuerat. Quod si tantum fuerat illud Adae peccatum, ut expiari non posset, nisi per mortem Christi, quam expiationem habebit ipsum homicidium quod in Christum commissum est, tot et tanta scelera in ipsum vel in suos commissa ? Numquid mors innocentis Filii in tantum Deo Patri placuit, ut per ipsam reconciliaretur nobis, qui peccando commisimus, propter quod innocens Dominus est occisus ? . . . Haec et his similia non mediocrem movere quaestionem nobis videntur, de redemtione scilicet vel justificatione nostra per mortem Domini nostri Jesu Christi.

Solutio.—Nobis autem videtur quod in hoc justificati sumus in sanguine Christi, et Deo reconciliati, quod per hanc singularem gratiam nobis exhibitam, quod Filius suus nostram susceperit naturam, et in ipso nos tam verbo quam exemplo instituendo usque ad mortem perstitit, nos sibi amplius per amorem astrinxit : ut tanto divinae gratiae

Paradise by the taste of a single apple ? For, the more amply sins were multiplied by mankind, the more amply God might justly have been angry with mankind. For, if that sin of Adam had been so great that it could not be expiated but by the death of Christ, what expiation shall that murder have which was committed against Christ, with so many and so great crimes committed against Him or His followers ? Did the death of His innocent son so far please God that through it He should be reconciled with us, who committed that crime on account whereof our innocent Lord was slain ? . . . It seemeth to us that these and similar thoughts raise no small question in us, namely, that of our redemption or justification through the death of our Lord Jesus Christ.

The solution.—Now to us it seemeth that hereby we are justified in Christ's blood, and reconciled unto God, that through this singular grace shown unto us, that His Son took upon Himself our nature, and therein persevered even unto death, teaching us alike by word and by example, He hath bound us to Himself more closely through love ; so that our true love, kindled by so great a gift of divine grace, may now fear

accensa beneficio, nil jam tolerare propter ipsum vera reformidet caritas. Quod quidem beneficium antiquos Patres etiam hoc per fidem exspectantes, in summum amorem Dei, tanquam homines temporis gratiae, non dubitamus accendisse, cum scriptum sit : " Et qui praeibant, et qui sequebantur, clamabant dicentes : Hosanna filio David, etc." Justior quoque, id est, amplius Dominum diligens quisque fit post passionem Christi quam ante, quia amplius in amorem accendit completum beneficium quam speratum. Redemptio itaque nostra est illa summa in nobis per passionem Christi dilectio, quae nos non solum a servitute peccati liberat, sed veram nobis filiorum Dei libertatem acquirit ; ut amore ejus potius quam timore cuncta impleamus, qui nobis tantam exhibuit gratiam, qua major inveniri, ipso attestante, non potest : " Majorem hac, inquit, dilectionem nemo habet, quam ut animam suam ponat pro amicis suis." De hoc quidem amore Dominus alibi ait : " Ignem veni mittere in terram, et quid volo nisi ut ardeat ? " Ad hanc itaque veram caritatis libertatem in hominibus propagandam se venisse testatur. Quod diligenter attendens Apostolus in sequentibus ait : " Quia caritas

to suffer nothing for His sake. And we doubt not that the Fathers of old, looking forward by faith to this gift, were kindled to the highest love of God, even as the men of the Time of Grace, since it is written : " And they who went before, and they who followed after, cried saying, *Hosanna, Son of David,*" etc. Therefore every one who loveth the Lord becometh more righteous (that is, more a lover of the Lord) after Christ's passion than before ; since a gift completed doth kindle us more to love than one hoped-for. Thus our redemption is that utmost love in us through the passion of Christ, which not only freeth us from the servitude of sin, but gaineth for us the true liberty of the sons of God ; so that we fulfil all rather through love than through fear of Him who hath shown us such great grace that (by His own assurance) no greater can be found. " Greater love," saith He, " hath no man than this, that a man lay down his life for his friends." Concerning this love, indeed, the Lord saith elsewhere : " I am come to send fire upon the earth ; and what will I, if it be already kindled ? " Thus He beareth witness that He is come to propagate this true liberty of love upon earth. The Apostle, giving diligent attention to this, saith in the following

Dei diffusa est in cordibus nostris per Spiritum sanctum qui datus est nobis. Ut quid enim Christus, etc." Iterum : " Commendat autem suam caritatem Deus in nobis. Quoniam cum adhuc, etc."

verses : " Because the love of God is shed abroad in our hearts by the Holy Ghost which is given unto us ; for why did Christ ? " etc. Again, "But God commendeth His love toward us, in that, yet," etc.

XIV. MONASTIC SCHOOLBOYS

From the Burgundian abbey of Noyers, about A.D. 1116 (Chevalier, *Cart. Noyers*, p. 448).

Notum sit omnibus catholicae Ecclesiae fidelibus, quod quidam vir nobilis, nomine David de Monteilo, parrochianus ecclesiae quae dicitur Sarinniacus, in infirmitate positus, cernens se esse propinquum mortis, vocavit ad se abbatem Nuchariensem, Gaudinum nomine, rogavitque eum ut eum faceret monachum ad succurrendum, et totius beneficii ecclesiae Nuchariensis participem faceret. Dedit autem isdem David omnem decimam quam habebat, ubicumque esset, in parrochia tota Sarinniacensis ecclesiae, Deo et Sanctae Mariae ac monachis de Nuchariis, tali convenientia, ut filium ejus, qui tunc

Be it known to all the faithful of the Catholic Church, that a certain noble man, David de Monteil by name, parishioner of the church called Serrigny, being fallen into sickness and seeing himself nigh unto death, hath called to himself the Abbot of Noyers, Gaudin by name, and hath besought him to make him a monk *ad succurrendum,*[1] and participant in all the benefits of the abbey of Noyers. So he gave to the said David all the tithes that he possessed, wheresoever they might be, in the whole parish of Serrigny, to God and St. Mary and the monks of Noyers, on this condition, that his son, who was then but little,

---

[1] It was common for dying men to give considerable endowments for the privilege of being clothed in the cowl before death and buried in it. See the extract from Caesarius of Heisterbach concerning the Landgraf Ludwig.

parvus erat, monachi nutrirent et eum cum [ad] aetatem venerit, a presbytero capellae de Gentiaco litteras discere facerent ; haberetque isdem presbyter de Gentiaco pro insinuatione pueri medietatem illius decimae quam David dabat, et aliam medietatem haberent monachi de Sarinniaco, et si monachi de Sarinniaco aut monachus qui ad Gentiacum manserit, puerum voluerint insinuare, habeant illam partem decimae quam dabat presbytero ; et si puer monachus voluerit esse, apud Nucharios pro hac decima recipiatur ; et si noluerit monachus esse, monachi tamen in perpetuum omnem decimam David possideant.

should be brought up by the monks, and that, when he came to that age, they should cause him to learn letters [1] from the priest of the chapel of Gency ; and that the said priest of Gency should have, for the boy's teaching, half of those tithes which David gave, and the monks of Serrigny the other half ; and if the monks of Serrigny or the monk who dwelt at Gency,[2] wish to teach the boy, then they should have that part of the tithes which he gave to the priest ; and, if the boy wished to be a monk, he should be received at [the abbey of] Noyers for those tithes ; and, if he would not be a monk, yet the monks should possess in perpetuity all David's tithes.

From the abbey of Weihenstephan in Bavaria (*Monumenta Boica*, ix. 485).

Anno ab incarnatione Domini MCCVIII, pridie Kal. Marcii Dominus Eberhardus venerabilis Abbas de communi consensu et voluntate fratrum, certa quantitate pecunie data, Ruodigero puero, magistri Alberti cognato, prebendam contulit eo modo,

In the year of the Incarnation 1208 (Feb. 28) the lord Eberhard, our venerable Abbot, by the common consent and will of the brethren, [in consideration of] a certain quantity of money given, granted a prebend [3] to the boy Roger, of Master Albert's kindred, on this condition, that

---

[1] *Litterae* nearly always means Latin letters. [2] Noyers had dependent cells at Serrigny and Gency. It seems plain that Gency had only one single monk : this was not infrequent, in spite of repeated decrees that two at least must always reside in a cell, for decency's sake. [3] *i.e.* a free place in the abbey : board, lodging, and raiment.

quod istic stare debeat sine monachali habitu per decem annos ; expletis vero X. annis monachalem habitum reverenter si voluerit assumat, si vero renuerit absolutus ab hoc loco libere recedat.

he should stay here without monastic habit for ten years ; then, after the ten years, he should reverently take, if he would, the monastic habit ; if on the other hand he renounced it, he should freely depart from this place.

XV. HYMNS

Here, again, we may begin with what Dante tells us (*Purgatorio*, viii. 1) :

" 'Twas now the hour that turns back the desire of those who sail the seas and melts their heart, that day when they have said to their sweet friends adieu, and that pierces the new pilgrim with love, if from afar he hears the chimes which seem to mourn for the dying day ; when I began to annul my sense of hearing, and to gaze on one of the spirits, uprisen, that craved a listening with its hand. It joined and lifted up both its palms, fixing its eyes towards the east, as though 'twere saying to God : ' For aught else I care not.' ' *Te lucis ante* ' so devoutly proceeded from its mouth, and with such sweet music, that it rapt me from my very sense of self. And the others then sweetly and devoutly accompanied it through the entire hymn, having their eyes fixed on the supernal wheels."

Hymnus

Te lucis ante terminum
Rerum Creator poscimus :
Ut pro tua clementia
Sis praesul et custodia.

Thee, ere the close of light, Creator of all things, we beseech that, of Thy mercy, Thou shouldst be our Captain and Guardian.

Procul recedant somnia,
Et noctium phantasmata :
Hostemque nostrum comprime,
Ne polluantur corpora.
Praesta, Pater piissime,
Patrique compar Unice,
Cum Spiritu Paraclito
Regnans per omne saeculum.
    Amen.

Let dreams recede afar, and the phantasms of the night ; and restrain our Enemy, that our bodies be not polluted. Grant this, O most loving Father, and Thou the Father's only compeer, reigning with the Spirit, the Comforter, world without end.

Once more we come to Dante, who has parodied this great hymn in his *Inferno* (XXXIV. 1 : " Vexilla regis prodeunt inferni ").

Vexilla Regis prodeunt,
Fulget Crucis mysterium
Quo carne carnis conditor
Suspensus est patibulo.
    Confixa clavis viscera,
Tendens manûs, vestigia,
Redemptionis gratiâ
Hic immolatur hostia.
    Quo vulneratus insuper
Mucrone diro lanceae
Ut nos lavaret crimine,
Manavit undâ et sanguine.
    Impleta sunt quae concinit
David fideli carmine
Dicendo nationibus,
Regnavit a ligno Deus.
    Arbor decora et fulgida,
Ornata Regis purpurâ,
Electa digno stipite
Tam sancta membra tangere ;
    Beata cujus brachiis
Pretium pependit saeculi ;

The royal banners forward go ; there shineth the mystery of the Cross, whereby in flesh the maker of flesh was hanged and gibbeted. Here is the victim sacrificed, His vitals pierced with nails, stretching His hands and feet for the sake of [our] redemption. By which [mystery] moreover, wounded by the dire edge of the lance, He gushed forthwith water and blood to wash us from guilt. [Then] was fulfilled that which David sang in faithful song, saying to the nations *God hath reigned from the wood.*[1] O tree comely and glorious, adorned with the King's purple, chosen from a worthy stock to touch so holy limbs ! Blessed, on whose arms the Price of the World hung ; being

---

[1] Ps. xcvi. 10, *A.V.*; *Vulg.*, xcv. 10. The words *a ligno* are neither in the Vulgate nor in our *A.V.*; but they occur in Greek, Coptic, and pre-Vulgate Latin versions.

Statera facta corporis,
Praedam tulisti tartari.

   Fundis aroma cortice,
Vincis sapore nectare,
Jucunda fructu fertili
Plaudis triumpho nobili.

   Salve ara, salve victima,
De passionis gloriâ,
Quâ vita mortem pertulit
Et morte vitam reddidit.

   O Crux, ave, spes unica,
Hoc Passionis tempore
Auge piis justitiam
Reisque donâ veniam.

   Te summa, Deus, Trinitas,
Collaudet omnis spiritus :
Quos per Crucis mysterium
Salvas, rege per saecula.

made a balance of [His] body, thou didst take away the prey of hell.[2] Thou pourest sweet odour from thy bark, thou excellest nectar in sweet savour, jocund with fertile fruit thou clappest thy hands in noble triumph. Hail, altar ! hail, victim ! from the glory of that passion whereby life bore death and by death restored life. O hail, Cross, our only hope ! At this Passion-season, increase righteousness for the pious and grant pardon to the guilty. Thee, God, sub-limest Trinity, let every spirit praise together ; do Thou govern, world without end, those whom Thou savest through the mystery of the Cross.

This time we turn to Chaucer. In the *Prioress's Tale* (B. 1743) the "litel clergeoun" sang this hymn, *O alma Redemptoris*, daily as he went down the street.

Alma Redemptoris mater, quae pervia caeli
Porta manes et stella maris, suc-curre cadenti
Surgere qui curat populo. Tu quae genuisti
Naturâ mirante tuum sanctum genitorem,
Virgo prius ac posterius, Gabrielis ab ore
Sumens illud *Ave* peccatorum miserere.

   Kindly Mother of the Re-deemer, who standest as open Door of Heaven and as Star of the Sea, succour Thy falling people who are careful to arise. Thou who, to the admiration of Nature, hast borne Thine own holy Begetter, Virgin before and after, taking that *Hail !* from Gabriel's mouth, have mercy on [us] sinners.

[1] For this legalistic doctrine of a ransom paid to the Devil for man's soul, which reaches its most realistic form in the so-called *Processus Belial*, see my *Five Centuries of Religion*, vol. i., App. 5.

St. Ambrose [390]

Splendor paternae gloriae,
De luce lucem proferens,
Lux lucis, et fons luminis
Dies dierum illuminans,

Verusque sol, illabere
Micans nitore perpeti ;
Jubarque Sancti Spiritûs
Infunde nostris sensibus.

Votis vocemus et Patrem,
Patrem perennis gloriae,
Patrem potentis gratiae,
Culpam releget lubricam,

Informet actûs strenuos,
Dentem retundat invidi,
Casûs secundet asperos,
Donet gerendi gratiam,

Mentem gubernet et regat
Casto fideli corpore ;
Fides calore ferveat,
Fraudis venena nesciat.

Christusque nobis sit cibus.
Potusque noster sit fides :
Laeti bibamus sobriam
Ebrietatem Spiritûs.

Laetus dies hic transeat :
Pudor sit ut diluculum,
Fides velut meridies,
Crepusculum mens nesciat.

Aurora cursûs provehit :
Aurora totus prodeat
In Patre totus Filius
Et totus in Verbo Pater.

Splendour of the Father's glory, bringing forth light from light, light of light and fount of illumination, day that givest light to day, and true sun, do thou creep upon us, shining with everlasting lustre, and pour into our senses the ray of the Holy Spirit. Let us invoke with our voices the Father also, Father of perennial glory, Father of potent grace. May He banish impure guilt, and mould our toilsome deeds ; may He blunt the tooth of the envious, and bring prosperity into our rough mischances ; may He govern and rule our mind, while our body is chaste and true ; may faith glow with heat, and ignore the venom of fraud. And may Christ be our food and faith our drink : gladly may we drink the sober intoxication of the Spirit. May this day pass in gladness : let shamefastness be as the dayspring and faith as the midday ; let the mind know no twilight. The dawn bringeth forward our courses : may dawn come forth in full flood, all the Son in the Father, and all the Father in the Word.

Abailard [1130]

O quanta qualia sunt illa sabbata,
Quae semper celebrat superna curia !

O how great and of what kind are those Sabbaths which the Court of Heaven keepeth ever-

Quae fessis requies, quae merces fortibus,
Cum erit omnia Deus in omnibus !
Vere Jerusalem est illa civitas,
Cujus pax jugis est summa jucunditas ;
Ubi non praevenit rem desiderium
Nec desiderio minus est praemium.
Quis Rex, quae curia, quale palatium,
Quae pax, quae requies, quod illud gaudium,
Hujus participes exponant gloriae,
Si quantum sentiunt possunt exprimere.
Nostrum est interim mentem erigere
Et totis patriam votis appetere,
Et ad Jerusalem a Babyloniâ
Post longa regredi tandem exsilia.
Illic, molestiis finitis omnibus,
Securi cantica Sion cantabimus,
Et juges gratias de donis gratiae
Beata referet plebs tibi, Domine.
Illic ex Sabbato succedet Sabbatum ;
Perpes laetitia Sabbatizantium ;
Nec ineffabiles cessabunt jubili,
Quos decantabimus et nos et angeli.
Perenni Domino perpes sit gloria,

more ! What rest for the weary, what reward to the brave, when God shall be all in all ! Truly Jerusalem is that city whose peace is unbroken and whose sweetness is beyond compare ; where desire forerunneth not the thing itself, nor is reward less than desire. What King, what Court, what Palace ! What peace, what rest, what [shall be] that joy, let those expound who are partakers in this glory, if they can express as much as they feel. Ours is it, meanwhile, to upraise our mind and to pant for our homeland with all our prayers, and to return at last to Jerusalem after our long Babylonian exile. There, when all our troubles are ended, we shall sing care-free the songs of Sion ; and, Lord, Thy blessed people shall bring Thee undying thanks for Thy gifts of grace. Then shall Sabbath succeed to Sabbath ; unbroken [shall be] the joy of the Sabbath-keepers [1] ; nor shall those ineffable rejoicings cease which both we shall sing and the angels. To the Eternal Lord be perpetual praise, from whom and

---

[1] The Church's law against " servile works " on Sunday was, in theory, as strict in the Middle Ages as in later times.

Ex quo sunt, per quem sunt, in quo sunt omnia.

Ex quo sunt, Pater est ; per quem sunt, Filius ;

In quo sunt, Patris et Filii Spiritus.

through whom and in whom are all things. He from whom they are, is the Father ; through whom, the Son ; in whom, the Spirit of Father and Son.

St. Thomas Aquinas [1250]. The perfection of lapidary conciseness and force.

Pange, lingua, gloriosi
  Corporis mysterium,
Sanguinisque pretiosi,
  Quem in mundi pretium
Fructus ventris generosi
  Rex effudit gentium.

Nobis datus nobis natus,
  Ex intactâ Virgine,
Et in mundo conversatus
  Sparso verbi semine,
Sui moras incolatûs
  Miro clausit ordine.

In supremae nocte cenae
  Recumbens cum fratribus,
Observatâ lege plenê
  Cibis in legalibus,
Cibum turbae duodenae
  Se dat suis manibus.

Verbum-Caro panem verum
  Verbo carnem efficit,
Fitque sanguis Christi merum ;
  Et si sensus deficit,
Ad firmandum cor sincerum
  Sola fides sufficit.

Tantum ergo sacramentum
  Veneremur cernui,
Et antiquum documentum
  Novo cedat ritui :

Sing, O my tongue, the mystery of the Glorious Body and the Precious Blood which, for the price of the world, was shed by the King of the Nations, the fruit of that generous womb. Given to us and born for us of a pure Virgin, and conversing in the world while He scattered the seed of His word, He closed in wondrous order the continuance of His indwelling [amongst us]. On the night of His last supper, reclining with His brethren, after fully keeping the Law in the matter of lawful foods, He gave Himself as food, with His own hands, to the twelvefold assembly. The Word-Flesh, with a word, made true bread into flesh, and Christ's blood became wine ; and, if our sense fail, yet faith alone sufficeth to uphold the sincere heart. Therefore let us revere this so great Sacrament, bowing [on our knees] ; and let the Old Covenant yield to the new rite ; let

Praestet fides supplementum
Sensuum defectui.

Genitori Genitoque
Laus et jubilatio,
Salus, honor, virtus quoque
Sit et benedictio :
Procedenti ab utroque
Compar sit laudatio.

faith afford a prop to the failing
of our senses. To Father and
Son be praise and jubilation,
health, honour and virtue and
blessing : and equal be the praise
to Him that proceedeth from
both.

Evening Hymn

Rerum Deus tenax vigor,
Immotus ini te permanens,
Lucis diurnae tempora
Successibus determinans,

Largire lumen vespere,
Quo vita nusquam decidat,
Sed praemium mortis sacrae
Perennis instet gloria.

Praesta, Pater piissime,
Patrique compar Unice,
Cum Spiritu Paraclito
Regnans per omne saeculum.

O God, abiding energy of [all]
things, remaining unmoved in
Thyself, and guiding in their
succession the times of daily
light, grant us that light at eventide, whence life may never fail,
but eternal glory come upon
[us], the reward of a holy death.
Grant it, O most loving Father,
and Thou, His only compeer,
reigning with the Spirit, the
Comforter, throughout all the
ages.

Dies irae, dies illa
Solvet saeclum in favillâ,
Teste David cum Sibyllâ.

Quantus tremor est futurus
Quando judex est venturus,
Cuncta strictê discussurus !

Tuba mirum spargens sonum
Per sepulcra regionum
Coget omnes ante thronum.

Mors stupebit et Natura
Cum resurget creatura
Judicanti responsura.

Liber scriptus proferetur
In quo totum continetur

That Day of Wrath, that
[great] day, shall dissolve the
world in ashes, witness David
and the Sibyl. What shall be
the shudder when the Judge shall
come, to make strict inquiry into
all things ! The trumpet, scatter-
ing its stupendous notes throughout the tombs of the nations,
shall compel all before the
Throne. Death shall be amazed,
and Nature, when Creation shall
arise to answer the Judge. The
written book shall be brought
forth, wherein is contained all

Unde mundus judicetur.

Judex ergo cum sedebit,
Quicquid latet apparebit ;
Nil inultum remanebit.

Quid sum miser tunc dicturus,
Quem patronum rogaturus,
Cum vix justus sit securus ?

Rex tremendae majestatis,
Qui salvandos salvas gratis,
Salvâ me, fons pietatis.

Recordare, Jesu pie,
Quod sum causa tuae viae,
Ne me perdas illâ die.

Quaerens me sedisti lassus ;
Redemisti, crucem passus ;
Tantus labor non sit cassus.

Juste Judex ultionis,
Donum fac remissionis
Ante diem rationis.

Ingemisco tamquam reus ;
Culpâ rubet vultus meus :
Supplicanti parce, Deus.

Qui Mariam absolvisti
Et latronem exaudisti,
Mihi quoque spem dedisti.

Preces meae non sunt dignae ;
Sed tu bonus fac benignê
Ne perenni cremer igne.

Inter oves locum praesta,
Et ab haedis me sequestra,
Statuens in parte dextrâ.

Confutatis maledictis
Flammis acribus addictis,
Voca me cum benedictis.

Oro supplex et acclinis :
Cor contritum quasi cinis :

wherefrom the world shall be judged. When therefore the Judge shall sit, whatsoever hideth shall appear ; nought shall remain unavenged. What shall I then say, poor wretch ? What patron shall I beseech, when scarce the righteous man is secure ? King of awful majesty, who savest freely those that shall be saved, save Thou me, O fount of pity ! Remember, pitiful Jesu, that I am the cause of Thine [earthly] pilgrimage ; cast me not away on that day. In search of me didst Thou sit in weariness ; Thou didst redeem me and suffer the Cross ; let not so great labour be in vain. Just Judge of vengeance, give me the gift of remission before the Day of Vengeance. I groan as a guilty thing ; my face reddeneth with guilt ; spare Thy suppliant, O God ! Thou who didst absolve Mary [Magdalene], and hear the [Penitent] Thief, to me also hast Thou given hope. My prayers are unworthy ; but Thou, the Good, of Thy benignity, make that I burn not in everlasting fire. Grant me a place among the sheep, and part me from the goats, setting me on the right-hand side. While the accused are confounded, and condemned to bitter flames, call Thou me with the blessed ! I pray, suppliant and bending [before Thee] ; my heart is

Gere curam mei finis.
Lacrimosa dies illa
Qua resurget ex favillâ
Judicandus homo reus :
Huic [1] ergo parce, Deus.
Pie Jesu Domine,
Donâ eis requiem.

crumbled as ashes ; have Thou a care for mine end ! Tearful is that day whereon guilty man shall arise from dust to be judged : spare him therefore, O God. Jesu, pitiful Lord, grant them rest.

XVI. INNOCENT III

The Fourth Ecumenical Council of the Lateran (1215) was the greatest that had ever been held in the west. Innocent III. in his opening sermon took his text from Luke xxii. 15. He desired before he died to start, if not complete, two things : a successful crusade to the Holy Land, and a reform of Christ's Church. (Text from Migne. *P.L.*, cols. 217, 674.)

Desiderio desideravi hoc pascha manducare vobiscum, antequam patiar, id est antequam moriar.

Quia " mihi vivere Christus est, et mori lucrum," non abnuo, si dispositum est a Deo, bibere calicem passionis, sive pro defensione fidei Catholicae sive pro subsidio Terrae Sanctae, sive pro statu ecclesiasticae libertatis mihi fuerit propinatus : quanquam desiderem in carne permanere, donec consummetur opus incoeptum. Verumtamen non mea, sed Dei voluntas fiat. Et ideo dixi vobis : *Desiderio desideravi hoc pascha manducare vobiscum antequam patiar.* . . . Tem-

With desire I have desired to eat this Passover with you before I suffer ; that is, before I die.

Because for me to live is Christ, and to die is gain, I do not shrink (if God so dispose) from drinking the cup of suffering, whether it be poured out to me for defence of the Catholic faith or for the succour of the Holy Land, or for the state of ecclesiastical liberty ; albeit I would desire to abide in the flesh until the work which I have begun be finished. Yet not my will, but God's, be done. And therefore have I said unto you : *with desire have I desired to eat this*

---

[1] The poet counts this as a dissyllable.

pus enim est, sicut beatus apostolus ait, ut judicium incipiat a domo Domini. Nam omnis in populo corruptela principaliter procedit a clero : quia, si sacerdos, qui est unctus, peccaverit, facit delinquere populum. Quippe dum laici vident turpiter et enormiter excedentes, et ipsi eorum exemplo ad iniquitatem et scelera prolabuntur, cumque reprehenduntur ab aliquo, protinus se excusant, dicentes : " Non potest filius facere, nisi quod viderit patrem facientem ; " et : " Sufficit discipulo, si sit sicut magister ejus." Impletum est illud propheticum : " Erit sicut populus, sic sacerdos : " quinimmo, " erubesce, Sidon, ait mare." Hinc etiam mala provenerunt in populo Christiano. Perit fides, religio deformatur, libertas confunditur, justitia conculcatur, haeretici pullulant, insolescunt schismatici, perfidi saeviunt, praevalent Agareni. De transitu autem aeternali Dominus : " Beati sunt servi illi, quos

Passover with you before I suffer. . . . For it is time (as the blessed Apostle saith) that judgment should begin from the house of the Lord. For all corruption among the people proceedeth principally from the clergy : for, if the anointed priest sinneth, he maketh the people to fall into sin. In truth, while the lay folk see them transgressing foully and enormously, they themselves also, after their example, fall into iniquity and crime ; and, when any man rebuketh them, they forthwith excuse themselves, saying : " The son cannot do save as he seeth his father doing," and : " It sufficeth for the disciple if he do as his master." That word of the prophet is fulfilled : " As the people is, so shall the priest be " ; and again, further : " Be thou ashamed, O Sidon, for the sea speaketh." Hence also have evils come forth among Christian folk. Faith is dying ; Religion [1] is deformed ; liberty is confounded ; justice is trodden under foot ; heretics swarm ; schismatics grow confirmed [in their schism] ; the treacherous rage ; the Hagarenes [2] prevail. Yet concerning the everlasting passage [3] the Lord saith : " Blessed are those

---

[1] In its common sense of " The Religious Orders," *i.e.* " Monasticism."
[2] *i.e.* the Saracens. [3] This first portion expresses the Pope's first heart's desire, for a fresh Crusade to the Holy Land. A very common word for this was *Passagium.*

cum venerit Dominus, invenerit vigilantes. Amen, dico vobis, quia praecinget se, et faciet illos discumbere, et transiens ministrabit eis." De hoc transitu sane martyres gloriantur in Psalmo, dicentes : " Transivimus per ignem et aquam, et induxisti nos in refrigerium." Hoc *pascha* prae caeteris *desidero manducare vobiscum* in regno Dei. . . . Hac ultima manducatione praecipue desidero manducare vobiscum hoc pascha, ut transeamus de labore ad requiem, de dolore ad gaudium, de infelicitate ad gloriam, de morte ad vitam, de corruptione ad aeternitatem ; praestante Domino nostro Jesu Christo, cui est honor et gloria in saecula saeculorum. Amen."

servants, whom the Lord when he cometh, shall find watching. Amen I say to you, that he will gird himself, and make them sit down to meat, and passing will minister unto them." Concerning this passage, indeed, the martyrs exult in the Psalms : " We have passed through fire and water, and thou hast brought us out into a refreshment." That Passover, above all others, I desire to eat with you in the Kingdom of God. . . . By this last eating, above all, I desire to eat with you this Passover, that we may pass from labour to rest, from pain to joy, from unhappiness to glory, from death to life, from corruption to eternity, by the gift of our Lord Jesus Christ, to whom is honour and glory, world without end. Amen.

A BENEDICTINE GLIMPSE

Abbot Thomas Marleberge of Evesham describes how he contended at the Roman Court, under Innocent III., for the freedom of his abbey from the bishop's jurisdiction. (*Chronicon Abbatiae de Evesham*, R.S., p. 189, an. 1206.)

Proferens rotulum nostrum incepi legere attestationes quae ad hoc faciebant. Et dominus papa, taedio affectus, conversus

Bringing forth our roll, I began to read the attestations which made for that [contention]. And the lord Pope,

ad adversarium nostrum dixit, "Num opus est lectione attestationum? num praescripserunt?" Et dixit magister Robertus, "Revera praescripserunt." Et dominus papa, "Ut quid ergo laboramus?" Et adversarius, "Pater sancte, nos didicimus in scholis, et haec est opinio magistrorum nostrorum, quod non currit praescriptio contra jura episcopalia." Et dominus papa, "Certe et tu et magistri tui multum bibistis de cerevisia Anglicana quando haec didicistis." Et quum magister Robertus adhuc idem affirmaret, iterum idem audivit responsum.'

touched with weariness, turned to our adversary and said : "Is it necessary to read the attestations? Have they pleaded prescription?" And Master Robert, [the Bishop's advocate] said : "In truth they have pleaded prescription." Then said the lord Pope : "To what end, therefore, do we labour the point?" And the adversary : "Holy Father, we have learned in our schools, and this is the opinion of our masters, that no prescription holdeth good against episcopal rights."[1] Then said the lord Pope : "Surely both thou and thy masters had drunk much of your English ale when ye learned this." And, when Master Robert again affirmed the same, he heard the same answer again."

A FRANCISCAN VIEW

A Franciscan View (Salimbene's *Chronicle*, *Mon. Germ. Hist.*, xxxii., p. 31.)

Salimbene de Adamo, son of a noble at Parma, was born in 1222. His Chronicle, largely autobiographical, extends to 1287 at least. At sixteen he ran away from home to join the Friars : "I and my brother Guido destroyed our house in all hope of male or female issue

---

[1] That was indeed the earlier law : but Innocent, following other Popes almost as great and masterful as himself, was fast creating that papal omnicompetence which led to grievous complaints in the fifteenth century, and to revolution in the sixteenth.

by entering into Religion, that we might build it in heaven." In that Order he saw many cities, had many experiences, and knew many distinguished people. He is almost as frank as Pepys, and as valuable for the picture of the great thirteenth century, so long as we make allowance for his personal equation. The nearest approach, as yet, to a full translation of this bulky book may be found in my *From St. Francis to Dante* (1907).

Anno Domini MᵒCCXVI obiit Innocentius papa tertius apud Perusium mense Iulii, et in episcopali ecclesia iacet sepultus. Floruit et viguit ecclesia suo tempore, retinens principatum super imperium Romanum et super cunctos reges et principes universe terre. Verumtamen principium maledictionis et dissensionis inter Romanum imperium et ecclesiam ipse fuit cum suis imperatoribus Octone quarto et Frederico secundo, quem exaltavit et filium nominavit ecclesie. . . . Verumtamen excusari potest Innocentius papa, quia bona intentione Octonem deposuit et Fredericum exaltavit, iuxta illud Ps. : *Hunc humiliat et hunc exaltat.* Et nota, quod Innocentius papa fuit audax homo et magni cordis. Nam aliquando mensuravit sibi tunicam Domini inconsutilem, et visum fuit sibi, quod Dominus parve fuisset stature ; quam cum induisset, apparuit grandior ipso.

In the year 1216, Pope Innocent III. died at Perugia in the month of July, and he lieth buried in the cathedral church. The Church flourished and throve in his days, holding the lordship over the Roman Empire and over all Kings and Princes of the whole earth. Yet he himself was the beginning of cursing and discord between the Roman Empire and the Church, with his Emperors Otto IV. and Frederick II., whom he exalted and entitled Son of the Church. But Pope Innocent may be excused, for that his intentions were good in deposing Otto and setting up Frederick, according to that verse of the Psalm, " he humbleth this one, and exalteth this other." And note that this Pope was a bold man and stout of heart. For once he measured on his own person the Seamless Coat of our Lord, and he thought how the Lord must have been of small stature ; yet when he had put on the coat, it seemed too great for him ; so he feared

Et sic timuit et veneratus est illam, ut decens fuit. Item solitus erat aliquando librum tenere coram se, cum populo predicabat. Cumque quererent capellani, cur homo sapiens et litteratus talia faceret, respondebat dicens : " Propter vos facio, ut exemplum dem vobis, quia vos nescitis et erubescitis discere." Item homo fuit, qui *interponebat suis interdum gaudia curis* ; unde cum quadam die quidam ioculator de Marchia Anconitana salutasset eum dicens :

> *Papa Innocentium,*
> *Doctoris omnis gentium,*
> *Salutat te Scatutius*
> *Et habet te pro dominus,*

respondit ei : " Et unde est Scatutius ? " Cui dixit :

> *De castro Recanato,*
> *Et ibi fui nato.*

Cui Papa :

> *Si veneris Romam,*
> *Habebis multam bonam,*

id est " bene faciam tibi." Fecit papa quod gramaticus docet : *Per quemcumque casum fit interrogatio, per eumdem debet fieri responsio.* Quia enim malam gramaticam fecit ioculator, malam gramaticam audivit a papa. Hic dum quadam die populo predicaret, consideravit quendam scolarem verba sua deridentem. Et finita predicatione habuit eum seorsum secreto in camera sua et quesivit ab eo, cur de verbis divinis risisset, cum sint animabus

and venerated the relic, as was seemly. Moreover he would sometimes keep a book before him when he preached to the people ; and when his chaplains asked why he did this, being so wise and learned a man, he would answer and say, " I do it for your sakes, to give you an example : for ye are ignorant and yet are ashamed to learn." Moreover, he was a man who mingled his business at times with mirth, as this example may show. One day a minstrel of the Mark of Ancona saluted him, saying : " Pope Innocent, Teacher of all nations, Scatuzio saluteth thee and holdeth thee for lord." And when the Pope asked, " Whence art thou then, Scatuzio ? " he answered : " Of the town of Recanati, and there was I born." To whom the Pope said : " If thou comest to Rome thou shalt have much good." The Pope did as the Grammarian telleth us : *By whatsoever case the question is asked, by that same should the answer be given.* For, because the minstrel spake bad grammar, he heard bad grammar from the Pope. One day as this Pope preached to the people, he saw how a certain scholar mocked at his words. So when his sermon was ended he had him apart into his chamber and asked him why he had laughed

salvandis utilia. Et respondit scolaris, quod verba, que dixerat, verba erant ; ipse vero opera demonstrare sciebat, ut mortuos suscitare et demonibus imperare. Et cognovit papa eo manifestante, quod nigromanticus esset, et quod Toleti studuerat, et rogavit eum, quod quendam suum amicum defunctum ei resuscitare deberet, ut cum eo haberet familiare colloquium et de statu anime sue ab eo posset inquirere. Et elegerunt locum desertum et secretum in Roma ; ad quem papa quasi sub occasione spatiandi accessit, et precepit sociis, ut ab eo diverterent et expectarent, quousque iret ad eos. Et crediderunt, quod descenderet *ad requisita nature*, et fecerunt ut dixerat. Suscitavit igitur ei Besmantie archiepiscopum sub illa pompa et vana gloria, qua solitus erat venire ad curiam. Nam primo veniebant pueri, qui hospicia prepararent, postea somarii in magna copia cum thesauris, deinde domicelli ad ministrandum docti, demum milites, subsequenter ipse cum capellanis multis. Cumque ab eo quereret nigromanticus, quo tenderet, dixit, quod ad curiam

at the Word of God, which is profitable for salvation of souls. The scholar answered that what the Pope had said was mere words, but that he himself could show deeds, as for example raising of the dead and authority over demons. So the Pope learned plainly from him that he was a necromancer who had studied at Toledo : wherefore he besought him to raise a certain dead friend of his own, with whom he would fain speak and hear of his soul's health. So they chose a desert and secret spot in Rome, whereunto the Pope went as though he walked abroad for air ; and when he was come thither he bade his attendants pass on and tarry until he came again to them. They therefore did as he had bidden, believing that he went down into this place at the call of nature. So the scholar raised up before his eyes the Archbishop of Besmantova, with the same pomp and vainglory with which he was wont to come to Court. First came his servants to make ready his lodging, then a great multitude of sumpter-mules with his treasures, then his squires to wait on him, and then his knights, and himself last of all with many chaplains round him. The necromancer asked him whither he went : and he made answer, " To the Court,

ibat ad papam Innocentium, amicum suum, qui eum videre volebat. Cui scolaris ait : " Hic est Innocentius amicus tuus, qui a te vult cognoscere, qualiter tibi sit." Cui ille dixit : " Male michi est, quia damnatus sum propter pompam et vanam gloriam meam et alia, que commisi, peccata, nec penitentiam feci, et ideo cum demonibus sum deputatus et cum his *qui ad infernum descendunt*." Finitis igitur hinc inde colloquiis mutuis, disparuit visio, et papa ad socios est reversus.

to my friend Pope Innocent, who would fain see me." Then said he, " Here is thy friend Innocent, who would know from thine own mouth how it standeth with thee." He answered, " It is ill with me ; for I am damned by reason of my pomp and vainglory and my other sins : and I did no penance : wherefore I am doomed to dwell with devils and with those who go down to hell." When therefore these speeches were ended on either side, the apparition vanished and the Pope went back to his attendants.

XVII. LOVE LYRICS

Carmina Burana—" Benediktbeuern Songs," is the modern title of a folio MS. which was preserved for centuries at the monastery of that name in Bavaria, but which was not in the catalogue, " probably on account of the not entirely irreproachable nature of its contents." These date almost entirely from the twelfth and thirteenth centuries, and contain pious verse and prose, satirical, bacchanalian, and amatory. The following poem is perhaps the finest of its kind which has come down from the Middle Ages ; it has been suggested that it may be Abailard's. The last three stanzas (here omitted) wander off into the repetitions and irrelevancies which so often disfigure medieval lyrics, in default of that sort

EXAMPLES

of critical public which finally fixed the Italian sonnets
and thus compelled compression and symmetry.

(1)

Dum Diane vitrea
sero lampas oritur,
et a fratris rosea
luce dum succenditur,
dulcis aura zephyri,
spirant omnes etheri ;
nubes tollit,
sic emollit
vi chordarum pectora,
et inmutat
cor, quod nutat
ad amoris pignora.
Letum iubar hesperi
gratiorem
dat humorem
roris soporiferi
mortalium generi.

(2)

O quam felix est
antidotum soporis,
quod curarum tempestates
sedat et doloris !
Dum surrepit clausis
oculorum poris,
ipsum gaudio equiparat
dulcedini amoris.

(3)

Morpheum [1] in mentem
trahit inpellentem
ventum lenem
segetes maturas,
murmura rivorum
per arenas puras,
molendinorum,
qui furantur somno
lumen oculorum.

(4)

Post blanda Veneris
Commercia
Lassatur cerebri
Substantia
Hinc caligant mira novitate
Oculi nantes in palpebrarum rate
Hei ! quam felix transitus amoris ad soporem
Sed suavior regressus ad amorem !

[1] The Editor prints *Morpheus*, but indicates his doubts.

While Diana's crystal lamp ariseth at eventide, and while she is kindled with her brother's rosy light, all the heavens breathe with the breeze of sweet Zephyr ; she chaseth the clouds ; thus doth she soften [men's] breasts with the power of harp-strings, and so change the heart that it inclineth to the pledges of love. The gladdening ray of Hesperus giveth the more grateful moisture of drowsy dew to the race of mortals.

O how happy is the antidote of sleep, which calmeth the tempests of cares and pain ! While it stealeth over the closed pores of our eyes, it doth equal in joy the sweetness of love.

It bringeth Morpheus to our mind : [and] the gentle breeze bending the ripening corn, the murmur of mill-streams over clean sand, which steal unto sleep the light of our eyes.

After the soft commerce of Venus the substance of the brain is wearied ; hence the eyes grow dim with a marvellous change, swimming in the vessel of the eyelids. Ha ! how happy is the passage from love to sleep, but sweeter the return to love !

(1)

Sic mea fata canendo solor,
ut nece proxima facit olor.
Roseus effugit ore color,
blandus inest meo cordi dolor.
Cura crescente,
labore vigente,
vigore labente,
miser morior.
Hei morior, hei morior, hei morior !
Dum quod amem cogor, sed non amor.

(2)

Si me dignetur quam desidero,
felicitate Iovem supero.
Nocte cum illa si dormiero,
si sua labra semel suxero,
mortem subire,
placenter obire,
vitamque finire
libens potero,
hei potero, hei potero, hei potero,
tanta si gaudia recepero.

(3)

Ubera cum animadverterem
optavi manus ut involverem,
simplicibus mammis ut alluderem.

Sic cogitando sensi Venerem,
sedit in ore
rosa cum pudore,
pulsatus amore,
quod os lamberem,
hei lamberem, hei lamberem, hei lamberem,
luxuriando per characterem.

(1) So do I solace my fate with song, as doth the swan when death is at hand. The ruddy glow hath fled from my face, soft pain is lodged in my heart. My care increaseth, my travail stirreth, my vigour faileth ; poor wretch, I die. Ah ! I die, while I am compelled to love, yet am not beloved.

(2) If she deigneth whom I long for, I surpass Jove in felicity. If I may sleep with her by night, if I may suck her lips, I can gladly suffer death, depart with a good grace, and end my life. Ah ! I can, if I get such joys.

(3) When I beheld her breasts, I wished to entangle my hands in them, that I might play with her naked paps ; thus in thought I felt love. The rose sat in her face with shame, that I, smitten with love, should lap her lips. Ah ! lap, revelling by occult art.[1]

XVIII. THE CHRONICLER'S HOME

Salimbene was born in 1222 at Parma, in a house at the corner by that Baptistery which is one of the city's glories. (*M.G.H.*, xxxii. 34.)

Solita erat mater mea michi referre, quod tempore istius magni terremotus iacebam in cunabilis, et ipsa accepit duas sorores meas, sub qualibet ascella unam (erant enim parvule), et	My mother was wont to tell me how at the time of that earthquake I lay in my cradle, and how she caught up my two sisters, one under each arm, for they were but babes as yet. So,

---

[1] The obscurity of these last lines must be confessed. It seems that *os* is to be taken in both senses, *face* and *mouth* ; and perhaps *character* has here its force of a cabalistic sign or spell.

me in cuna dimisso cucurrit ad domum patris et matris et fratrum suorum. Timebat enim, ut dicebat, ne baptisterium super eam caderet, quia ibi iuxta erat domus mea. Et ex hoc non ita clare diligebam eam, quia plus debebat curare de me masculo quam de filiabus. Sed ipsa dicebat, quod aptiores erant sibi ad portandum, cum essent grandiuscule.

Avus domni Iacobi dictus est domnus Guidolinus de Ençola, homo stature mediocris, dives et inclitus valde et multum ecclesiasticus, quem mille vicibus vidi. Hic separavit se a ceteris de Ençola, qui habitabant in burgo Sancte Christine, et venit et habitavit iuxta matricem ecclesiam, que est virginis gloriose. In qua qualibet die missam audiebat et totum diurnum offitium atque nocturnum temporibus oportunis. Et tempore, quo in ecclesiastico offitio occupatus non erat, sedebat cum vicinis suis sub porticu communi iuxta palatium episcopi et loquebatur de Deo vel loquentem de Deo audiebat libenter. Non patiebatur, quod aliquis puer prohiceret lapides contra baptisterium vel contra

leaving me in my cradle, she ran to the house of her father and mother and brethren, for she feared (as she said), lest the Baptistery should fall on her, since our house was hard by. Wherefore I never since loved her so dearly, seeing that she should have cared more for me, her son, than for her daughters. But she herself used to say that they were easier for her to carry, being better grown than I.

The grandfather of the Lord Jacopo was called the Lord Guidolino da Enzola, a man of middle stature, rich and most renowned and devoted beyond measure to the Church, whom I have seen a thousand times. He separated himself from the rest of the family, who dwelt in the Borgo di Santa Cristina, and came and dwelt hard by the Cathedral Church, which is dedicated to the glorious Virgin, wherein he daily heard mass and the whole daily and nightly offices of the Church, each at the fit season ; and, at times when he was not busied with the offices of the Church, he would sit with his neighbours under the public portico by the Bishop's Palace, and speak of God, or listen gladly to any who spake of Him. Nor would he ever suffer children to cast stones against the Baptistery or the

maiorem ecclesiam ad destruendum celaturas et picturas. Quod cum videret, egre ferebat et veloci cursu ibat et cum corigia verberabat eos, ac si pro custodia deputatus fuisset ibidem, cum tamen non faceret hoc nisi pro zelo Dei et amore divino, quasi diceret illud propheticum : *Zelus domus tue comedit me.* Porro iste dominus supradictus preter viridarium et turrim et palatium, in quo habitabat, habebat multas alias domos et furnum et cellarium vinarium. Et semel in qualibet ebdomada fiebat pauperibus omnibus, qui de tota civitate venire volebant, caritas generalis de pane et faba cocta et vino iuxta domum suam in via, ut vidi oculis meis *non semel neque bis.* Iste dominus supradictus multum fuit fratrum Minorum amicus et precipuus benefactor, implens quod Ecclesiasticus docet : *Congregationi pauperum affabilem te facito.*

Cathedral to destroy the carvings or paintings ; for when he saw any such he waxed wroth and ran swiftly against them and beat them with a leather thong as though he had been specially deputed to this office ; yet he did it for pure godly zeal and divine love, as though he said in the Prophet's words, " The zeal of thy house hath eaten me up." Moreover, this said lord, besides the orchard and town and palace wherein he lived, had many other houses and an oven and a wine cellar ; and once every week, in the road hard by his house, he gave to all the poor of the whole city who would come thither a general dole of bread and sodden beans and wine, as I have seen, not once or twice only, with mine own eyes. He was a close friend of the Friars Minor, and one of their chief benefactors, fulfilling the precept of Ecclesiasticus : " Make thyself agreeable ·to the congregation of the poor."

XIX. FRANCISCAN HYMNOLOGY

Salimbene in *M.G.H.*, xxxii. p. 181, under the year 1247.

Frater Henricus Pisanus fuit pulcher homo, mediocris tamen stature, largus, curialis, liberalis et alacer ; cum omnibus bene conversari sciebat condescendendo et conformando se moribus sin-

Brother Henry of Pisa was a comely man, yet of middle stature, free-handed, courteous, liberal, and ready. He knew well how to converse with all, condescending and conforming

gulorum, fratrum suorum gratiam habens et secularium, quod paucorum est. Item sollemnis predicator et gratiosus clero et populo fuit. Item sciebat scribere, miniare—quod aliqui illuminare dicunt, pro eo quod ex minio liber illuminatur—notare, cantus pulcherrimos et delectabiles invenire, tam modulatos, id est fractos, quam firmos. Sollemnis cantor fuit. Habebat vocem grossam et sonoram, ita ut totum repleret chorum. Quillam vero habebat subtilem, altissimam et acutam, dulcem, suavem et delectabilem supra modum. Meus custos fuit in Senensi custodia et meus magister in cantu tempore Gregorii pape noni. . . . Multas cantilenas fecit frater Henricus et multas sequentias. Nam illam litteram fecit et cantum :

"Christe Deus, Christe meus
    Christe rex et domine ! "
ad vocem cuiusdam pedisseque, que per maiorem ecclesiam Pisanam ibat cantando :
    " E s'tu no cure de me,
    E nos curaro de te."
Item de resurrectione Domini fecit sequentiam, litteram et cantum, scilicet :
    Natus, passus Dominus
        resurrexit hodie.
Secundum vero cantum, qui ibi

himself to each man's manners, gaining the favour both of his own brethren and of secular persons, which is given but to few. Moreover, he was a preacher of great weight and favour with both clergy and people. Again, he was skilled to write, to miniate (which some call *illuminate*), for that the book is illuminated with the scarlet *minium*), to write music, to compose most sweet and delightful songs, both in harmony and in plain-song. He was a marvellous singer ; he had a great and sonorous voice, so that he filled the whole choir ; but he had also a flute-like treble, very high and sharp ; sweet, soft, and delightful beyond measure. He was my Custos in the Custody of Siena, and my master of song in the days of Pope Gregory IX. . . . Brother Henry made many songs and many anthems. For he made both letter and chant of " Christ divine, Christ of mine, Christ my King and Lord," after the voice of a certain maidservant who went through the cathedral of Pisa singing : " And if thou carest not for me, I will care no more for thee." Again, he made an anthem of the Lord's Resurrection, both letter and chant, to wit : " Our born and suffering Lord is risen to-day." Now the second air of these words, that

est, id est contracantum, fecit frater Vita ex ordine fratrum minorum de civitate Lucensi, melior cantor de mundo tempore suo in utroque cantu, scilicet firmo et fracto. Vocem habebat gracilem sive subtilem et delectabilem ad audiendum. Non erat aliquis adeo severus, qui non eum libenter audiret. Coram episcopis, archiepiscopis, cardinalibus et papa cantabat et libenter audiebatur ab eis. Si quis loqueretur, cum frater Vita cantaret, statim Ecclesiastici verbum resonabat ibidem Eccli. xxxii. : *Non impedias musicam.* Item si quando cantabat philomena in rubo vel sepe, cedebat isti, si cantare volebat, et ascultabat eum diligenter nec movebatur de loco, et postmodum resumebat cantum suum, et sic alternatim cantando voces delectabiles et suaves resonabant ab eis. Ita curialis de cantu suo fuit, quod nunquam se excusavit, nec occasione vocis lese sive a frigore impedite vel aliqua alia de causa, quando fuit ad cantandum rogatus. . . . Item hunc fratrem Vitam domnus Phylippus archiepiscopus Ravennas assumpsit, ut esset de familia sua . . . tum quia de contrata sua erat, tum quia frater minor, tum etiam quia optime cantare et dictare

is, the counterpoint, was composed by Brother Vita of the city of Lucca, and of the Order of Friars Minor, the best singer in the world of his own time in both kinds, namely, in harmony and in plain-song. He had a thin or subtle voice, and one delightful to hear. There was none so severe but that he heard him gladly. He would sing before Bishops, Archbishops, and the Pope himself ; and gladly they would hear him. If any spoke when Brother Vita sang, immediately men would cry out with Ecclesiasticus, " Hinder not music." Moreover, whenever a nightingale sang in thicket or hedge, it would cease at the voice of his song, listening most earnestly to him, as if rooted to the spot, and resuming its strain when he had ceased ; so that bird and friar would sing in turn, each warbling his own sweet strains. So courteous was he in this that he never excused himself when he was asked to sing, pleading that he had strained his voice, or was hoarse from cold, or for any other reason. . . . Moreover, the Lord Philip, Archbishop of Ravenna, took this Brother Vita to be of his household, both because he was one of his own country, and because he was a Friar Minor, and because he knew so well to sing and compose. He died at

sciebat. Mediolani obiit, in loco fratrum Minorum sepultus. Macilentus homo fuit et gracilis et in statura maior quam frater Henricus. Vox eius magis pertinebat ad cameram quam ad chorum. Pluries exivit ordinem et pluries rediit, ita tamen quod intrabat ordinem sancti Benedicti ; et quando redire volebat, semper parcebat ei papa Gregorius nonus et propter amorem beati Francisci et propter dulcedinem cantus sui. Nam quadam vice ita delectabiliter cantavit, quod quedam monacha, que eum ascultabat, ut sequeretur eum, se per fenestram deiecit. Sed non potuit, quia ex casu illo sibi tibiam fregit. Non fuit talis illa ascultatio, de qua dicitur Canticorum ultimo : *Que habitas in ortis, amici ascultant : Fac me audire vocem tuam.* Ideo bene dixit frater Egidius Perusinus— non quia de Perusio fuerit, sed quia ibi diu vixit et vitam finivit, homo extaticus et totus divus, quartus in ordine frater computato beato Francisco. — Dixit enim : *Magna gratia est non habere gratiam.* Et loquebatur de gratiis non gratis datis, sed acquisitis, propter quas non nulli frequenter male faciunt facta sua. Sane frater Henricus Pisanus in-

Milan, and was buried in the Convent of the Friars Minor. He was slender and lean of body, and taller of stature than Brother Henry. His voice was fitter for the chamber than for the choir. Oft-times he left the Order, and oft-times returned ; yet he never left us but to enter the Order of St. Benedict ; and when he wished to return Pope Gregory IX. was ever indulgent to him, both for St. Francis's sake, and for the sweetness of his song. For once he sang so enchantingly that a certain nun, hearing his song, threw herself down from a window to follow him ; but this might not be, for she broke her leg with the fall. This was no such hearkening as is written in the last chapter of the Song of Songs, " Thou that dwellest in the gardens, the friends hearken : make me hear thy voice." Truly, therefore, spake Brother Giles of Perugia (not that he was of Perugia, but that there he lived and ended his days—a man given to ecstasies and rapt in divine contemplation, the fourth Brother admitted to our Order, after St. Francis—), truly he spake, " It is a great grace to have no graces at all," speaking here of graces not given freely by God, but acquired, by reason whereof some men are frequently led into evil. . . . In truth Brother Henry of Pisa was my

timus meus amicus fuit et talis vere, qualem describit sapiens in Proverbiis xviii. : *Vir amabilis ad societatem magis amicus erit quam frater*. Nam et ipse fratrem habebat in ordine contemporaneum michi, et ego fratrem contemporaneum sibi ; et longe plus me diligebat, ut dixit, quam germanum et proprium fratrem ; et cum dicat Ecclesiasticus xiii. *Vestigium cordis boni et faciem bonam difficile invenies et cum labore*, hoc in eo locum habere nullatenus potuit. Hic factus fuit minister in Grecia, que est provintia Romanie, et michi obedientialem litteram dedit, per quam possem, si michi placeret, ire ad eum et esse de provintia sua, cum quocumque socio voluissem. Insuper et promisit michi Bibliam se daturum ad alios libros multos. Sed non ivi, quia eodem anno, quo pervenit illuc, ultimum diem clausit. Obiit autem in quodam provinciali capitulo celebrato Corinthi. In quo loco sepultus requievit in pace. Prophetavit autem sive futura predixit audintibus fratribus qui in capitulo erant, dicens : " Nunc dividimus libros decedentium fratrum, sed poterit esse, quod usque ad breve tempus dividentur et nostri. Revera ita factum fuit quia in eodem capitulo fuerunt libri sui divisi."

intimate friend, and such as he of whom the Wise Man saith, " A man amiable in society shall be more friendly than a brother"; for he himself also had a brother in the Order of my age, and I a brother of his age ; yet he loved me far more, as he said, than his own blood-brother. And whereas Ecclesiasticus saith, "The token of a good heart and of a good countenance thou shalt hardly find, and with labour," yet this could in no wise be said of him. He was made Minister of Greece, which is the Province of Roumania, and gave me a letter of obedience, whereby, if it pleased me, I might go to him and be of his Province, with a companion of my own choice. Moreover, he promised that he would give me a Bible and many other books. But I went not, for he departed this life in the selfsame year wherein he went thither. He died at a certain Provincial Chapter, celebrated at Corinth, where also he was buried and hath found rest in peace. Moreover he foretold the future in the hearing of the Brethren who were in that Chapter, saying, " Now are we dividing the books of departed Brethren ; but it may be that within a brief while our own too shall be divided." And so it came to pass ; for in that same Chapter his books were divided.

XX. A PAPAL LEGATE

After Innocent III. the Papacy became less spiritual and more definitely political. Salimbene knew intimately one of Innocent IV.'s legates, Archbishop Philip of Ravenna.

Cum autem pervenimus ad hostium ecclesie, invenimus ibi conversum cum thuribulo fumigante. Et incensato legato, accepit thuribulum de manu ipsius et thuricavit quemlibet fratrem ecclesiam introeuntem dicendo : " Del incenso ali frati me. Del incenso ali frati me. Del incenso ali frati me ! " Quod erat dicere : " De incenso fratribus meis." Post hec ivimus ad scalam, et ascendendo et postea descendendo et exeundo apodiabat se super me causa honoris et utilitatis, et ego sustentabam brachium dextrum eius, et archidiaconus Ravenne sinistrum. Et ecclesia in solario erat ; et totus conventus illarum dominarum numero LXX duarum congregatus ibidem. Et celebrata sollemniter missa et expeditis consiliis et negotiis omnibus egressi de monasterio invenimus ignem copiosum paratum. Et statim pulsabatur ad nonam. Et exuens se legatus dixit : " Omnes vos

When therefore we were come to the door of the church, we found there a lay-brother with a smoking censer, and when he had censed the Legate the latter took the censer from his hands, and censed each friar as he entered the church, saying thrice, " *del incenso ali frati me, del incenso ali frati me, del incenso ali frati me*," which being interpreted is, " Of incense to my Brethren." Then we went to the stairs, and he leant on me, for honour's sake and for help, both in mounting and descending ; so that I held up his right arm, and the Archdeacon of Ravenna his left. And the church was on an upper floor, and the whole convent of those ladies, to the number of seventy-two, was there gathered together ; and after Mass had been solemnly celebrated, and all our counsel and business was ended, we went out from the convent and found a plenteous fire kindled. And forthwith the bell ran to Nones, and the Legate took off [his robes], and said,

invito ad prandendum mecum." Credo, quod dixit bene decies Tusice loquendo : " Mo ve c'envito, e si vece revito." Quod erat dicere : " Invito vos ad prandium et iterum reinvito." Verumtamen ita erant fratres illi timidi et verecundi, quod non potui ducere mecum nisi duos. Alii iverunt ad domum fratrum ad comedendum.

Porro domnus Philippus archiepiscopus Ravennas, qui fuit legatus domni pape, cum esset in villa que appellatur Argenta iuxta Padum et deambularet per palatium suum, ibat cantando aliquod responsorium vel antiphonam ad laudem virginis gloriose ab angulo palatii ad alium angulum, et in quolibet tempore estivo bibebat, quia in quolibet palatii angulo enghestariam optimi et precipui vini habebat in frigidissima aqua. Fuit enim magnus potator et aquam in vino nolebat, propter quod et tractatum Primatis, quem fecit de non miscenda aqua vino, optime diligebat, quem forte in hoc libro ponemus causa solatii ad noticiam aliquorum.

" I invite you all to dine with me." I believe that he said full ten times over in the Tuscan tongue, " *mo c' vece envito, e si vecere vito*," which is as much as to say, " I invite you to dinner, and again I reinvite you." Nevertheless those brethren were so fearful and shamefaced that I could not bring with me but two ; the rest went to eat in the Convent of the Brethren.

Moreover, this Lord Philip, Archbishop of Ravenna, who was the Lord Pope's Legate, when he was in his villa called Argenta beside the Po, and when he went to and fro through his palace, was wont to go singing some responsory or antiphon in praise of the glorious Virgin, from one corner to another of that palace. And in summer time he would drink at each corner ; for at each corner of the palace he had a pitcher of excellent and noble wine in the coldest water. For he was a mighty drinker, and loved not water with his wine, wherefore also he loved much the Treatise which Primas wrote against mixing water with wine, which perchance we will put into this book, for the sake of pastime, for some folk to note

Incipit tractatus Primatis de non miscenda aqua vino.

Denudata veritate succinctaque brevitate ratione varia

Dico, quod non copulari debent, immi separari que sunt adversaria.

Cum in scypho reponuntur, vinum [et] aqua coniunguntur, sed talis coniunctio

Non est bona, nec laudari debet, immo nuncupari melius confusio.

Vinum sentit aquam secum, dolens inquit : " Quis est mecum ausus te coniungere ?

Exi, surge, vade foras ! non eodem loco moras debes mecum facere.

Super terram debes teri et cum terra commisceri, ut in lutum transeas.

Vilis et inverecunda rimas queris, ut inmunda mundi loca subeas." . . .

. . . . .

. . . Audiens hec obstupescit aqua, deflens obmutescit, geminat suspiria.

Vinum clamat : " Quare taces ? Patet res, quod victa iaces rationis nescia."

Ego quidem disputator, huius

Here beginneth the treatise of Primus, that water should not be mixed with wine.

In naked truth, and with succinct brevity, for various reasons I say that things which are contraries should not be conjoined, but rather separated. Wine and water, when they are poured into the goblet, are [indeed] conjoined ; but such a conjunction is not good, nor should it be praised : nay, rather called *confusion*. The wine feeleth the water by its side, and saith in grief : " Who hath dared to couple me with thee ? Go forth, arise, depart hence ! thou oughtest not to tarry in the same place with me. Thou shouldst be ground upon the earth and commingled with earth, that thou mayest pass into clay. Vile and shameless, thou seekest crevices in order to slink into the unclean places of the world."

The dialogue continues thus to a considerable length, until at last :

Water, hearing this, was dumbfoundered, wept and held her peace, and reduplicated her sighs. Wine cried, " Wherefore art thou dumb ? The matter is plain, that thou liest conquered, knowing no reason." I for my part, the discusser and summar-

cause terminator, omni dico populo :

Qui est miscens, execretur et a Christo separetur in eterno seculo ! Amen.

Familiam habebat terribilem et ferocem ; et omnes reverebantur fratres Minores sicut apostolos Christi, cognoscentes quod dominus eorum intime diligeret nos. Erant enim bene XL homines armati, quos semper secum ducebat, ut essent capitis sui custodes et totius persone ; et timebant eum sicut diabolum. Nam Icilinus de Romano parum plus timebatur. Dabat enim suis maximas penitentias. Cum enim quadam die de Ravenna iret Argentam, quod est archiepiscopale castrum, quendam de suis ligari fecit cum fune et demergi in aquam, et sic ligatum ad navem traxerunt per aquas vallivas, ac si esset unus sturio. Oblitus enim fuerat salem accipere. Alia vice quendam alium fecit ligari ad magnam perticam et iuxta ignem volvi. Cum autem illi de familia ex quadam pietate et compassione ipsum deflerent videndo crudele spectaculum, dicebat eis : " Miseri, iam fletis." Et sic precepit eum removeri ab igne. Verumtamen

izer of this case, say to all people, " He who is a mixer, let him be accursed and separated from Christ, world without end. Amen."

He had a terrible and savage household, yet they all revered the Friars Minor as apostles of Christ, knowing that their lord loved us dearly. For they were full forty men-at-arms, whom he ever led with him, to be guardians of his life and his whole person ; and they feared him as they feared the Devil. Nay, Ezzelino da Romano was scarcely more feared : for he gave his servants most grievous punishments. One day as he went from Ravenna to Argenta (which is the Archiepiscopal castle), he caused one of his servants to be bound with a rope and plunged into the water, and thus they dragged him bound to the ship through the wallowing waves, as though he were a sturgeon, because he had forgotten to bring salt. Another time he caused a certain other servant to be bound to a great pole and turned [as on a spit] before the fire ; and when the men of his household wept for him with pity and compassion, seeing this cruel sight, the Legate said to them, " Poor wretches ! Do ye weep so soon ? " and so bade that he should be taken

multas anxietates et calefactiones sustinuit. Amanatum vero, quendam Tuscum gastaldum suum, coniecit in vincula, et in carcere comederunt eum mures. Imponebat enim ei, quod dissipasset bona sua. Multas alias crudelitates exercuit in his qui erant de familia sua, ut se vindicaret et illis penitentiam daret et aliis timorem incuteret.

away from the fire. Yet the man had already borne bitter anguish of soul and much roasting. Moreover, the Legate cast into chains a certain Amanato, his steward, a Tuscan ; and the rats devoured him in the prison, for he accused him of having wasted his master's goods. Many other cruelties he practised on those who were of his household, for his own vengeance and their punishment, and to strike fear into others.

XXI. GERALD THE WELSHMAN

Giraldus Cambrensis (1147–1223) was descended through his mother, Nest, from the last of the Welsh kings, and through his father from the Norman conquerors. He was vain, but had much to be proud of ; his uncle was Bishop of St. Davids ; he himself was once elected to the bishopric by the canons, though he failed to get royal and papal consent ; he had risen to an archdeaconry at the age of twenty-eight, and became one of the most prominent writers of his age. His two books on Wales are translated in *Everyman's Library*. He never lets a story lose by the telling ; we cannot always take him literally ; yet the following instances of clerical Latin can be even outdone from cold business documents.

Priests' Latin (Gemma Ecclesiastica, CHAPTER XXXV. ; R.S. II. p. 341).

Qualiter autem evangelia sacramque scripturam hodie presbyteri parochianis suis exponant

Now we will show by some examples how priests nowadays expound the Gospels and Holy

per exempla quaedam osten-
demus. Exemplum de presbytero, qui, sermonem faciens ad
populum de sancto Barnaba,
inter caetera, dixit : " Bonus vir
erat et sanctus, sed tamen latro
fuerat," auctoritatem sumens de
evangelio hoc, scilicet, " erat
autem Barrabas latro ; " inter
Barnabam et Barraban male distinguens. Item exemplum de
sacerdote, qui, sermonem faciens
de muliere Cananea, dixit eam
partim canem sese, partim mulierem, inter Cananeam et cani-
nam non bene distinguens.

Item exemplum de presbytero,
qui, festum Simonis et Judæ
denuntians, dixit : " Alterum
bonum virum et sanctum fuisse,
alterum vero proditorum Christi,
nec ei honorem aliquem vel diei,
propter ipsum, sed propter so-
cium ejus deferendum." Hic
etiam æquivocatione deceptus,
inter Judam et Judam male dis-
tinxit.

Item exemplum de presbytero,
qui sermonem faciens de evangelio ubi legitur : " De pisce
asso et favo mellis ; " dicebat
enim quod comedit Dominus de
pisce asinino et fabis mellitis ; et
cum quaereretur ab eo quisnam
piscis erat ille, respondit, quod
sicut est piscis marinus qui a cane,
et alius qui a lepore denominatur,
quia fere singulis terrarum bestiis
pisces in mari assimulantur, sic et
ab asino quoddam piscis genus

Scripture to their parishioners.
One example is of the priest
who, preaching to the people
concerning St. Barnabas, said
among other things : " He was
a good man and holy ; yet he
had been a robber," taking his
authority from that Gospel passage : " now Barrabas was a
robber," and distinguishing ill
between Barnabas and Barrabas.
Another example is of the priest
who, announcing the feast of
Simon and Jude, said " that one
was a good and holy man, but
the other the betrayer of Christ,
nor should we give any honour
unto him or unto the day on his
account, but for his companion's
sake." He also, deceived by the
equivoque, distinguished ill between one Judas and another.
Again, there is the case of the
priest who, preaching on that
Gospel text where we read " of
a broiled fish and a honey-
comb " ; for he said that our
Lord ate of ass-fish and honeyed
beans ; and when he was asked
what kind of fish that was, he
answered that, as there is one
sea-fish called after the dog, and
another after the hare, since
almost all beasts on earth have
their like in the sea, so one kind
of fish is called after the ass ; but

denominatur, sed in partibus istis non reperitur.

Item exemplum de illo qui loquens de manifestatione facta ad mare Tiberiadis, illud quod ibi legitur, " Viderunt prunas positas," exposuit, de fructu arboris quae prunus vocatur.

Item exemplum de illo qui, clerico suo quaerenti quid esset *altera* respondit quia piscis erat regius in partibus illis, quod et probavit per illud : " Mittite in dexteram navigii rete et invenietis altera."

Item exemplum de presbytero, qui, sermonem faciens de illo evangelio, " Duo debitores erant," in quo legitur " alii donavit quingenta, alii quinquaginta," etc., exposuit de eodem numero, scilicet quinquagenario ; cui praepositus villae ait, " Neutri ergo plus quam alteri donavit cum utrique L. nec plura." Presbyter autem, se deprehensum sentiens, subintulit : " sed alii denarii Andegavenses erant, alii vero sterlingi."

Item exemplum de presbytero, qui sermonem faciens de hoc evangelio, " Occidit Herodes omnes pueros a bimatu et infra," sic exposuit, " ab una provincia in aliam provinciam," *bimatum* unam provinciam construens et *infra* aliam.

it is not found in these parts. Again, the example of him who, speaking of the appearance [of Christ] showed at the sea of Tiberias, at the place where we read " they saw hot coals lying," expounded it concerning the fruit of the tree called *plum*. Again, of him who, when his clerk asked him what *altera* was, replied that it was a royal fish in those parts, which also he proved by those words, " Cast the net on the right side of the ship ; and you shall find." Another example of the priest who, preaching on that Gospel text " there were two debtors," wherein we read " to one he gave five hundred, and to another fifty," expounded them as of the same number, that is, fifty. The reeve of the village said unto him : " So he gave to neither more than to the other, for he gave each fifty and no more." So the priest, finding himself caught, added : " But one set of pence were of the Anjou mint, while the others were sterling."

Another, of the priest who, preaching on this Gospel text : " Herod slew all the children that were in Bethlehem, and in all the borders thereof, from two years old and under," expounded it thus, " from one province to another," construing *bimatum* as one province and *infra* another.

Item exemplum de presbytero, qui, exponens illud de vita sancti cujusdam, " Omnem substantiam suam trifariam divisit," *trifariam* exposuit Gallice, *tine de farine*, hoc est, vas farinæ.

Item exemplum de presbytero denuntiante festum* sancti Johannis ante portam Latinam, et dicente : " Quoniam Johannes ille primo Latinam linguam in Angliam portavit ; " sic enim exposuit *ante*, id est, primo *portam*, portavit, Latinam supple *linguam.*

Item exemplum de presbytero qui locum illum Evangelii : " Si quis vobis aliquid dixerit, dicite quia Dominus his opus habet ; " de pectoris herba exposuit in hunc modum : " Dicite quia Dominus habet herbam illam quæ vocatur hisopus."

Item exemplum de illo qui hoc vocabulum " Apocalypsis " clerico suo quaerenti sic exposuit, alludens Anglico tam appellativo quam proprio, *sacculus Lipsi.*

Item exemplum de illo qui quæsivit a magistro Johanne Cornubiensi quis esset *busillis ?* putabat enim proprium nomen regis vel alicujus magni viri fuisse. Interroganti autem magistro Johanni ubinam hoc, et in

* Ed. R.S. has *bestiam.*

Again, of him who, expounding the text from the life of one saint, " He divided all his substance into three parts," expounded *trifariam* in French, *tine de farine*, that is, " barrel of flour."

Again, the priest who announced the feast of St. John before the Latin Gate, and said : " Because that John was the first to bring the Latin tongue into England " ; for thus he expounded : *ante*, that is " first," " he carried the Latin," with *tongue* understood.

Again, of the priest who thus expounded that passage of the Gospel, " If any man shall say any thing to you, say ye, that the Lord hath need of them," concerning the pectoral herb,[1] in this fashion : " Say that the Lord hath that herb which is called hyssop."

Again, there is the example of him who, in answer to his clerk's question, thus expounded the word " Apocalypse " (alluding to the English, appellative and proper noun) as " Lipsy's poke."[2]

Again, that man who asked Master John of Cornwall who *Busillis* might be ? for he thought it was the proper name of a King or some great man. So when Master John asked him where

[1] Hyssop, according to the herbals, is " cleansing for the breast and the lungs." [2] *i.e.* " pocket," a form which survives in the proverbial " buy a pig in a poke " (Fr. *poche*).

237

qua scriptura inveniretur, respondit quoniam in missali ; et currens propter librum suum, ostendit ei 'in fine columnæ paginae unius scriptum *in die*, in principio vero alterius columnae *bus illis*, quod recte distinctum facit " in diebus illis." Quo viso, magister Johannes dixit ei : " Quoniam de divina pagina hoc erat principium, videlicet evangelii, se velle in crastino in publico scholae suae auditorio istud inquiri." Quo facto, cum sequutus esset omnium risus, ostendit magister, hinc occasionem sumens, exemplis variis quantum accidat in clero dedecus et scandalum ex ignorantiae tenebris et illiteraturae. . . . Non solum autem in minoribus sacerdotibus, sed etiam in majoribus, abbatibus scilicet, prioribus, magnis ecclesiarum decanis, episcopis, et archiepiscopis tales interdum defectus invenies. Audivi auribus meis quendam abbatem verba Domini ad mulierem Samaritanam sic recitantem : " Quinque viros habuisti, et qui nunc habes non est tuum vir." Et iterum cuidam clerico pauperi Hibernico eleemosynam petenti, sic respondentem audivi : " Ubi sunt vaccas tuas." . . . Johannes Cumin, qui postmodum archi-

this was found, and in what book, he answered that it was in the Missal ; and, running for his book, he showed him at the end of the column of one page *in die*, and at the beginning of the next column *bus illis* ; which, rightly arranged, makes " in those days " (Mark i. 9). When Master John saw this, he said to him that, since this was the beginning of the divine page, that is of the Gospel, he himself would on the morrow put that question in the public audience of his own school. When this was done, and when a general laughter followed, the master took occasion therefrom to show by various examples how much disgrace and scandal accrueth to the clergy from the darkness of their ignorance and illiteracy.

Yet not only among the lower priesthood, but even among the greater, such as abbots, priors, great deans of churches, bishops and archbishops, thou shalt sometimes find such defects. I have heard with mine own ears a certain abbot recounting thus the Lord's words to the woman of Samaria : " Thou hast had five husbands, and he whom thou now hast is not thy husband." And again, to a poor clerk of Ireland who begged for alms, I heard him answer thus : " where are thy cows." . . . John Cumin, who afterwards

episcopus Dublinensis in Hibernia factus est . . . retulit de quodam abbate, quem vidit in curia Romana coram Alexandro III. et cardinalibus super illiteratura similiter a monachis suis accusatum, et de canone missæ probatum hoc loco : " Vere dignum et justum est, æquum et salutare," qui cum exposuisset " Vere dignum et justum est," " *Veraiment dignum et juste*," veniens ad æquum, dixit : " ' Equum,' *ceo est cheval*, et ' salutare ' *saillavit*." Et cum putarent multi eum deponendum, quia tamen bonus dispensator erat, et domui suæ bene praepositus, judicio summi pontificis obtinuit et abbas remansit. . . . Item exulante beato Thoma Cantuariensi missi sunt antistites Angliae, qui magis eloquentes et literati reputabantur, ad summum pontificem Alexandrum III., qui tunc in Francorum regno fuerat, ad causam Anglorum regis fulciendam et archipraesulis infirmandam ; qui cum ad hoc astarent et rationes fabricatas etiam et excogitatas allegarent, non fuit unus qui babarismum [*sic*] vel soloecismum in tanta audientia non incurreret.

became Archbishop of Dublin in Ireland, . . . related concerning a certain abbot whom he saw at the Roman Court, accused likewise by his own monks of illiteracy before Alexander III. and his Cardinals, and tested from the Canon of the Mass in that passage, " it is truly meet, right, just and salutary." He, having expounded *vere dignum et justum est* as " truly dignum and justu," coming to *aequum*,[1] said " ' Equum,' that is, *horse*, and ' salutare,' *he jumped*. And, while many thought that he should be deposed, yet because he was a good steward [of goods], and in good authority over his house, he gained by the judgment of the Supreme Pontiff, and remained Abbot. . . .

Again, when St. Thomas of Canterbury was in exile, English bishops who were accounted most[2] eloquent and learned were sent to Pope Alexander III. (who was then in the realm of France) to support the cause of the King of England and weaken that of the Archbishop. When these men stood up for that business and alleged reasons which they had also invented and thought out, there was not one who did not fall into some barbarism or solecism in so great an audience.

---

[1] Giraldus himself, like all of his day, doubtless spelt *aequum* as *equum*.
[2] Common use of comparative for superlative.

Alpes itaque transcendens, et Italiam ac Tuscaniam transcurrens, circa festum Sti. Andreae Romam pervenit ; et accedens ad pedes papae sc. Innocentii III. qui tunc praesidebat, et papatus ejus anno secundo, vi. libros suos, quos ipse studio magno compegerat, ei presentavit ; dicens etiam inter caetera : " Praesentant vobis alii libras, sed nos libros." Libros autem illos papa, quia copiose literatus erat et literaturam dilexit, circa lectum suum indivisos per mensem fere secum tenuit, et elegantia ac sententiosa verba cardinalibus advenientibus ostentabat ; deinde vero singulis cardinalibus singulos precario concessit. *Gemmam* autem *Sacerdotalem* prae caeteris dilectam a se separari non permisit.

So, crossing the Alps and passing through Italy and Tuscany [Giraldus] came to Rome about St. Andrew's day ; and, coming to the feet of the Pope —that is, of Innocent III., who then ruled, and in the second year of his papacy—he presented to him his six volumes, which he had composed with great zeal, saying unto him among other words : " Others present pounds to you, but we bring books." So the Pope, who was abundantly literate and loved literature, kept those books by him, about his bed, for about a month, and showed the Cardinals who came to him their elegant and sententious words : then, indeed, he granted them on loan, one by one, to one Cardinal at a time. But my *Gemma Sacerdotalis* he loved beyond the rest, and suffered it not to be parted from him.

XXII. CISTERCIAN STORIES

Caesariaus of Heisterbach was probably a native of Cologne : certainly he was novice-master at the Cistercian abbey of Heisterbach, across the Rhine from Godesberg. He wrote (about 1230) a book of Homilies and a Dialogue of Miracles, from which the following extracts are taken. The interlocutors are a novice-master and a novice. This book, of singular value for religious and

EXAMPLES

social life, has been translated in two volumes by H. von E. Scott and C. C. S. Bland. (Text from J. Strange, 1851.)

Monachus : Ex relatione cuiusdam viri religiosi cognovi ; Lodewicum Lantgravium, patrem Hermanni Lantgravii, qui ante hos duos annos defunctus est, in errorem periculosum non solum propriae animae, sed et subditorum substantiae decidisse. Qui cum esset praedo ac tyrannus maximus, duras et plurimas in sibi commissum populum faciens exactiones, plurimas ecclesiarum sibi usurpans possessiones, cum propter haec et multa alia mala a viris religiosis corriperetur, qui ei proponebant in confessione poenam malorum gloriamque electorum, verbum miserabile respondit : Si praedestinatus sum, inquit, nulla peccata poterunt mihi regnum coelorum auferre ; si praescitus, nulla bona mihi illud valebunt conferre. Et, sicut mihi dicere solitus est nonnus Conradus senex monachus noster, de Thuringiae partibus oriundus, versiculum illum Psalmistae : *Coelum coeli Domino, terram autem dedit filiis hominum,* loco proverbii ad suam excusationem arguentibus se proponebat : erat siquidem literatus, et ob hoc amplius induratus. Et cum ei

Monk. I learned from the mouth of a certain Religious that the Landgraf Ludwig, father to Landgraf Hermann, who died this two year since, fell into an error grievous not only for his own soul but also for the substance of his subjects. For, since he was a robber and a very great tyrant, who laid hard and most numerous exactions upon the people committed unto him, and usurped very many Church possessions, when he was rebuked for these and many other evils by men of Religion, who put before him in confession the punishment of the wicked and the glory of the elect, he answered with this wretched word : " If I be predestinate, no sins will be able to take from me the Kingdom of Heaven ; if I am foreknown, no good deeds will avail to bestow it upon me. And (as old Dom Conrad, our monk, who came from Thuringia, was wont to tell me), he was wont to quote as a proverb, in his own excuse to those who rebuked him, that word of the Psalmist : *The heaven of heaven is the Lord's, but the earth he has given to the children of men ;* for he was a man who could read Latin, and the more hardened on that account.

dicerent viri timorati : Domine, parcite animae vestrae, desinite peccare, ne Dominus peccatis vestris provocatus peccatorem in peccatis occidat ; iterum respondit : Cum venerit dies mortis meae, moriar, non illum potero bene vivendo extendere, neque male vivendo praevenire. Volens illum pius Dominus a tanto errore misericorditer revocare et reducere ad mentem, infirmitate periculosa coepit eum flagellare. Vocatus est medicus eius, vir bonus et discretus, et non solum in physica, sed etiam in theologia non mediocriter literatus. Cui Princeps dixit : Ut vides, infirmus sum valde ; adhibe curam, ut possim convalescere. Memor medicus erroris illius, respondit : Domine, si venit dies mortis vestrae, non vos poterit cura mea morti subtrahere ; si vero moriturus non estis de infirmitate ista, superflua erit medicina mea. Et ille : Quomodo sic respondes ? Si mihi non fuerit adhibita curae diligentia et diaeta proposita, potero tam a me ipso quam ab aliis imperitis negligi, et ante tempus mori. Audito hoc verbo physicus multum hilaris effectus, data occasione respondit : Domine, si creditis vitam vestram

So, when Godfearing men said unto him : " Spare your soul, cease from sin, lest God, provoked by your sins, should slay the sinner in his sins," he answered again : " When my death-day cometh, I shall die : I cannot extend it by living well, nor anticipate it by living ill." So the kind Lord, willing mercifully to recall him from so great error and to bring him to his senses, began to chastise him with a perilous sickness. His physician was called, a good and discreet man, and not only in physic but also of no mean learning in theology. To him the Prince said : " As thou seest, I am very sick : apply thy care that I may be able to recover." The physician, mindful of that error, made answer : " My lord, if thy death-day be come, my care cannot withdraw you from death ; but if you are not destined to die of this sickness, my medicine will be superfluous." Then said he : " How answerest thou thus ? If careful diligence be not applied to me, and diet put before me, I may be neglected as much by myself as by other inexperienced folk, and die before my time." The physician, hearing this word, was made very joyful, and (the occasion thus given) he answered : " My lord, if you believe that your life may be

posse protelari virtute medicinae, quare hoc credere renuitis de poenitentia et operibus institiae, quae sunt antidota animae? Sine his anima moritur, sine his ad sanitatem quae est in futura vita, nemo pervenit. Considerans Lantgravius pondus verborum, et quia rationabiliter perorasset, dixit ei : De cetero medicus esto animae meae, quia per tuam medicinalem linguam Deus liberavit me a maximo errore. *Novicius :* Numquid non bene vixit postea Princeps iste? *Monachus :* Minime. Promisit verbis, quod non implevit factis. Qualis eius finis fuerit, cum quanta sarcina peccatorum obierit, poena tormentorum illius in sequentibus te docebit. Revertamur igitur ad praecedentia, quia longam hanc evagationem fecit interrogatio tua.

Monachus. Lodewicus Lantgravius maximus tyrannus fuit, de quo supra dictum est in distinctione prima capitulo tricesimo quarto. Hic cum moriturus esset, praecepit amicis suis dicens : Mox ut mortuus fuero, cucullam ordinis Cisterciensis mihi induite, et ne hoc fiat me vivente diligentissime cavete. Obedierunt illi ; mortuus est et cucullatus. Quod ubi miles quidam vidit, commilitones yro-

prolonged by the power of medicine, why do you refuse to believe this of penitence and works of righteousness, which are remedies for the soul? Without these the soul dieth ; without these no man cometh to the health which is in the life to come." The Landgraf, considering the weight of his words and that he had spoken reasonably, said unto him : " Henceforth thou shalt be the physician of my soul ; for through thy healing tongue the Lord hath freed me from the greatest error." *Novice.* Did not that Prince live well afterwards? *Monk.* By no means. He promised in word that which he fulfilled not in deed. What his end was, and with what a load of sins he died, the pains of torments in my following [pages] will teach thee.

Monk. The Landgraf Ludwig was a most evil tyrant, of whom I have spoken above in the thirty-fourth chapter of my first section. When he was about to die, he commanded his friends, saying : " As soon as I am dead, put the cowl of the Cistercian Order upon me, and take most diligent care that this be not done while I live." They obeyed ; he died and was becowled. When a certain knight saw this, he spake ironically

nice allocutus est dicens : Vere non est similis domino meo in omni virtute. Quando miles erat, non habuit parem in actibus militiae ; factus vero monachus, omnibus factus est forma disciplinae. Videte quam diligenter custodit silentium suum. Nec unum quidem verbum loquitur. Anima vero eius cum educta fuisset de corpore, principi daemoniorum praesentata est, sicuti cuidam manifestissime revelatum est. Sedente eodem tartarico super puteum, et scyphum manu tenente, huiusmodi verbis Lantgravium salutavit : Beneveniat dilectus amicus noster ; ostendite illi triclinia nostra, apothecas nostras, cellaria nostra, sicque eum reducite. Deducto misero ad loca poenarum, in quibus nihil aliud erat nisi planctus, fletus, et stridor dentium, et reducto, sic princeps principem affatur : Bibe amice de scypho meo. Illo valde reluctante, cum nihil proficeret, imo coactus biberet, flamma sulphurea de oculis, auribus, naribusque eius erupit. Post haec sic infit : Modo considerabis puteum meum, cuius profunditas sine fundo est. Amotoque operimento, eum in illum misit, et

to his fellow-knights, saying : "Truly there is none like unto our lord in all virtues ! When he was a knight, he had no peer in warlike deeds ; but, now that he is become a monk, he is become a model of discipline to all. See how diligently he keepeth his silence : he speaketh not even a single word !" Yet, when his soul was drawn forth from the body (as was revealed most clearly to a certain man), he was presented to the Prince of the demons. As that Hell-prince sat over the pit, and held a goblet in his hand, he greeted the Landgraf in these words : "Welcome be our beloved friend ; show him our feasting-couches, our store-chambers and our cellars, and bring him back." When the poor wretch had been brought to the places of torment, wherein was nought but wailing and weeping and gnashing of teeth, and brought back again, then said Prince to Prince : "Drink, friend, from my goblet." Though he struggled hard, since nought availed, but he must drink perforce, then a sulphurous flame burst forth from his eyes and ears and nostrils. After this the Devil spake thus : "Now shalt thou inspect my pit, the depth whereof is bottomless. So the cover was removed, and he sent him therein and replaced the cover.

removit. Ecce iste est puteus in quo eum clericus vidit, sicut praedictum est in praefato capitulo.

Monachus. Retulit mihi Daniel Abbas Sconaviae, militem quendam honestum et in militia nominatum, in Campo factum fuisse monachum. Hic cum alium quendam militem, aeque in armis strenuum, in saeculo amicum habuisset, et die quadam ad conversionem eum hortatus fuisset ; respondit ille magnae pusillanimitatis verbum : Vere, amice, ego forte venirem ad ordinem, si non esset una res quam timeo. Interrogante monacho, quaenam esset res illa ; respondit miles : Vermiculi vestimentorum. Pannus enim laneus multos vermiculos nutrit. Tunc ille subridens ait : Och fortem militem ! Qui in bello diaboli non timuit gladios in militia Christi timere debet pediculos ? Auferent tibi nunc pediculi regnum Dei ? Ille licet ad haec verba tunc tacuerit, tempore tamen modico emenso, effectu respondit. Nam et ordinem tam verbis quam exemplo illius provocatus intravit. Contigit ut postea hi duo convenirent

Lo ! that is the pit wherein the cleric saw him [in vision], as I have said before in the aforesaid chapter.

Monk. Daniel, Abbot of Schönau, told me how a certain honourable knight, renowned in war, had been made monk at Camp. Since this man had for friend in the world another knight, equally valiant in arms, and had exhorted him one day to take the cowl,[1] that man answered him in a word of great faintheartedness : "Truly, friend, I would perchance come to the Order, were it not for one thing which I fear." The monk asked what that thing might be ; and the knight replied : "The vermin of your garments." For our woollen cloth nourisheth many vermin.[2] Then said the other, smiling, "Oh, the valiant knight ! He who, in the devil's wars feared no swords, must fear lice in Christ's warfare ! Shall lice now take from thee the Kingdom of God ? " Though the other held his peace at that word, yet when a little time had elapsed he answered in effect ; for he entered our Order, provoked both by the other's words and by his example. It befel that these two

---

[1] *Conversio*, in medieval Latin, means nearly always the taking of monastic vows. [2] The early Cistercians, like most of the stricter Orders, insisted on absence of linen, and on sleeping in the same garments as were worn by day.

Coloniae in ecclesia beati Petri. Monachus vero Campensis cum alterum regulariter salutasset, subridens adiecit : Quid est, frater ? Timesne adhuc vermiculos ? Ille bene recordans unde talis interrogatio haberet originem, et ipse subridendo respondit verbum bonum, verbum memoria dignum : Crede mihi, frater, et hoc pro certo scias, quia si essent omnes vermiculi omnium monachorum in uno corpore, non me de ordine morderent. Quo verbo audito, ille multum aedificatus est, multis illud ad aedificationem recitans. Vides quantae fortitudinis factus sit is, qui ante conversionem nimis fuerat pusillanimis ? Unde hoc, nisi ex divinis consolationibus, quae sunt in ordine ?

In ecclesia sancti Gereonis Martyris civitatis Coloniensis nostris temporibus canonicus quidam exstitit, Werinboldus nomine, genere nobilis, dives satis in stipendiis ecclesiasticis. Hic tantae simplicitatis fuit, ut nullius rei summam caperet, nisi quantum ex paritate numeri vel imparitate colligere posset. Cum tempore quodam multas haberet pernas in coquina sua pendentes, ne aliqua ei subtrahi posset,

met afterwards in the Church of St. Peter at Cologne. When the monk of Camp had saluted the other in regular fashion, he added with a smile : " How is it, brother : dost thou still fear the vermin ? " He, well remembering whence this question arose, and smiling himself, answered with a good word, a memorable word : " Believe me, brother, and know this for certain, that if all the vermin of all the monks were in one body, they should not bite me away from the Order." The other, hearing that word, was much edified, and repeated it to many for their edification. See how valiant that man became, who before his conversion had been so faint-hearted. Whence cometh this, but from the divine consolations which are in our Order ?

At the church of the martyr St. Gereon, in the city of Cologne, there was in our days a certain canon named Werinbold, of noble race and very rich in ecclesiastical revenues. He was of such simplicity that he grasped not the sum-total of anything except so far as he could infer it from the evenness or oddness of the number. When, once upon a time, he had many hams hanging in his kitchen, lest any should be stolen

intravit, et in hunc modum eas numeravit : Ecce perna et eius socia, ecce perna et eius socia, sicque de ceteris. Una ex illis nequitia servorum subtracta, cum iterum intrasset, et praedicto modo suas pernas numerasset, impares inveniens exclamavit : Unam ex pernis meis perdidi. Cui servi subridentes responderunt : Domine, bene invenietur. Illoque educto, cum una iterum subtracta numerum parificassent, et sic inductus secundo eas numerasset, paresque reperisset, satis iocunde dicebat illis : Eia vos domini, nimis diu poteram tacuisse.

from him, he went in and numbered them in this fashion : " Here is a ham and its mate, here is a ham and its mate," and so on with the rest. When, by the wickedness of the servants, one had been removed, having entered again and numbered his hams in the aforesaid fashion, he found them uneven, and cried : " I have lost one of my hams ! " His servants smiled, and answered : " Master, it shall be found well enough." So they led him out and made the number even ; and so he was brought in and numbered them for a second time ; and, finding them even, he said unto them most joyfully : " Ha, my masters, I might have held my peace too long."

XXIII. A PULPIT ANECDOTE

From *A Selection of Latin Stories* [for preachers]. (Percy Soc., Vol. VIII., ed. Thos. Wright, p. 14).

De quodam alio homine audivi, quod cum ejus uxor nunquam vellet obedire illi, ipse simulavit se ire ad nundinas, et uxori suae dixit, " Quicquid vis, facias ; hoc solo excepto, quod in foramine isto digitum non ponas." Cum autem homo ille recederet, ac si ad nundinas

I have heard of another man that, since his wife would never obey him, he feigned to go to the fair, and said to his wife : " Do whatsoever thou wilt, with this single exception that thou thrust not thy finger into this hole." So when this man withdrew, as though he were to go

iturus esset, abscondit se in quadam vicina domo. Uxor autem ejus cogitare coepit, " Quare inhibuit mihi maritus meus quod in foramine isto digitum non mitterem : certe digitum mittam, ut probem quare istud prohibuit mihi." Et ipsa cum magno impetu digitos suos immittente in foramine, clavi acutissimi quos maritus ejus in foramine posuerat digito ejus infixi sunt, et prae angustia coepit clamare, ita quod ejus maritus et vicini concurrerent. Cui maritus ejus ait, " Quare non credidisti mihi, et mandatis meis obedire noluisti ? Praeciperam enim tibi ut quicquid velles faceres, dummodo in foramine isto digitum non poneris." Et ita uxorem malam castigavit, ut alia vice praeceptis ejus aquiesceret.

to the fair, he hid himself in a neighbouring house. So his wife began to think : " Wherefore hath my husband forbidden me, that I should not thrust my finger into this hole : surely I will thrust my finger, that I may prove wherefore he hath forbidden me." And, as she thrust her fingers [sic] with great force into the hole, some pointed nails which her husband had placed in the hole ran into her finger, and she began to cry aloud in anguish, so that her husband and the neighbours ran together. So her husband said unto her : " Wherefore didst thou not believe me, and wouldst not obey my commands ? For I had bidden thee do whatsoever thou wouldest, provided only that thou thrust not thy finger into that hole." And thus he chastised his evil wife, so that another time she might conform to his commands.

XXIV. OUR GREATEST CHRONICLER

Matthew Paris was a St. Albans monk from 1217, the year after Innocent III. died, to his own death in 1259, the year when the choir of Westminster Abbey was consecrated. He is the greatest of English, and many would say of all European chroniclers. He was far from unprejudiced ; his bugbears were the foreign usurers

and prelates thrust into England by the workings of the Roman machine, and all rivals or adversaries of his own Benedictine Order. Yet, even on these points, the witness of cold-blooded documents can convict him of no more than polemical exaggeration.

The Papal Legate Otto and the Scholars of Oxford; A.D. 1238
(R.S. III. p. 481).

Tunc vero temporis dominus legatus cum Oxoniam advent-asset, et honore summo, prout decuit, reciperetur, hospitatus est in domo canonicorum, scilicet abbatia de Oseneie. Clerici vero scholares eidem xenium honorabile in poculentis et esculentis transmiserunt ante prandii tempus. Et post prandium, ut eum salutarent et reverenter visitarent, ad hospitium suum venerunt. Quibus advenientibus, janitor quidam transalpinus, minus quam deceret aut expediret facetus, et more Romanorum vocem exaltans, et januam aliquantulum patefactam tenens, ait, " Quid quaeritis ? " Quibus clerici, " Dominum legatum, ut eum salutemus." Credebant enim confidenter, ut essent honorem pro honore recepturi. Sed janitor, convitiando loquens, in superbia et abusione introitum omnibus procaciter denegavit. Quod videntes clerici, impetuose irruentes intrarunt ; quos volentes Romani reprimere, pugnis et virgis caedebant ; et dum

So at that time, when the Lord Legate had come to Oxford, and was received with utmost honour, as befitted, he was lodged in the house of the [Austin] canons, that is in Oseney abbey. The scholar-clerks sent him, before dinner, an honourable gift of food and drink ; and, after dinner, they came to his lodging to greet and visit him with reverence. At their arrival, a certain Italian doorkeeper, less courteous than was proper or expedient, and raising his voice after the Roman fashion, and holding the door ajar, said : " What seek ye ? " To which the clerks [answered] : " The Lord Legate, in order to greet him " : for they confidently believed that they would receive honour for honour. But the doorkeeper, speaking insultingly and in pride and abuse, denied entrance wantonly to them all. The clerics, seeing this, rushed impetuously and entered in ; and the Romans, wishing to restrain them, smote them with fists and rods ; and

objurgantes ictus et convitia geminarent, accidit quod quidam pauper capellanus Hyberniensis ad ostium coquinae staret, et ut quippiam boni pro Deo acciperet, instanter, more pauperis et famelici, postulaverat. Quem cum magister coquorum legati (frater legati erat ille, et ne procuraretur aliquid venenosum, quod nimis timebat legatus, ipsum ipsi officio praefecerat, quasi homini specialissimo) audivit, nec exaudivit, iratus in pauperem, projecit ei scilicet in faciem aquam ferventem, haustam de lebete ubi carnes pingues coquebantur. Ad hanc injuriam, exclamavit quidam clericus de confinio Walliae oriundus, " Proh pudor ! ut quid haec sustinemus ? " Et arcum, quem portavit, tetendit, (dum enim tumultus accreverat excitatus, clericorum aliqui arma, quae ad manus venerunt, arripuerant,) et ipse missa sagitta corpus coci, quem clerici satirice Nabuzardan, id est, principem coquorum, vocabant, transverberavit. Corruente igitur mortuo, clamor excitatur. Ad quem stupefactus legatus, et nimis perterritus

while, with objurgations, they were multiplying strokes and contumely, it befel that a certain poor Irish chaplain stood by the kitchen door, and had begged earnestly, as a poor famishing fellow, that he might receive some food for God's sake. When the Legate's cookmaster (he was the Legate's brother, and the latter had promoted him to that very office lest anything poisonous should be administered, which the Legate greatly feared) heard him, yet heard him not out, being incensed against the poor man, he even cast into his face some hot water, drawn from the cauldron wherein fat flesh was seething. At this insult, a cleric whose house was in the Welsh border cried " For shame ! wherefore do we suffer this ? " So he drew the bow that he carried (for while the tumult and excitement had increased, some of the clerics had caught up the arms which came to hand) and he, letting fly the arrow, transpierced the body of the cook, whom the clerics named satirically Nabuzardan, to wit, Prince of the Cooks.[1] So he fell dead and a clamour arose. The Legate, dismayed at this, and greatly terrified with a fear

---

[1] The commentators thus interpreted the name of Nabuzardan, the general of the army (4 Kings xxv. 8 ; Jer. xxxix. 9). As that man destroyed the walls of Jerusalem, so " the Prince of Cooks " (that is, Belly or Gluttony) destroys the walls of the soul. (Hugo de S. Caro on Jeremiah xxxix. 10.)

timore qui posset in constantissimum virum cadere, in turrim ecclesiae indutus capa canonicali se recepit, seratis post terga ostiis. Ubi cum noctis opacae conticinium tumultum pugnae diremisset, legatus, vestimentis canonicalibus exutis, equum suum optimum ascendit expeditus, et ducatu eorum qui vada secretiora noverunt, amnem, qui proximus erat, licet cum periculo, transivit, ut ad protectionem alarum regis ocius avolaret. Clerici enim furia invecti legatum etiam in abditis secretorum latebris quærere non cessabant, clamantes et dicentes ; "Ubi est ille usurarius, simonialis, raptor reddituum, et sititor pecuniae, qui, regem pervertens, et regnum subvertens, de spoliis nostris ditat alienos ? " Insequentium autem adhuc clamores cum fugiens legatus audiret, dixit intra se :

"Cum furor in cursu est, currenti cede furori."

which may fall even upon the most steadfast man,[1] took refuge in the church tower, clad in his canonical cope, and the doors were locked behind his back. Then, when the silence of dark night had done away with the tumult of the fight, the Legate doffed his canonical robes and mounted with all speed his best courser ; then, under the guidance of those who knew the more secret fords, he crossed, though not without peril, the river which ran hard by, in order to flee away swiftly to the protection of the King's wings. For the clerics, transported with fury, ceased not to search for the Legate even in the hidden lairs of the privy chambers, crying aloud and saying : "Where is that usurer, simoniac, robber of revenues and thirster for money, who, perverting the King and subverting the kingdom, enriches foreigners with our spoils ?" But the fleeing Legate, hearing yet the cries of his pursuers, said within himself : "When madness rides apace, do thou yield to the riding madness."

A Benedictine View of Franciscans and Dominicans ; A.D. 1243 (R.S. IV. p. 279).

Et ne mundus turbinibus undique multiplicatis vacare videre-

And, less the world should seem to be free from whirlwinds

---

[1] This is a stock phrase of the law-courts for a man pleading that he had signed or acted under compelling force.

tur, inter fratres Minores et Prædicatores controversia eisdem temporibus ventilata, multos, eo quod viam perfectionis, videlicet paupertatis et patientiae, videbantur elegisse, movit in admirationem. Asserentibus enim Praedicatoribus se fuisse priores, et in hoc ipso digniores, habitu quoque honestiores, a praedicatione merito nomen et officium se sortiri, et Apostolica dignitate verius insigniri, respondent Minores, se arctiorem vitam et humiliorem pro Deo elegisse, et iccirco digniorem, quia sanctiorem, et ab ordine Praedicatorum ad ordinem eorum fratres posse et licenter debere, quasi ab inferiori ad ordinem arctiorem et superiorem, transmigrare. Contradicunt eis in faciem Praedicatores, asserentes, quod licet ipsi Minores nudi pedes et viliter tunicati cinctique funiculis incedant, non tamen eis esus carnium, etiam in publico, vel dieta propensior, denegatur, quod fratribus est Praedicatoribus interdictum ; quapropter non licet ipsis Praedicatoribus ad Minorum ordinem, quasi arctiorem et digniorem, avolare, sed potius e converso. Sic igitur, sicut inter Templarios et Hospitalarios in

multiplied on every side, a controversy which was ventilated in those same days between the Friars Minor and Preachers moved many men to amazement, seeing that they seemed to have chosen the way of perfection : that is, of poverty and patience. For, while the Preachers asserted that they had been first in the field, and by this very fact more worthy, and more honourable in their dress, that they deservedly took their name and office from preaching, and were more truly distinguished by apostolic dignity, the Minors answered that they had chosen for God's sake a stricter and humble life, and therefore more worthy as being holier ; also, that brethren might lawfully pass from the Order of Preachers into their own, as from a lower Order to one stricter and higher. The Preachers gainsay these to their face, asserting that, although the said Minors go barefooted and with coarse frocks and girt with ropes, yet flesh-eating and richer diet are not forbidden to them even in public, as to the Preaching Friars : wherefore it is not lawful for the said Preachers to fly off to the Order of Minors, as to one stricter and worthier, but rather conversely. Thus therefore, even as between Templars and Hospitallers in the

Sancta Terra, sic et inter illos, humani generis inimico zizania seminante, ortum est discordiae enorme scandalum, et quia viri literati sunt et scolares, universali ecclesiae nimis periculosum, in indicium magni judicii prae foribus imminentis. Et quod terribile est et in triste praesagium, per trecentos annos vel quadringentos, vel amplius, ordo monasticus tam festinanter non cepit praecipitium, sicut eorum ordo, quorum fratres, jam vix transactis viginti quatuor annis, primas in Anglia construxere mansiones, quarum aedificia jam in regales surgunt altitudines. Hi jam sunt, qui in sumptuosis et diatim ampliatis aedificiis et celsis muralibus thesauros exponunt impreciabiles, paupertatis limites et basim suae professionis, juxta prophetiam Hyldegardis Alemanniae, impudenter transgredientes. Morituris magnatibus et divitibus, quos norunt pecuniis abundare, diligenter insistunt, non sine ordinariorum injuriis et jacturis, ut emolumentis inhient, confessiones extorquent et occulta testamenta, se suumque ordinem solum commendantes et omnibus aliis praeponentes. Unde nullus fidelis, nisi Praedicatorum et

Holy Land, so also among those [Friars] the Enemy of the human race hath sown tares and a huge scandal of discord hath arisen : and, because they are men of letters, and scholars, this is highly perilous for the Church Universal, in token of the Great Judgment imminent at our doors. And (which is a fearful thing, and a melancholy presage) during the last three or four hundred years or more, the monastic Order of Monks hath had no such rapid downfall as their Order ; for their brethren, scarce four and twenty years ago, set up their first dwellings in England, the buildings whereof rise now to royal heights. These, nowadays, are those who, within costly buildings amplified from day to day, and lofty walls, spend untold treasures, transgressing impudently (as St. Hildegardis of Germany prophesied) the bounds of poverty and the foundation of their profession. They diligently haunt the deathbeds of great and rich folk, whom they know to abound in money, not without injury and loss to the ordinaries, in order that they may gape after gain, extort confessions and hidden testaments, commending only themselves and their own Order, and putting them before all others. Wherefore none of the faithful now thinks himself in a state of

Minorum regatur consiliis, jam credit salvari. In adquirendis privilegiis solliciti, in curiis regum et potentum consiliarii, et cubicularii, et thesaurarii, paranimphi et nuptiarum praelocutores, papalium extorsionum executores, in praedicationibus suis vel adulatores, vel mordacissimi reprehensores, vel confessionum detectores, vel incauti redargutores. Ordines quoque auctenticos et a sanctis patribus constitutos, videlicet a Sanctis Benedicto et Augustino, et eorum professores contempnentes, prout in causa ecclesiae de Scardeburc, in qua Minores turpiter ceciderunt, patuit, suum ordinem aliis praeponunt. Rudes reputant, simplices, et semilaicos, vel potius rusticos, Cistercienses monachos ; Nigros vero, superbos et epicuros.

salvation unless he be guided by the counsels of Preachers and Minors. They are busy in acquiring privileges, counsellors and chamberlains and treasurers in the courts of kings and powerful folk ; bridemen and procurers of marriages, executors of papal extortion ; in their sermons either flatterers or most bitter backbiters, or revealers of confessions or rash reprehensors. Moreover they despise the authentic Orders, founded by holy fathers, namely Saints Benedict and Augustine, with those who profess them (as was plain in the case of the church of Scarborough, wherein the Minors had an uncomely fall) and put their own Order before others. They count the Cistercian monks as rough, simple, half-layfolk,[1] or rather clowns ; the Black Monks [of St. Benedict and Cluny] they count as proud and luxurious.

XXV. A MODEL STUDENT

S[t.] Richard Wych, afterwards Bishop of Chichester (1245–53). From *Acta Sanctorum*, April 3 (Vol. I. p. 278).

Postea cum Richardus totam hereditatem a fratre pacifice obtinuisset, amici ejus carnales de

Afterwards, when Richard had obtained the whole heritage peaceably from his brother, his

---

[1] *Laicus* has nearly always the further hint of *uneducated*.

quadam nobili et generosa puella ei matrimonialiter copulanda tractare coeperunt. Quod cum frater ejus intellexisset, et jam Richardum dictam nobilem puellam cum multis bonis recepturum, de collatione terrae suae poenituit, et coepit contristari. Richardus autem hoc intelligens, dixit fratri suo : Non carissime frater, non propter hoc turbetur cor tuum : nam adeo curialis, ut fuisti erga me, ero et erga te. Ecce restituo tibi terram et chartam : sed et puellam, si sibi et amicis suis placuerit : numquam enim os ipsius deosculatus sum. Confestim igitur reliquit Richardus tam terram quam puellam, et omnes amicos, et ad studium Universitatis primo Oxoniae, deinde Parisiis se transtulit, ubi Logicam addidicit. Tantaque fuit discendi affectio, quod de victu aut vestitu parum aut nihil curavit. Nam, sicut narrare consueverat, ipse, et duo socii ejus existentes in camera, non nisi unicam habebant cappam, et tunicam tantum ; et quilibet eorum lectum infimum. Exeunte ergo uno cum cappa ad lectionem audiendam, reliqui in camera residebant ; et sic alternatim exierunt : panisque et parum de vino cum potagio eis pro cibo sufficiebat. Non enim

friends in the flesh began to treat for marrying to him a noble and well-born maiden. When his brother had learned this, and that Richard would now receive the said noble maiden with many possessions, he repented of having given his land, and began to be sad. But Richard, perceiving this, said to his brother : " No, dearest brother, let not thy heart be troubled on this account : for as courteous as thou hast been to me, so will I be to thee. Lo, I restore to thee the land and the title-deed ; nay, and the maiden also, if it please her and her friends ; I have never kissed her mouth. So Richard hastily left both [his father's] lands and the lady, and all his friends, and betook himself first to the University of Oxford and then to that of Paris, where he learned logic also. Such was his love of learning, that he cared little or nothing for food or raiment. For, as he was wont to relate, he and two companions who lodged in the same chamber had only their tunics, and one gown between them, and each of them a miserable pallet. When one, therefore, went out with the gown to hear a lecture, the others sat in their room, and so they went forth alternately ; and bread with a little wine and pottage sufficed for their food. For their poverty never suffered carnes aut pisces, nisi in die Dominica, vel die solenni, vel sociorum seu amicorum praesentia, eorum paupertas ipsos comedere permisit : et tamen saepe retulit, quod nunquam in vita sua tam jucundam, tam delectabilem duxerat vitam.

them to eat flesh or fish, save on the Sunday or on some solemn holy day or in presence of companions or friends ; yet he hath oftentimes told me how, in all his days, he had never after led so pleasant and delectable a life.

XXVI. THE FRIARS CONQUER THE UNIVERSITIES

Thomas Cantimpratanus, a Dominican Friar and suffragan Bishop, wrote his *Bonum Universale de Apibius* about A.D. 1250. We must read it with the definite discount that a Friar here criticizes the old-fashioned teachers ; but his words are borne out to a great extent not only by Roger Bacon, from the Franciscan standpoint, but by impartial and irrecusable documents. His book is unfortunately almost unprocurable ; the modern Dominican edition, advertised for many years past, has not yet appeared. This extract is from Book II. c. 10 (ed. 1597, page 145). He is describing the great quarrel at Paris University.

Summa autem in supradictis magistris et aliis secularibus clericis inuidiae causa fuit, quod Fratres Parisiis plures, et prope omnes litteratiores, in scholis auditores habebant, et in regimine praeeminebant. Videbant enim scholares quod Magistri seculares, sicut viri diuitiarum, dormierunt somnum suum, duce-

Now the main cause of envy among the aforesaid masters and the secular clergy was this that the Friars at Paris had more hearers in the schools, and almost all the better educated hearers, and were pre-eminent in teaching. For the scholars saw that the secular masters, as men of wealth, slept their sleep and

bantque in bonis dies suos. Et cum vespere multiplicitate ferculorum obruerentur et potuum, et postea vigilare non possent nec studere, et per hoc nihil inuenirent in manibus quod proferrent, sequenti mane solennem diem constituebant auditoribus in condensis : et sic per ineptas vacationes, quibus sua clerici inaniter expendere se dolebant, optato priuabantur studio. Maiore enim corporis sarcina, ut Seneca dicit, animus eliditur, et minus agilis est : deinde copia ciborum subtilitas impeditur. Mirum est enim aliquid fortiter dici ab homine mollitiem professo. Fratres autem Praedicatores siue Minores, sicut viri pauperes, in magna sobrietate refecti, vigilare poterant et studere, et per consequens inuenire quae auditoribus essent digna. Istud, in summa, occasio fuit, quod in Magistris secularibus, secundum vulgare prouerbium, calceus pedem presserit.

lived their days in good things. So, seeing that in the evening they were overwhelmed with a multiplicity of dishes and of drinks, and after this they could neither keep awake nor study, and through this they found nothing in their hands to produce, therefore next morning they " appointed a solemn day, with shady boughs," [1] for their hearers ; and thus, through foolish vacations, whereby the clergy mourned that they themselves were spending their money in vain, they were deprived of the study they desired. For, as Seneca saith, by a greater burden of body the mind is crushed and becometh less active : then subtlety is clogged by abundance of food. For it is a marvel that anything should be stoutly spoken by a man professed to luxury. But the Friars Preachers or Minors, as poor men, fed in great soberness, were able to wake and study, and consequently to find things worthy of their hearers. That, in brief, was the occasion why among the secular masters, as the vulgar proverb hath it, the shoe pinched the foot.[2]

---

[1] They decreed extra holidays. The quotation is from Ps. cxvii. 27, *Vulg.* ; the *A.V.* (Ps. cxviii. 27) gives quite a different sense. [2] In MS. 37 of Balliol College Library is a commentary on the Psalms by one Odo, probably not the great Franciscan Archbishop of Rouen, Eudes Rigaud. The author there speaks (folio 4) of certain elderly theologians at the universities to whom he applies the story of Abishag in I Kings i. 1–4. So (he says) such old men sleep with Theology, but know her not.

XXVII. THE ABBOT'S FEAST

In 1319 Bishop Stapeldon, visiting the nunnery of Polsloe, enjoined that the nuns should speak as little as possible. "And in words as brief as may be, provided that the wishes of the speaker be understood ; and it is better that this should be in Latin than otherwise ; yet the Latin need not be well ordained according to the rules of grammar : as for instance in this form, *candela, liber, missale, gradale, panis, vinum, cervisia, est, non, sic,* and others after the same fashion." In other words, so long as the word is intelligible the inflexions may be neglected. (*Reg. Stapeldon,* p. 316). This may go far to explain the following satirical complaint of a mere rank-and-file man against his monastic superiors, written in a Latin which anticipates the *Epistolae Obscurorum Virorum.* One version has "Gloucester"; but the Leicester version must be the more correct, for in both versions the cloisterer speaks of himself and his brethren as "canons"; *i.e.* Augustinians. With that one change, I print from E. du Méril, *Poésies Populaires Latines* (1847), page 214. It dates probably from the early fourteenth century. I give only the first few lines as a specimen.

Quondam fuit factus festus, et vocatus ad commestus, Abbas, Prior de Leycestrus, cum totus familia.	Once a feast was made, and invited to the banquet were the Abbot and Prior of Leicester, with their whole household.
Abbas est in sede sursum, et Prioris juxta ipsum ; ego miser stetit dorsum, inter rascalilia.	The Abbot was seated on high, and the Prior beside him ; I, poor wretch, stood behind among the riff-raff. Blood-red

Vinum venit sanguinatis ad Prioris et Abbatis ; nihil nobis paupertatis, sed ad dives omnia.	wine came to the Prior and Abbot : nothing to us of the poor folk, but all to the rich.
Abbas bibit ad Prioris : date vinum ad majoris, possit esse de minoris, si se habet gratia.	The Abbot drank to the Prior : give wine unto the great folk ; it may be [the same] with the lesser folk if our bounty may so extend. It is not good to drink
Non est bonum sic potare, et conventus nihil dare ; quia volunt nos clamare durum in capitula. . . .	thus, and give nought to the community ; for they will accuse us hard in chapter-house. . . .

XXVIII. THE PEASANTS' REVOLT

John Gower, Chaucer's friend, describes in his *Vox Clamantis* a world of decay and discomfort ; like practically all other satirists, he is convinced of human degeneracy. His pessimism was increased by the fact that, during the Peasants' Revolt of 1381, he was compelled to take shelter in the woods in order to escape the fate of neighbouring landlords. It is in that long passage that his indignation is fiercest, and lays the heaviest strain upon his verse.

Book I., l. 843.

Hec sibi rusticitas furiens statuebat, ut omnis Et vetus et iuuenis que valet arma ferat : Hi palos veteres gestant, qui sunt veterani, Aut contos, cicius quam sibi desit onus.	The raging peasantry had made this decree for itself, that all should bear arms who could, both young and old. These, who are ancient, bear ancient hedge-stakes or poles, rather than that they should lack some burden. Even those who are wearied with

Membra leuant baculis fessique [1]
    senilibus annis,
Quos, velut est ouium, tussis
    eundo notat.
Rusticus hic veniens fert euer-
    samque [2] pharetram,
Hic fractos arcus, hic sine luce
    facem ;
Quique colum baiulat non se
    reputauit inermem,
Debilis armatus sic furit ipse
    senex.
Rusticitate tamen iuuenilis quos
    furit etas
Quicquid adest manibus asperi-
    ora gerunt ;
Ascia, falx, fede quas roderat
    atra rubigo,
Gestantur, que [3] suo cuspide colla
    secant.
Quem vagina tegit ensem vix
    dimidiata,
Gestat et ingenuos rusticus inde
    ferit :
Est ibi vanga loco gladii, baculus
    velut hasta
Vibratur, que [4] simul prompta
    securis adest.
Arcus ibi multus fumo que [5]
    etate retortus,
Et sine tunc pennis multa sagitta
    volat :
Tribula, furcula tunc quasi rum-
    phea rite feruntur,
Fertur et ut gladius malleus ipse
    ferus.

elderly years raise their arms with cudgels, men who are marked as they go along by a cough like the cough of sheep. Here comes a peasant and carries even a quiver upside-down : this man carries broken bows, this [other], an unkindled torch ; and he who beareth a distaff thought himself not unarmed ; so doth even the feeble grey-beard rage in arms. Meanwhile, in the peasantry, those whom youthful age driveth to fury bear rougher weapons, whatsoever cometh to hand. The axe is born, and the sickle, which dark rust had foully eaten, and cut [the bearer's] neck with their point. The boor beareth a sword covered by scarce half a sheath, and therewith he smiteth the gentlefolk. There is spade in lieu of sword, a club is brandished as a lance, and at the same time an axe is ready at hand. Many a bow is there, twisted by smoke and age, and then flieth many an unfeathered arrow ; flails and pitchforks are then borne duly as lances, and even the fierce hammer is borne as a sword.

[1-5] Gower enjoys a bad pre-eminence even among medieval versifiers for his abuse of the enclitic *que*. But even he can seldom elsewhere be caught offending five times in twenty-two lines.

Ibid., l. 1430.

Silua vetus densa [et] nulla vio-
lata securi
Fit magis ecclesiis tunc michi
tuta domus.
Tunc labor insolitus sic me las-
sauit, ut egros
Vix passus potui ferre vel hic vel
ibi :
Si potui, volui sub eodem cortice
condi,
Nulla superficies tunc quia tuta
fuit ;
Perque dies aliquot latitans,
omnemque tremescens
Ad strepitum, fugi visa pericla
cauens.
Glande famem pellens mixta
quoque frondibus herba
Corpus ego texi, nec manus una
mouet :
Cura dolor menti fuerat, lacri-
meque rigantes
In fundo stomachi sunt alimenta
quasi.

An ancient thick wood, untouched by any axe, became
then a safer abode for me than
the church [sanctuaries] then did
the unwonted labour so weary
me, that I could scarce bear my
tottering steps hither or thither.
. . . If I could, I would fain
have been hidden under the very
bark [of a tree], since no surface
was then safe ; and, hiding a
few days, and starting at every
sound, I fled, guarding against
the perils that I saw. Banish-
ing hunger with acorns, and
with grass mingled with leaves,
I covered my body, nor did one
hand move. Care pained my
mind, and streaming tears were
as it were food at the bottom of
my stomach.

XXIX. A MODEL SCHOOL

Ambrogio Traversari, General of the Order of Camal-
doli, was one of the greatest churchmen who favoured
the Renaissance in Italy. His style marks a constant
effort to go back to Cicero. He was equally interested
in the collection of Greek MSS. and in the education of
children. The following passage is from a letter to the
Roman Court, in which he tries to interest his friend,

Pope Eugenius IV. (1431–47), in a new educational foundation at Florence. (Mehus, *Epistolae Ambrosii Camaldulensis*, page 136, No. 106, dated 1435.)

Sed missa haec facio. Venio ad rem. Grata fuisse Pontifici quae de puerorum diligentissima institutione scripsimus nihil miratus sum, quum sciam illius animum ad pietatem pronum hisce narrationibus pasci solere. Sed certe nihil fictum a nobis scriptum est, nihil simulatum. Gaudent primores Civitatis plerique filios suos in eo ludo nutriri, et in ista schola christianae virtutis educari, in qua nihil praeter pietatem discitur, nihil praeter bonos mores hauritur. Praefectus huic societati (sic enim vulgariter dicitur) vir fidelis, laicus licet, magna infantes ac pueros cura summoque studio piis exercet operibus, doctrinisque salutaribus imbuit. Profitentur perfectam continentiam, et in saeculari habitu, vulgares licet exerceant artes, otiosis abstinent verbis, ne dicam scurrilibus aut turpibus, et saepe inter sceleratorum obscaenos sermones innocui, non secus atque in camino Babylonis tres illi pueri, durant, ne alienae malitiae illos contingat incendium. Nullum genus ludi

But I pass over these things and come to the point. I am nowise surprised that the Pope should have been pleased with that which I wrote concerning that most diligent education of boys ; for I know that his mind, inclined to kindness, is wont to feed upon such narratives. But assuredly I have written nothing feigned, nothing simulated. Many patricians of the city [of Florence] rejoice that their own sons are brought up in that school, and educated in that seminary of Christian virtue, wherein nought is learned but piety, nought but good manners. The Superior of this Society (for thus it is named in common speech) is a faithful person, though a layman ; with great care and the utmost zeal he trains the infants and boys, and imbues them with salutary doctrines. They profess perfect continence ; and, in secular dress, although they practise common handiworks, yet they abstain from idle words—not to speak of buffooneries or foul speech ; and often they endure unscathed among the filthy talk of wicked folk, even as those famous three children in the Babylonian furnace. They permit no kind of

admittunt, neque modo ludos ipsi non exercent, sed spectasse piaculum putant. Dominicis ac festis diebus, quibus major lasciviendi licentia usurpatur, in unum omnis coeunt, et post salubria monita vel psalmos recitant vel hymnos pariter concinunt ; ibique si quis ab instituto tramite vel leviter forte detorsit, poenitentiam agit, confiteturque reatum. Ita instituti et imbuti parentum repetunt domos, ibique religionis specimen prae se ferentes familiae reliquae ad bonam frugem exemplo atque incitamento sunt. Constitutus est sacerdos persona gravis et electa ad eos audiendos atque ad poenitentiam iniungendam ; nam saepi ex instituto suo et confitentur, et communicant. Quam laetus ex hac exercitatione prodeat fructus obscurum esse non potest. Sive enim isti in saeculo permanere delegerint, gustum supernae gratiae, quem in tenera aetate perceperunt, servant, atque ad Magistratus quosque civitatis electi justitiam prae ceteris colunt. Sive, quod saepissime fit, religionem profiteri maluerint, hac veluti præexercitatione edocti minus vitae

game ; and not only do they themselves practise no games but they regard it as a sin to have looked on. On Sundays and Holy-days, wherein a greater licence of sportiveness is customary, they gather all together and, after salutary monitions, they either recite psalms or sing hymns in harmony ; and there whosoever may chance to swerve aside, be it but lightly, from the prescribed track, he doth penitence and confesseth his fault. Thus educated and imbued they come back to their parents' houses ; and there, showing forth a model of religion, they are to the rest of the household an example and incitement to good fruit. A priest, a grave and elect person, is appointed to hear them and enjoin their penance ; for, according to their institution, they frequently confess and communicate. It cannot but be manifest, how happy is the fruit produced by such discipline. For, whether those pupils choose to remain in the world, they retain that taste of heavenly grace which they have received in their tender years, and, when elected to any magistracies in the City, they follow righteousness beyond the rest. Or if (as cometh very often to pass) they prefer to profess [cloistered] Religion, having been taught by this rehearsal (so

quavis austeritate deterrentur, evaduntque facile in bonos viros. Ista mihi jampridem explorata nescio quo pacto inter familiares sermones exciderit enarrare Pontifici. Diversorium isti sibi in expositorum infantium hospitali delegerunt ; quia et remotus est locus, et huic exercitationi adcomodatus. Verum in ipsius habitaculi reparatione impendendae pecuniae quum non satis subpeterent, oratus a magistro ludi, hanc inopiam Pontifici commendavi, gratulorque non infructuosam fuisse commendationem meam.

to speak), they are the less deterred by any austerity of life, and develop easily into good men. These things I have discovered long since, but I know not how it hath slipped my memory to tell them to the Pope in our familiar talks. These folk have chosen themselves an abode in the Hospital for Foundling Children, since the place is retired, and well fitted for this discipline. But, seeing that we have not enough money to meet the expense of repairing that habitation, at the prayer of the Headmaster I have brought this poverty to the Pope's notice, and am glad that my recommendation has not been fruitless.

XXX. PAPAL INFALLIBILITY

Cardinal Nicholas of Cues (Cusanus, 1401–64) may perhaps be called the last great medieval thinker, since his successors belong rather to the Renaissance. He was also the leader of the last general fight for monastic reform in Germany, before the crash came. His *De Concordantia Catholica* is a bold attempt to work out a healthy constitution for the Church, after the medieval theory of Microcosm and Macrocosm, the analogy between Man's body and the Universe. He came perilously near to pantheism : the pantheist Giordano Bruno (*d.* 1600) harked back to him as *il divino Cusano*. This book, written for the Council of Basel, was as

definitely anti-infallibilist as the decree of Constance had already been, and as Bossuet was to be later on with his *Déclaration du Clergé Français*. Aeneas Sylvius, another anti-infallibilist at Basel, recanted when he himself became Pope : but Cusanus, though the Council's intestine quarrels drove him finally over to the Papal side, never publicly reconciled himself to the doctrine of Infallibility. I have summarized his *Dialogus de Pace* in my *Medieval Thought*, pp. 201ff.

Ecce quod, licet omnem quæstionem de sede Apostolica exortam definire habeat universale Concilium, hoc tamen ob primatiam et reuerentiam capitis, cum conuenienti reuerentia, et non audacter sententiam dicendo, facere debet. Quare manifestum est ex his, universale Concilium simpliciter supra Papam esse, nec amplius de hoc opus est exempla producere, quum habeamus uaria decreta sacri Basiliensis Concilii, et etiam Constantiensis, quomodo Papa dicatur subesse Conciliis. Et licet Constantiense tantum in tribus casibus loquatur, clarum est quod omnes canones facti, aut amplius factibiles, ad ipsos reducuntur. Nonne in quinta sessione huius Basiliensis Concilii fuit definitum, nullum

See now that, although [this] Ecumenical Council [of Basel] has to define the whole question that has arisen concerning the Roman See, yet, by reason of the primacy and reverence for the Head, it must do this with proper reverence and without pronouncing its sentence audaciously. For it is plain from these [foregoing conclusions] that the Ecumenical Council is simply above the Pope, nor is there any need for producing further examples concerning this matter, since we have various decrees of the Holy Council of Basel, and also of that of Constance, [recording] how the Pope is said to be subject to the Councils. And, although the Council of Constance speaketh of three cases only, yet it is clear that all the decrees made, or that can afterwards be made, are reduced to those [three cases]. Was it not defined, in the fifth session of this Council of Basel,

per se uel procuratorem incorporatum, extra locum Concilii etiam auctoritate Apostolica trahi posse. Quare hoc ? nisi quia hoc cadere posset in praeiudicium Concilii. Si ergo auctoritas Romani Pontificis in particulares personas, quando praesumit[ur] hoc uergere posse in praeiudicium Concilii, non potest, quis dubitat totum Concilium supra Papam esse ? Talia plura decreta sunt huius Concilii, quae hoc probant, scilicet citationem et monitionem Papae et huiusmodi. . . . Clare patet, Ecclesiam supra Petrum esse, sicut supra illam est Christus. . . . Quare concluditur uniuersale Concilium rite adunatum, licet graduationes inter se habere possit quoad iudicia, est tamen semper maioris auctoritatis, et minoris fallibilitatis, quam Papae tantum. Ex quo sequitur corollarie, universale Concilium etiam in alio quam haeresis casu Papam deponere posse. Sicut hoc etiam de Benedicto 12 et Joanne 23 legitur.

that no man might be drawn [into court], whether by himself or through his official proxy, outside the Council hall, even by Papal authority ? Wherefore was this decreed, except that such a proceeding might be prejudicial to the Council ? If therefore the authority of the Roman Pontiff hath no power over particular persons, when there is a presumption that this might tend to prejudice of the Council, who doubteth that the Council as a whole is above the Pope ? Many such decrees have been passed by this Council, proving this point, namely, [the right of] citing and admonishing the Pope, and so forth. . . . It is clear and plain that the Church is above Peter, even as above her is Christ. . . . Wherefore we conclude that an Ecumenical Council, duly assembled, although it may have gradations within itself, yet, in the matter of judicial decisions, hath always greater authority and less fallibility than the Pope alone. Wherefrom follows the corollary that an Ecumenical Council, even in another case than that of heresy, can depose a Pope, as indeed we read concerning Benedict 12 and John 23.[1]

---

[1] It had been admitted in Canon Law, from time immemorial, that a heretical Pope was subject to a Council's judgment. The practically universal belief was that Honorius I. had been so condemned by the Council of Constantinople in 680. See my *Medieval Panorama*, p. 33.

XXXI. AN OXFORD CHANCELLOR

Thomas Gascoigne held this office longer, perhaps, than any one else. He had strong opinions of his own : Lollardy was one of his bugbears, but he was equally opposed to his contemporary Bishop Pecock, who attempted to confute the Lollards by taking them on the ground of their own appeal to the Bible. His *Liber Veritatum* was written about A.D. 1450 : a valuable selection from this very lengthy book was published by Prof. J. E. T. Rogers in 1881. Like almost all other medieval writers, he exaggerates wherever he deals with statistics ; but in the main he is borne out by contemporary evidence. His attitude towards Indulgences, for instance, is borne out by Cusanus.

Nota, Cancellarie, quod in Oxonia ex purgationibus admissis indifferenter multiplicantur perjuria, et hoc experientia plurium probavi. . . . Purgatio Oxoniae occasio est intolerabilis nequitiae ; ubi enim forma laborat et evidentiae notoriae, statim reus offert se purgationi suae, ad jurandum se non esse nec fuisse reum in crimine sibi imposito, nec consensu nec opere nec verbo, nec villanus Oxoniae audet objicere contra purgantem, et causa est metus mortis vel mutilationis ; quod, si objiceret contra false purgantem seipsum,

Note, O Chancellor, that perjury is multiplied at Oxford by the facility of allowing purgation, as I know from the experience of very many. . . . Purgation at Oxford is an occasion of intolerable wickedness ; for when a man has no case, and the evidence is notorious the accused forthwith offers himself for purgation, to swear to his present and past innocence of the crime imputed to him, either in consent or word or deed, and no townsman of Oxford dares to object to his purgation for fear of death or mutilation : for if he did so object against the man falsely purging himself, then the purga-

tunc purgans se et sibi adhaerentes ipsum occulte mutilabunt vel occident.

tor and his abettors would take occasion secretly to mutilate or slay him.

Rome and Firstfruits (Lib. Ver., 13.)

Roma enim singularis et principalis ferus vastavit vineam ecclesiae, elecciones episcoporum sibi ipsis reservando, ut nulli conferant ecclesiam episcopalem alicui nisi prius solvant annata seu primos ecclesiae vacantis fructus et redditus. Item destruxit vineam ecclesiae Dei, in pluribus, elecciones omnium episcoporum in Anglia cassando. Item destruit ecclesiam malos promovendo secundum quod rex et ipse consentiunt. Item Roma ut ferus vastavit in hoc ecclesias quod omnes elecciones episcoporum in ecclesiis cathedralibus factas cassavit, statuendo quod omnes elecciones episcoporum pertineant camerae apostolicae, i.e. eleccioni papae et suorum cardinalium. Item quod Roma non vocat aliquem episcopum nisi quem papa et cardinales eligunt in episcopum vel in archiepiscopum praehabitis et solutis Romae prius fructibus millibus marcharum, et eciam solutis primis, i.e. donis ad curtesanos Romanos seu papales.

For Rome, the singular and principal wild beast, hath laid waste the vineyard of the Church, by reserving to herself the elections of bishops, so that they confer an episcopal see upon no man unless they first pay *annates*, or the first fruits and revenues of the vacant see. Again, she hath destroyed the vineyard of God's Church in many ways, by quashing the election of all Bishops in England. Again, she destroyeth the Church according as the King and he [the Pope] consent. Again Rome, like a wild beast, hath herein laid the churches waste, that she hath quashed all elections of Bishops made in cathedral churches, decreeing that all elections of Bishops should pertain to the Apostolic Camera; that is, to the device of the Pope and his Cardinals. Them, that Rome calleth no man Bishop but him whom the Pope and Cardinals elect as Bishop or Archbishop, when the first fruits of a thousand marks have first been earmarked and paid in Rome, and also when *primes* have been paid; that is, gifts to the Roman or Papal courtiers.

UNIVERSITY DISCIPLINE

A cleric was generally allowed by the ecclesiastical courts to appeal to the process of *compurgation*. By this, he swore on the gospels to his own innocence, and produced a number of others to swear that, to the best of their knowledge, he was telling the truth. Practically all University students were clerics, and Gascoigne here records solemnly in the Chancellor's book, as a warning to future Chancellors, his own estimate of this time-honoured procedure. (*Munimenta Academica*, R.S. II. p. 536.)

Clerical Ignorance (Lib. Ver., p. 201).

Novi enim jam in ecclesia valde viciosos et fatuos ex nativitate exaltari, ita quod unus habet septem praebendas et magnum archidiaconatum centum librarum, et nunquam per viginti annos aliquam earum personaliter visitavit ; sed unus vir, nuptus et armiger, omnia bona praebendarum et archidiaconatus illius annuatim recipit et secum retinet et habet xx libras annualis pensionis a praefato stulto ; et alius secularis habet x libras, et alius secularis habet x libras, et alius secularis x libras, et alius mundanus centum solidos ; et ipse nullum denarium habet, nisi secundum voluntatem praedicti secularis, qui omnia bona praefati archidiaconi recipit, et ipsum archidiaconum exhibuit per xx

For now in the Church I have known very vicious and foolish men exalted by reason of their birth, so that one hath seven prebends, and a great archdeaconry of £100, and never for twenty years hath he personally visited any one of them ; but a married man, a squire, receiveth yearly all the revenues of the prebends and the archdeaconry and keepeth them by him, and hath £20 annual pension from the aforesaid fool ; and another layman hath £10, and another £10, and another £10, and another worldly fellow £5 ; and he himself hath not a penny but by the will of the aforesaid layman, who receiveth all the goods of the said archdeacon, and hath maintained the said

annos in domo alterius ad communas ebdomadales xvjᵈ ; et audivi, ego doctor et professor sacrae paginae, eundem archidiaconum dicentem, anno Domini 1440 : " Non curo de clerimonia, ego enim majora habeo quam magni doctores, et ego credo ita bene sicut illi ; credo enim tres Deos esse in una persona, et credo quicquid Deus credit." Haec absurda ego, Cancellarius Oxoniae, audivi personaliter ab ore ejus. Deus scit quod non mencior.

archdeacon for twenty years in another man's house at 16d. weekly commons [1] ; and I myself, Doctor and Professor of Divinity, have heard that same archdeacon saying, in the year of our Lord 1440, "I care not for book-learning, for I have more than the great doctors, and I believe as well as they ; for I believe that there are three Gods in one Person, and I believe whatsoever God believeth." Those absurdities did I, Chancellor of Oxford, hear in person from his mouth. God knoweth that I lie not.

Indulgences and Money (*Lib. Ver.*, p. 123).

Consimiliter jam moderni peccatores dicunt, " Non curo quae et quot mala fecero coram Deo, quia facillime et citissime habeo remissionem plenariam cujuscunque culpae et poenae per absolucionem et indulgenciam concessam michi a papa, cujus scripturam et concessionem emi pro 4 denariis, vel pro sex denariis, vel per lusum ad pilam ;" isti enim qui concedunt literas indulgenciarum discurrunt per regiones et dant aliquando literam pro duobus denariis, aliquando pro bono haustu vini vel serevisiae, aliquando pro lusu ad pilam si

In like fashion sinners say nowadays : " I care not what or how many evils I do before God, for I can get at once, without the least difficulty, plenary remission of any guilt or sin whatsoever through an Indulgence granted me by the Pope, whose written grant I have bought for fourpence, or for the stake of a game of ball " ; for, indeed, these granters of letters of Indulgence run about from place to place and sometimes give a letter for twopence, sometimes for a good drink of wine or beer, sometimes to pay their losses at a game of ball, some-

---

[1] Fellows of Oxford and Cambridge Colleges, about this time, were commonly allowed from 10d. to 1s. per week for commons.

vincantur, aliquando pro actu meretricio, aliquando pro amore carnali. Petrus enim de Monte qui, circa annum Domini 1440, collegit pecunias plurimas pro indulgenciis concessis a papa Eugenio, in recessu suo ab Anglia, quando intravit navem in mari, dixit doctori Vincencio Clement : " Per Deum ! " inquit, " papa Eugenius nunquam habebit unum denarium de illis saccis impletis pecunia, nisi prius miserit michi literas suas quod promisit michi archiepiscopatum mediolanensem." [1]

times for the hire of a prostitute, sometimes for fleshly love. And Pietro da Monte, who, about the year 1440, collected much money for Indulgences granted by Pope Eugenius, when he went on board his ship to leave England, said to Dr. Vincent Clement, " By God," he said, " Pope Eugenius shall never have a single penny of these sacks filled with money, unless he first send me letters of promise for the Archbishopric of Milan."

XXXII. THE IMITATION OF CHRIST

As to the authorship of the *Imitatio Christi* [1450], there seems no sufficient reason for doubting the testimony of Johann Busch, who was a younger contemporary of Thomas à Kempis, a member of the same Windesheim Congregation, and well known to Thomas's brother John. If the MSS. bear no name, not only is this common in the Middle Ages, but it is particularly appropriate to a book which, essentially, is far less the expression of one personality than a quintessence of quiet thought in the cloister, especially from St. Bernard onwards. The following extract (Bk. III. c. 5) is from the best text, that of C. Hirsche, who prints the book as it was originally arranged, in verses for chanting.

---

[1] For further evidence to the same effect, see my *Sectarian History*, p. 43.

Magna res est amor,
magnum omnino bonum
quod solum leve facit omne
    onerosum :
et fert aequaliter omne inaequale.
Nam onus sine onere portat :
et omne amarum dulce ac sapi-
    dum efficit.
Amor Jesu nobilis ad magna
    operanda impellit :
et ad desideranda semper per-
    fectiora excitat.
Amor vult esse sursum :
nec ullis infimis rebus retineri.
Amor vult esse liber,
et ab omni mundana affectione
    alienus :
ne internus ejus impediatur
    aspectus :
ne per aliquod commodum tem-
    porale implicationes susti-
    neat :
aut per incommodum succum-
    bat.
Nihil dulcius est amore :
nihil fortius,
nihil altius nihil latius :
nihil jucundius nihil plenius nec
    melius in caelo et in terra :
quia amor ex Deo natus est :
nec potest nisi in Deo super
    omnia creata quiescere.
Amans volat currit et laetatur :
liber est et non tenetur.
Dat omnia pro omnibus :
et habet omnia in omnibus :
quia in uno summo super omnia
    quiescit :
ex quo omne bonum fluit et
    procedit.

Love is a great thing, great
and altogether good ; by itself
it lightens everything burdensome ; and it bears evenly all
that is uneven. For it carries a
burden which is no burden, and
makes every thing that is bitter,
sweet and pleasant to taste. The
noble love of Jesus impels us to
do great things, and stirs him up
to be always longing for what is
more perfect. Love desires to
be aloft, and not to be kept back
by any of the lowest things.
Love desires to be free, and
estranged from all worldly
affections, lest its inward sight
should be hindered ; lest it
should suffer entanglement with
any temporal prosperity, or
be by any adversity subdued.
Nothing is sweeter than Love,
nothing more courageous, nothing higher, nothing wider, nothing more pleasant, nothing fuller
nor better in Heaven and earth ;
for Love is born of God, and
cannot rest but in God, above
all created things. He that
loveth, flieth, runneth, and re-
joiceth ; he is free, and cannot
be held in. He giveth all for all,
and hath all in all ; because he
resteth in One Highest above all
things, wherefrom all that is
good floweth and proceedeth.

Non respicit ad dona :
sed ad donantem se convertit super omnia bona.
Amor modum saepe nescit :
sed super omnem modum fervescit.
Amor onus non sentit :
labores non reputat,
plus affectat quam valet :
de impossibilitate non causatur :
quia cuncta sibi posse et licere arbitratur.
Valet igitur ad omnia :
et multa implet et effectui mancipat,
ubi non amans deficit et jacit.
Amor vigilat et dormiens non dormitat :
fatigatus non lassatur,
artatus non artatur,
territus non conturbatur :
sed sicut vivax flamma et ardens facula sursum erumpit secureque pertransit.
Si quis amat,
novit quid haec vox clamet.
Magnus clamor in auribus Dei est :
ipse ardens affectus animae,
quae dicit.
Deus meus, amor meus :
tu totus meus,
et ego totus tuus.
  Dilata me in amore :
ut discam interiori cordis ore degustare quam suave sit amare :
et in amore liquefieri et natare.

He respecteth not the gifts, but turneth himself above all goods unto the Giver. Love oftentimes knoweth no measure, but is fervent beyond all measure. Love feels no burden, thinks nothing of labours, aims at what is above its strength, pleads no excuse of impossibility ; for it thinks all things possible and lawful for itself. It is therefore strong enough for all things, and it fulfils many things, and warrants them to take effect, where he who loveth not faileth and lieth down. Love watcheth, and sleeping slumbereth not. Though weary, it is not tired ; though pressed, it is not straitened ; though alarmed, it is not confounded : but as a lively flame and burning torch, it bursteth forth upwards, and securely passeth through all. If any man love, he knoweth what is the cry of this voice. For it is a loud cry in the ears of God, the ardent affection of the soul itself, which saith, " My God, my Love, Thou art wholly mine, and I am wholly Thine." Enlarge Thou me in love, that with the inward palate of my heart I may taste how sweet it is to love, and to be dissolved, and to swim in Thy Love. Let me be pos-

Tenear amore,
vadens supra me prae nimio fervore et stupore.
Cantem amoris canticum,
sequar te dilectum meum in altum :
deficiat in laude tuo anima mea jubilans ex amore.
Amem te plus quam me,
nec me nisi propter te,
et omnes in te qui vere amant te :
sicut jubet lex amoris lucens ex te.

sessed by Love, mounting above myself, through excessive fervour and amazement. Let me sing the song of love, let me follow Thee, my Beloved, on high ; let my soul swoon in Thy praise, jubilant with love. Let me love Thee more than myself, nor love myself but for the sake of Thee ; and in Thee all that truly love Thee, as the law of Love commandeth, shining forth from Thyself.

XXXIII. A FREE PREACHER

The Franciscan, Michel Menot ([1440]–1518) was perhaps the boldest and most original of the *Libres Prêcheurs*—mission-preachers at Paris and other great cities—about the turn of the fifteenth century. He earned the title of *Lingua Aurea*. Like many others, he wrote down for his fellows, in Latin, what he and they would give from the pulpit in the vernacular. This first extract (with discount for nationalist jealousies) represents pretty exactly the truth about English wines in the Middle Ages. There is a good deal of evidence on our side (though this also must be discounted by the fact that *vinea* seems to be used sometimes for any kind of orchard) ; but there is no evidence for the theory that the monks carried on a really flourishing industry, killed by the Reformation. (Text from *Sermons Choisis de Michel Menot*, ed. J. Nève, 1924).

EXAMPLES

English Wine (p. 6).

Fuerunt Britones et Angli qui voluerunt portare Franciam in patriam suam, quia inveniebant vinum melius quam cervisiam. Sciebant se non posse semper manere in Francia, nec posse portare Franciam in patriam suam. Voluerunt portare sub-tilitates Francie : ceperunt pal-mites *et à Cornouailles et à Guingamp* voluerunt plantare vineam, similiter et in Anglia. Sed cum ibi fuerunt plantate, fuerunt *abastardis.* . . . Dicit lex quod quando pauper homo ponitur in tortura, gallice *en la geyne*, et ponitur ei vita ad duos digitos de morte, si in isto tormento confitetur omnia, et maiora quam fecerit, dicit lex quod nullius roboris sunt verba et nullius momenti seu valoris, nisi ablato tormento perseveraverit in illo verbo. O et quando eris in mortis tortura, dicis quod dices veritatem et omnia dices ? Ecce, hoc nullius est momenti nec appretiatur a Deo, quia coactus es illa dicere. Cum veniet tempus ieiunandi, dicetis : Non possum ieiunare.—Quare ? —Quia doleo caput.—Et unde ? —Quia lesi me *au talon.*—Ecce

There have been Bretons and Englishmen who would fain carry France into their own country, since they found wine better than beer. They knew that they could not always stay in France, nor carry France [bodily] into their own country. They wished to carry France's delicacies : they took cuttings and would have planted the vine *à Cornouailles et à Guingamp*, so also in England. But when they were planted there, they were bastardized. . . . The law saith that when a poor fellow is put to torture (in French, *en la gêne*) and his life is set at two fingers' breadth from death, if in that torment he confesseth, all and more than he ever did, the law saith that his words are of no force, and of no moment or worth, unless he persevere in that word when the torment hath been removed. O, and when thou shalt be on the rack of death, dost thou say [now] that thou wilt tell the truth and tell all ? Behold, that is of no moment, nor is it valued by God, for thou art compelled to say those things. When fast-time cometh, thou wilt say : " I cannot fast." Wherefore ? " Because my head aches." And how is that ? " Because I have hurt myself in the heel." Lo !

mirum quod chorisatis et luditis ad taxillos et transitis noctem in hoc, et mane dicitis : O maledicte *talon* qui sic mihi fecit vexationem ! O doleo caput. Claudatis fenestram. . . . Poeta : " Cum lupus languebat monachus tunc esse volebat.

Sed dum convaluit, peior quam ante fuit."

it is a marvel that ye dance and play at dice, and spend the night in this, and in the morning ye say : " O cursed heel, which so vexeth me ! O, my head aches ! Shut the window." . . . The poet saith : " When the wolf was sick, then he wished to be a monk ; but, when he grew well, he was worse than before."

Confession and Indulgence (p. 258).

Si predicator dicat vobis periculum damnationis in quo estis et quomodo arcus ire Dei est bene contra vos, et non expectat nisi horam ad mittendum sagittam ; O, non venit adhuc hora ut debeam penitere ; habeo satis spatii ; gratias Domino, non sum adhuc propinquus morti, quia etiam in articulo mortis non oportet habere nisi unum bonum suspirium et unum : " peccavi," et Dominus miserebitur creature. Sed dicis tu, socie optime : Non oportet aliud [1] ; sed tu computas sine hospite tuo ; non dicis si Deus dabit tibi illud bonum suspirium et an faciet tibi gratiam cogitandi de salute. . . . Habemus, dices, magnas indulgentias et pluries eas sum lucratus ; in

If the preacher telleth you of the peril of damnation wherein ye are, and how the bow of God's wrath is well [bent] against you, and how he awaiteth but the hour to let the arrow fly : " O, the hour is not yet come that I ought to repent ; I have space enough ; thank God ! I am not yet at death's door ; for even at the last gasp one need only have one good sigh and one *peccavi*, and God will have mercy on that which He hath created." But, my good fellow, thou sayest, " It needeth no more " ; but thou reckonest without thy host ; thou sayest not whether God will give thee that good sigh, and whether He will do thee the mercy of thinking about thy salvation. . . . Thou will say : " We have great indulgences, and oftentimes we have earned them ; in the hour

[1] I here punctuate differently from the editor, as the sense seems plainly to require.

hora mortis, faciam Deo oblationem de ipsis.—Tu enim es similis Balaam qui dicebat, [*Numeri* XXIII] : *Moriatur anima mea morte iustorum*, etc., tamen propter hoc non est salvatus. O, magnus abusus ! O, abyssus et perditio animarum infinitarum. (Clama :) Certifio vobis et puto dicere verum quod sunt mille et mille qui crediderunt eas acquisisse, qui tamen non lucrati sunt ; illarum medio putabant se ituros recto tramite ad paradisum et iverunt ad omnes diabolos.—Quomodo, Frater ? Nonne Papa potest nobis remittere penam pro peccatis debitam ?—Ita, supposito quod facias ea qui continentur in pargameno, quia verba in eis posita tantum valent quantum sonant. Ponitur ibi : *Omnibus vere confessis e contritis*. . . . Si sitis tales, promitto vobis quod tunc lucrabimini indulgentias. Creditis quod usurarii, latrones et avari, etc., sint contriti, qui adhuc remanent in fetore suorum peccatorum et qui morientur in illo miserabili statu ? Creditis quod illi qui habent cor plenum rancore contra proximum sint con-

of death I will make an offering thereof to God. But thou art like unto Balaam, who said [Numbers xxiii.] : " Let me die the death of the righteous, [and let my last end be like his "] ; yet for all that he was not saved.[1] O great abuse ! O gulf and perdition of souls beyond number ! (Cry aloud here [2]) : I certify unto you, and methinks I say true, that there are thousands and thousands who believe themselves to have gotten those [indulgences], yet who have not earned them ; by means of these they thought to go straightway to paradise, and they are gone to all the devils. " How is this, Brother [Michel] ? Cannot the Pope remit us the penalty due for our sins ? " Yes, supposing that thou doest that which is contained in the parchment ; for the words set therein are worth all that they say. It is set down there, *To all who are truly confessed and contrite*. . . . If ye be such, I promise you that ye will then earn the indulgences. Do ye believe that usurers, robbers and avaricious men, and the like, are contrite ? men who yet remain in the stench of their sins and who will die in that wretched state ? Do ye believe that those are contrite who have their heart full of rancour against

---

[1] See Bishop Butler's famous sermon on this subject.   [2] A " stage direction " (so to speak) for the preacher.

triti ? (Practica et dilata de abusu harum indulgentiarum et contra caffardos qui decipiunt populos, dicentes eos esse absolutos a votis et peregrinationibus sanctorum. Dic de illis qui reliquias suas in taberna perdiderunt et stipitem inventum in sudario loco reliquiarum suarum dixerunt esse quo beatus Laurentius combustus fuerat.)

their neighbour ? (Emphasize and dilate here [1] concerning the abuse of these indulgences, and against the *cafards* [2] who deceive the people, saying that they are absolved from their vows and from pilgrimages to the saints. Tell of those men who lost their relics in the tavern, and said that the stick found in the napkin instead of their relics was that wherewith St. Laurence had been burned.) [3]

The Village Dance (pp. 269 ff. On the text of Exodus xxxii. 11).

Super hanc epistolam posset queri an chorizare sit semper peccatum mortale ? Ad hoc dicam vobis unam rationem veram et totam peremptoriam que talis est : Nullus punitur eternaliter nisi pro peccato mortali ; sed propter choreas iam multi damnati sunt eum diabolis omnibus et puniti pena eterna ; ergo chorea est peccatum mortale. . . . Auctoritas ponitur Iob xxi. : *Tenent tympanum [et citharam et gaudent ad sonitum organi. Ducunt in bonis dies suos] et in puncto ad inferna descendunt.* Quod attendens mater Ecclesia tales choreas valde arguit et pro-

Upon this text it might be asked whether dancing is always a mortal sin. To that I will tell you one reason, true and quite conclusive, which is this : No man is punished eternally but for mortal sin ; yet for dances many have now been damned with all the devils and punished with everlasting pains : therefore the dance is a mortal sin. . . . The authority is laid on Job xxi. [12] : " They take the timbrel and harp and rejoice at the sound of the organ. They spend their days in wealth, and in a moment go down to the grave." In consideration whereof Mother Church doth strongly rebuke and prohibit

---

[1] A " stage direction " (so to speak) for the preacher. [2] French for " religious impostor." [3] A story immortalized by Boccaccio (*Decam.*, Giorn. vi., Nov. 10.

hibet, patet in c. *Irreligiosa. De conseçra*, dist. iii. Et ultimum arrestum huius materie est quod omnes chorizantes diebus dominicis et festis semper male agunt. Non tamen, ut dicit Albertus super IIII., dist. xv., est semper peccatum mortale ; immo, ut dicit, choree possunt esse licite cum quibusdam circunstanciis et causis ; ut puta quando fuint tempore debito, ut tempore prandii, victorie, vel liberationis hominis, et in adventu amici a terra longinqua, dummodo non fiant in ipsis dissolutiones, nec fiant die dominico, vel festo, et maxime tempore misse, vesperorum et predicationis.

such dances, as is plain in [Gratian's *Decretum*, pars. III., dist. iii., c. i.] [1] And the final decision on this matter is that all who dance on Sundays and Holy-days always do ill. Yet (as Albert [the Great] saith [in his commentary upon Peter Lombard], Bk. IV., dist. xv.) it is not always a mortal sin ; nay, as he saith dances may be lawfully done in some circumstances and for some reasons ; as for instance when they are at a due time, as at the time of a feast, or a victory [in war], or the liberation of a man, and at the home-coming of a friend from a far-off land,[2] provided only that there be no dissipation therein, and that they are not done on a Sunday or Holy-day, and specially at the time of Mass or vespers or sermon.

---

[1] A decree of the 4th Council of Toledo.   [2] This sentence of Albert, repeated almost verbally by Aquinas and, later, by the friar who wrote *Dives and Pauper*, is the high-water mark of clerical tolerance for the dance in the Middle Ages. To begin with, the pagan unrestraint of the village dance was revolting to the ecclesiastical disciplinarian and the philosopher. Again, the Bible was inerrant, and wherever its meaning seemed plain there was no appeal against this. Now, men read prohibition into such texts as 1 Cor. x. 7 (taken with Exod. xxxii. 6) ; Isa. iii. 16 ; 1 Thess. v. 22. But, on the other hand, Miriam led the maidens of Israel in song and dance after the victory of the Red Sea (Exod. xv.) ; so also we have the " damsels playing with the timbrels " in Ps. lxvii. 25 (*A.V.* lxviii.) as the sequel of " let God arise and let His enemies be scattered." Again, when the Jews come back from their Babylonian captivity, " O virgin of Israel . . . thou shalt go forth in the dances " (Jer. xxxi. 4). Therefore the dance is allowed, by way of exception, " in a due time of joy, as at a wedding, or at the time of a victory, or of the delivrance of a man or of his country, or at the coming of a friend from a far-off land." So writes Albert the Great, who set the standard. (*Com. in Sent.*, lib. IV., dist. XVI., § 43 ; ed. 1641, vol. xvi., p. 357.)

INDEX OF PROPER NAMES

This applies to Sections I. and II. only, except that the **authors** represented in Section III. are indexed with numbers in **heavy type.**

PRINTED IN GREAT BRITAIN AT
THE PRESS OF THE PUBLISHERS